The Pastor's Wife

Sabina Wurmbrand

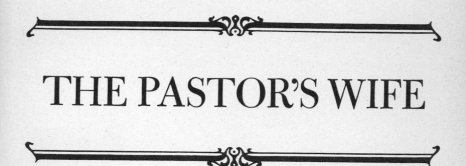

THE PASTOR'S WIFE

Edited by Charles Foley

LOGOS INTERNATIONAL

PLAINFIELD, NEW JERSEY

LOGOS EDITION 1973
LOGOS INTERNATIONAL
Plainfield, New Jersey

by arrangement with
The John Day Co.
New York, New York

Library of Congress Catalogue Card Number: 79-143216
International Standard Book Number: 0-88270-32-4
Printed in the United States of America

CONTENTS

In order to preserve certain people from identification by the Communist authorities, names of people and places have been deliberately disguised in this narrative.

S.W.

PART ONE

I Meet the Soviet Army

In the summer of 1944, when Hitler's Germany began to collapse, a million Soviet troops entered Rumania. As the first columns approached Bucharest we went to meet them on a No. 7 tram.

It was the last day of August. Cloudless and hot. The guns were silent. Somewhere across the fields, bells were pealing.

My husband Richard, as a wartime pastor, had known many Russians in Rumanian prison camps. They were by nature instinctively religious, he said, and not less so for twenty-five years drilling in atheism.

'We must go out and meet them,' said Richard. 'To speak to Russians about Christ is heaven on earth.'

When we dropped off at the suburban crossroads I saw a group of red flags, carried by local Communists who had come out of hiding to greet the 'glorious Red Army'. They looked at us in doubt. Most people were keeping out of the way of the liberators for the time being, although a big official reception had been prepared in Bucharest.

Richard was a striking young man. Tall and broad-shouldered, with a confident air that sprung from sureness in his faith. I stood beside him, half his height. Smiling, since the war was over now and we would all be friends again.

In a patch of shade two or three Rumanian officials waited. Nervously they rehearsed some words in Russian. They had come to make the age-old gift to the stranger—a loaf of bread, a handful of salt.

We gazed up the empty road, wondering what to expect. The Russians were our allies now. But also a conquering army with known tastes in rape and robbery.

In the distance appeared a boy on a bicycle, pedalling for dear life.

'They're coming,' he shrilled. 'The Russians are coming!'

The Communists fell into line. Up went the wilting red flags. The officials, who had been discussing plans for celebrations in the capital, stood like sacrificial victims under the hot sun. Roaring motor-cycles approached. Then the first tanks.

From their turrets sprouted red-starred helmets. The Communists quavered out the 'Internationale'. The macadamed road shook under the weight of the invaders. Great treads slowed and stopped.

The leading tank towered over us. Dusty grey scarred steel. A huge gun-barrel pointing skywards. As the welcoming speech ended an officer leant over and took the bread and salt which was held up. He stared at the black loaf as if it might explode. And laughed.

The young sergeant beside him caught my eye.

'Well, sweetheart,' he grinned. 'And what have you to offer?'

Few women were out on the streets that day. I said:

'I've brought you the Holy Bible.' I handed up a copy.

'Bread, salt and Bibles. All we want is a drink!' He guffawed and pushed back his helmet. The fair hair glittered in the sun. 'Thanks, anyway!' he said.

Metal tracks bit into the road. Engines belched black fumes. The column thundered past. We choked and wiped our eyes.

From the tram on the way home we saw Russians looting; wine-casks being rolled out on to the pavement; chickens, hams, sausages vanishing into sacks.

Soldiers pointed excitedly into the windows of suburban shops. Bucharest was then a sad shell of its old self but to these giant Russian children it was rich beyond belief.

Richard spoke to some of them when we got out, but the only answer was: 'Where can we find vodka?' So we returned home to make new plans. From these poor souls God had been stolen in exchange for the promise of an earthly paradise, which can never be fulfilled by human means alone.

One thing everyone knew: the Nazi terror was over at last. People hoped that the Russians would calm down and soon go their way in peace. Few guessed that a new and more lasting tyranny had begun. Certainly I did not know that we had just set out on a road that led to prison and would be marked by the graves of friends.

I didn't believe Richard when he warned me, before we married, 'You'll have no easy life with me.'

In those days we cared little about God. Nor, very much, about other people. We didn't want children. We wanted pleasure.

Then we became Christians. Richard worked for Norwegian and Swedish and British missions. He became a pastor. He played a role in the World Council of Churches. He preached in churches of many denominations, and in bars, brothels and prisons.

I was thirty-one years old when the Russians came, and by then Richard was a well-known preacher and author.

We suffered both as Jews and as Christians under the Rumanian fascists led by Marshal Antonescu, Hitler's puppet. Richard was arrrested three times. We were both among a group of seven Jews court-martialled on charges of holding 'illegal religious meetings'. A Rumanian woman came to the police station and told the officer: 'You have detained my Jewish brethren. It would be a privilege for me to suffer with them.'

It was enough. She was arrested and tried with us. God put many such friends on our way. They seemed like angels in the shape of men, working day and night for our good, appearing at every turning in our lives. God has thousands and thousands of such angels and he uses a multitude of them to make us what we are.

One was an influential priest within the Orthodox church, which was favoured by Antonescu. He spoke for us at our trial, saying we were his brothers in Christ. A German Baptist, Pastor Fleischer, and others, gave evidence for us, saying we did great work for Christianity. They risked their lives, and shamed the judges—who knew we were innocent—into acquitting us.

Each time Richard was in trouble there was a powerful trio that interceded for him: Pastor Solheim and his wife, and the Swedish Ambassador, von Reuterswärd, to whom they introduced us. Without their repeated interventions, Richard would have passed the whole Nazi era in prison. The Ambassador had considerable influence, since Marshal Antonescu used his neutral embassy to keep in contact with Moscow. (Antonescu's ally Hitler, after all, might lose the war.) Once when Richard was seized in a round-up of Jews and put to work with a labour gang, Reuterswärd's strong protests saved him. He helped us countless times.

Bucharest was lucky. Terrible pogroms occurred in the provinces. In one day at Iasi, 11,000 Jews were slaughtered. Perhaps in Bucharest there were the ten righteous people of whom the Bible speaks as being a reason for saving Sodom and Gomorrah. We heard that seven young girls had survived in Tassy with the Norwegian missionary, Sister Olga, who had brought them to Christ. How could we smuggle them into Bucharest before the next massacre? Jews were not permitted to travel.

A Christian friend in the police had the girls arrested and sent to the capital. We met the train and brought them to our home and safety. Another young man reached the capital from this district with his girl friend and stayed with us. What help and comfort they all were in years to come—especially the young man. He became my successor as pastor when I was arrested.

Where there's a will there's a way, and we willed this: we
could save these girls from the slaughter that threatened. But
so many people wished only not to be involved and failed in
their Christian duty and allowed thousands who might have
been saved to perish. There was no one to rescue the tens of
thousands of Jews deported from provincial towns, including my
own family who lived near the frontier town of Czernowitz. It
was winter. Many captives collapsed in the snow. Others died
of starvation. Soldiers massacred the rest. My parents, my
brother and three sisters, many friends and relatives never came
back. Even today the thought is like a wound; it bleeds whenever it is touched.

Jewish history is full of such traumatic events. Remembrance
of them is inscribed deeply in the heart of every Jew. This can
carry them beyond self, to weep with the multitudes from other
nations who mourn over similar tragedies.

Our only son Mihai was five years old by the time Nazism
was overthrown. He'd taken in more than a child would in normal times. Fear and death were everywhere. He missed nothing.
Our apartment was a gathering place and every night people
came to tell their troubles. He listened and learnt early of cruelty
and suffering. Richard taught him, told him stories. Mihai adored his father who, although always busy with his mission,
found time every day to speak and play with him. Once he explained how John the Baptist said that a man with two coats
should give 'to him that hath none'. 'You've got two suits, Daddy,'
said Mihai. 'So I have,' Richard replied. He'd just bought his
first new suit in years. 'You can give the new one to old Mr. Ionescu who always wears that smelly jacket.' Richard promised
he would and Mihai went content to bed. He always took what
he was told very seriously and drew his own conclusions. He
was very attentive to how his father worked on the hearts of
others. Sometimes the conversions produced by Richard's work
had side results for Mihai—he became a favourite with the converts, who brought him toys and candy.

During the war we had to move to a smaller apartment. Our
neighbours in the new block were violently anti-Jewish. This
hatred pervaded Rumania and even Christians, particularly
Christian prelates, played a role in exciting it. Few failed to suc-
cumb to the phobia.

In our courtyard were pasted big posters of Corneliu Codreanu,
the Iron Guard leader—a symbol of everything anti-semitic. And
JEW was stamped on our identity cards, as on our hearts. We
didn't feel very comfortable. But Richard went from neighbour
to neighbour breaking the ice. He had a confidence that souls

can be won for Christ, and a trust that was not easily dismayed by worldly cynicism or brutality. He could find the right word about the Saviour for different people or warn about the punishment of God without giving offence. He could charm or cajole, yet be very direct. His blue eyes could look into your soul.

Richard went to work strategically, first on our new landlord, then one by one on neighbours. He began by trying to make them laugh.

Mr. Parvalescu, on the third floor, exploded: 'You Jews have never done a damned thing that's any good!'

Richard, who was standing in their parlour, simply, replied: 'That's a fine sewing-machine. What's its make? A Singer! Hold on—wasn't that invented by a Jew? Mr. Parvalescu, if you really think the Jews are so useless, you'd better get rid of it!'

Across the landing from us was waspish, middle-aged Mrs. Georgescu, who raged about 'those Jews'. But soon she was confiding her woes to Richard. Her husband had left her. Her young son was wild. She feared he would catch venereal disease. Richard promised to speak to him.

'But even if he was to catch something,' said Richard, 'these things can be cured now. Although the remedy was invented by a Jew.'

He broke down their prejudice. Then he told them the Gospel message. Soon they began to change. We met a new politeness; then affection. Posters of Codreanu were replaced by Bible verses And in that small block, when hell raged outside, we lived as in another world of friendship and peace.

One new friend was a policeman with a motor-cycle. He drank and beat his wife, until Richard spoke to him and Christ gave him a new heart. Then he took Mihai for rides. A motor-cycle was a rarity in those days. Mihai was the happiest of boys.

When air-raids began we couldn't leave the city. Jews were not allowed to travel. But the policeman took Mihai out to stay with friends in the country until the worst was over. If they were challenged, Mihai was to give the fine old Rumanian name of 'Jon M. Vlad'. He was thrilled by the adventure.

Mihai heard much about cruelty and suffering but in this house he knew also great goodness. He was surrounded only by friends and from their love he learnt many lessons that were of great value to him later.

Anutza, one of my closest friends, called one day for coffee at our flat. Small and fair, pretty and gay, she came from Norway. And she talked like a flowing river.

'Oh these Russians! Have you heard about our new deal with

Moscow? They take all our wheat and in return we give them all our oil. Yesterday I saw a Red Army man with three wrist-watches on each arm. They take them from people in the streets as if they were collecting bus tickets!'

She laughed, but for the country it was no laughing matter. The Soviet Army looted goods worth thousands of millions of dollars. Then, on orders from the Kremlin, our navy, our merchant fleet, half the rolling stock and every car was carried off to Russia. The shops were empty. Endless queues waited everywhere. But Stalin said the Red Army would leave when Germany was finally beaten. Perhaps it would all be over soon.

'Oh, let's talk about something nice! Sabina, I heard you speak at the ladies' guild; what a lawyer the world lost in you! It was beautiful, and your husband's sermon was wonderful too. So much history and art and philosophy, and isn't two hours rather long? We in Norway aren't used to such long ones, although for myself I just wish he'd keep on and on.'

Anutza loved to chatter. She'd come to collect another pile of our church magazine, *The Friend*. The fascists had banned it. Now we were all working to put out issues.

Briefly we enjoyed a spell of religious freedom. The dictator Antonescu had been taken to Moscow, then brought back and shot. Orthodox church prelates who had exercised tyranny over Jews and Protestants had lost their absolute dominion.

At last we had a democratic government. To please the Russians, Communists filled a few posts. Scarcely anyone realized what lay ahead.

'After all,' they said, 'this is a country of twenty million people. We haven't got enough real Communists to fill a football stadium.'

All through the war we had worked to help victims of the Nazis—Jews in concentration camps, children left parentless by the massacres, Rumanian Protestants, who were greatly persecuted under Antonescu. We organized the first relief to Hungarian Jews and to another oppressed minority—the gypsies.

But now a new minority had been created. The hunter had become the hunted. German troops left behind in the retreat had to fend for themselves and many died.

We were utterly opposed to the Nazis: they had killed millions; they had devastated whole countries, leaving cities in ruins; our friends and relatives had been thrown into their furnaces. But now they were defeated and offered no danger. Most of the soldiers who remained were like ourselves, simply victims of war. They were starving and terrified. We could not refuse them help.

People said: 'You're taking foolish risks for the sake of murderers.'

'God is always on the side of the persecuted,' Richard answered. It was not only Martin Bormann and Co. who were being hunted like animals: it was also the silly boys who had paraded in Brown Shirts on Sunday afternoons and become soldiers by order. And not everyone was brave enough to prefer death to taking part in Nazi massacres. Anti-semitism had prevailed among Germans and Rumanians, but there existed also small groups who had risked their lives to help Jews. Why hate a whole people because of a Hitler and his many followers? Why not rather love this people for the sake of its saints and the few who resisted the tyrant?

The Bible tells us what it really means to be a Jew. The Biblical word for Hebrew (*Ivri*) means etymologically *to stand on the other side*. The first Hebrew was Abraham, and he was one in a real sense of the word, standing on the other side. When all men worshipped idols, Abraham worshipped the living God. When others are bent on revenge, on ways of doing more evil than their neighbour, God gives to some the ability to return good for evil.

Once three German officers hid in a tiny outhouse in our yard. It was a dark little garage, half-buried in snow. We fed them, and emptied their buckets at night. We hated their former atrocities. We ourselves had been the victims. But now we talked to them, trying to make them feel less like caged beasts.

One evening when I called, their captain said: 'I must tell you something that's on my mind. You know that it is death to shelter a German soldier. Yet you do it—and you are Jews! I must tell you that when the German army recaptures Bucharest, which it surely will, I'll never do for you what you have done for us.'

He looked at me strangely. I thought I should try to explain. Sitting down on an upturned box, I said: 'I am your host. My family were killed by the Nazis, but even so, as long as you are under my roof I owe you not only protection, but the respect due to a guest. You will suffer. The Bible says, "Whoso sheds man's blood, by man shall his blood be shed." I will protect you as much as I can from the police, but I cannot protect you from the wrath of God.'

'Humbug,' he answered.

He patted me on the shoulder. I drew back. His hand had shed innocent blood. He apologized: 'I did not mean it badly. I just wondered why a Jewess should risk her life for a German soldier. I do not like Jews. And I do not fear God.'

'Let us leave it,' I said. 'We remember a word of God in the

Old Testament, "Give love to strangers, for you, too, have been strangers in the land of Egypt".'

He seemed puzzled.

'That was thousands of years ago. What is it to you if your forefathers suffered in Egypt?'

I said: 'To God a thousand years are as one day. Wise men tell us we store the experience of past generations like memory-books. In our unconscious are written the events of the past. We don't know them, but they are determining our feelings and our judgements.

'And secondly, God says with good reason, love strangers; for in the last resort we are all strangers to each other ... even to ourselves.'

'Wait a minute!' said the officer. 'Jews have committed crimes against the German people and mankind. Honesty makes me tell you this to your face. But you must look on us as men who have committed crimes against the Jews. And you forgive them all?'

I answered very earnestly, 'Even the worst crimes are forgiven by faith in Jesus Christ. I have no authority to forgive. Jesus can do so, if you repent.'

The soft crunch of footsteps on loose snow came from the yard outside. I peered out through a crack. But it was only the deaf old janitor from next door. The captain lit one of the cigarettes Richard had found for them (although he himself hated smoking). He inhaled and passed the butt to his friend. He said:

'*Gnädige Frau,* I won't say I understand you. But perhaps if no one had this gift of returning good for evil you talk about, then there would never be an end to killing.'

When I stood up to leave, they rose and gave little formal bows. I put their laundry in my shopping bag and went out.

These men eventually crossed the frontier safely into Germany. But many thousands like them were rounded up and died after spending years in Soviet labour camps, together with Russian Christians who might have taught them further.

Every German at that time wanted to get rid of his Wehrmacht uniform. How proudly they had once worn those well-cut tunics, the badges and the medals. How hard it was now to accept in exchange the poor civilian clothes we offered.

It was at this time that Richard began to bring home Russian soldiers. He was determined to tell them about Christ. Others rightly believed the country should be rid of them.

'Do be careful, Sabina!' said Anutza. 'What will you do if the two armies meet in your home?'

We took care not to let that happen.

Richard began by entering Red Army barracks posing as a

black-market dealer in cheap watches. A group would gather round. After a time, he would lead the talk away from bargaining to the Bible.

'You haven't come for a watch,' an older man would say, 'you want to tell us about the saints.'

As Richard spoke, one would put a warning hand on his knee.

'Talk watches. The company informer's coming.'

The Red army was full of them. They spied on comrades and reported all they said. The young soldiers knew nothing about God. They had never seen a Bible, or been inside a church. Now I learnt why Richard said it was 'heaven on earth' to bring the Gospel to Russians.

I found some educated men who knew German or French. I told them the Creed.

'It begins with the words *I believe*. It isn't like a Party order that tells you what to think. It says that you must become an "I", a personality in your own right. You must think for your-selves.

'An army moves at the speed of the slowest truck. And if men advance in the mass, it will be at the rate of the slowest man. Christ calls you out of the mass. Man's greatest privilege is the right to say Yes or No, even to God.'

It was beautiful to see men awakening to Truth.

The work involved a great part of our church. Using dodges to mislead the censor, we printed thousands of Gospels in Russian. Red soldiers went about in groups. They were hard to approach. We invented manoeuvres. Troops moved in goods, boarded trains alongside them. When one train began to move wagons which sat for hours in sidings, waiting to move, we hastily handed out Gospels.

Red soldiers often slept in our spare room. Once six stayed, on the same evening, all boots and rifles. I had great trouble keeping the house free from lice. But it was the soldiers, rather than us, who were nervous. It was a long time since they'd lived in a house. How happy they were to be away from their noisy barracks for an hour. But that didn't stop their stealing. Two boys in uniform with country faces came to the door.

'D'you want to buy an umbrella?' they asked, offering three stolen samples.

'Ah, but we are Christians,' Richard replied. 'We don't buy, we have something to sell.' He invited them in. I brought them some milk to drink. Then the elder of them, who was fair-haired and hardly more than twenty, stared at me.

'Why, it was you who gave me the Bible!' he exclaimed.
In the same moment I recognized him.

'You're the sergeant from the first tank into Bucharest!' I said.
He had the Bible still, in his locker. He had read in it, and
settled a question that puzzled him.

Ivan told us over a meal how he had fought his way across
Eastern Europe. In his Company was a Jew who, like the rest of
them, had been brought up without religion.

'An older man in our unit used to rant at this Jew, "You killed
Christ." The Jew thought he was crazy. He'd been killing people
all the way from Stalingrad to Bucharest. How did he know
whom he had killed?'

The name of Christ was totally unknown to him.

Ivan brought the Jew to our home. Richard told them everything—from Adam to the Revelation. Stalin ceased to be their
God.

They came often to see us. When his regiment moved out,
Ivan left a farewell gift—a shining new electric stove.

I looked at Richard. We knew it had not been paid for.

'It's beautiful!' cried Anutza. 'Just what the Liebmanns need!'
This family had returned from Auschwitz, destitute. We sent
them the stove. It had been stolen out of gratitude for being
shown the way of Christ. A simple soul's love may show itself
in strange ways. If God were really to judge man for all his
deeds scarcely anyone would be saved. How good it was that
the blood of Jesus Christ covered even such sins.

Richard and his colleague at the Lutheran Church, Pastor
Magne Solheim, started a canteen to feed war victims. Our
flat, which was rather a guest-house, was always overflowing
with friends and strangers. Many were ex-convicts won for Christ
by the zealous work in prison of another friend, Milly. We never
sat down to luncheon on Sunday with less than a dozen people
around the table.

Young girls worked with us. They asked advice sometimes
about moral questions. One in particular I didn't know how to
answer correctly, because it had been my problem too.

At the age of seventeen I lived in Paris. For the first time, I
was free of parental control. I'd been brought up in a strictly
Orthodox Jewish family in a small town, hedged about with
prohibitions, inhibitions, rules. And now I was up at the university, and the first boy in my life took me out. He wanted to kiss
me, and I repelled him. I told him a little about how I'd been
brought up.

The boy asked simply: 'If you believe in God, wouldn't you
say that the same God made the hands and the lips? And if I

can touch your hand to mine, why is it wrong to touch your lips or to embrace you?'

Teachers, parents, no one had warned me of this question. I had no answer to it. And the boy was very appealing. So I altered my convictions to suit the gay life of Paris. An atheist is free to kiss and to behave as she likes.

His eyes and his hands were the brokers of sin. And as for my eyes and my heart, they were his handmaiden.

But conscience won't be stifled for ever. The problem nagged. Why should a girl keep herself pure? It is at the heart of many moral codes. But what purpose does it serve?

I did not know. Only many years later I learnt the answer.

A pastor's wife doesn't usually discuss sexual questions. Still less is she expected to experience such temptations herself. But both pastors and their wives are human. And in the past Richard and I had led such thoughtless, self-indulgent lives. We were converts, insecure about some things which lifelong Christians took for granted. Sexuality is vital to human nature, and in our marriage the stresses it caused were sometimes great. Richard was so good, so handsome and so brilliant that I feared all the adulation he was given might turn his head. Many girls fell in love with him, and to one he was much attracted. I must say she was lovely: it was a joy to look at her. I saw that Richard was being torn in two. Quietly, I tried to help him. Sin is often the result of occasion. It is a wife's duty to stay close to her husband in crises like these.

He said nothing, but one day, as he played a Christian hymn on the piano, he came to the words, 'I need you every hour'; and all the strings of the piano seemed to sing together, and he wept. I put my arms around him and said, 'Richard, you're not an angel, don't take it so hard. You are only a man. These things will pass.' They did pass. But when I was left alone for fourteen years after Richard's arrest, temptations came to me also. And to some I nearly yielded in my loneliness. Then I understood him better.

The Terror

My family grew overnight from one son to four—and three daughters. Thousands of orphaned Jewish children were returning from the concentration camps, often wrapped in paper for warmth, with only rags to wear. I love children. So we were happy to take in six. It was a joy to have them about the house.

Mihai was delighted. He said, 'But Mummy, you said I wouldn't be having any more brothers and sisters and look what I have now!'

They were lovely children, but so thin. And with such haunted eyes. What had they seen? All their relatives and friends had been killed.

Soon their hollow cheeks filled out. They began to laugh and play. The Russian soldiers loved them. They had families of their own, unseen for years. Often Russians talked to Mihai and the children in the street.

'Have a sweet,' they offered. And placed a hand on a small head. The children smiled and thanked them. And in turn they gave the soldiers Gospels.

It was dangerous for adults, but children were safe. Russians adore children, and many soldiers who would not otherwise have done so became aware of God. So Mihai began work as a missionary at the age of five.

Our church members went out almost nightly with posters to stick on walls, doors, sides of buses, in railway waiting rooms. Each carried Bible verses or a Christian message. Although friends were arrested for work among the Russians, none betrayed us. As fast as the Communists tore down the posters, we put them back. One of our workers Gabriella, was beautiful. She had no difficulties approaching Russian soldiers, and she gave Bibles to several high-ranking officers. But one day she was arrested and handed by the Soviets to the Rumanian militia. While she sat in prison awaiting trial a man came to her cell. He asked why she was there. As she explained a smile crossed his face. 'I'll try to help you,' he said. Soon a second stranger appeared and unlocked her cell. He led her out into the street by a side door.

'Now disappear—quickly!' She walked away, free, thanking God. The man was the recently-converted head of police.

We saw many miracles. A friend, Mrs. Georgescu, was ill, but wouldn't see a doctor. She belonged to a strict sect which disapproved of human medicine; it was for God to cure the sickness, they said. All her free time was spent in missionary work to the Russians. She was caught and taken before the Commandant, a petulant red-faced man. Suddenly, as he shouted at her, she had a violent haemorrhage. The officer saw the blood and paled. 'Throw her out!' he cried. Mrs. Georgescu was hustled out into the street. By God's will, she had escaped.

'My poor feet! I queued five hours in Victoria Street this morning and this is all I got.' Anutza had a little coffee and some greyish sausage in her bag, the first we had seen in weeks.

It was the anniversary of the Russian 'liberation'. For two days there was food in the shops. Then shelves were bare again, and windows displayed dusty cardboard meat, empty wine bottles. Rumania was faced by famine.

On top of Soviet looting and extortions ('war damage' claims) had come drought, shrivelling crops, leaving millions to exist on starvation level. People made soup from leaves and the roots of trees.

A section of the World Council of Churches sent food, clothes and money and we organized relief for the hungry. A canteen run by Pastor Solheim and Richard fed 200 each day in the church hall. Administrative work was heavy and the Communist government tried to sabotage the effort but we had many voluntary workers.

It was arranged that children in areas worst hit by famine should be brought to Bucharest to live in the houses of brethren. We took a small girl of six. She was thin as a lathe and came to us with only the clothes she wore. I gave her good food—to start with, cereal with sugar and milk. She wouldn't eat. She was a peasant girl and she wanted her own food: *mamaliga*, a sort of maize cake that was about all she knew. We had to speak very severely to make her taste our food. Slowly she began to put on weight.

We grew very fond of her. Once she said, 'You I will love until the autumn.' Then the new crop would come and she would return to her parents.

When the Russians occupied Budapest we needed someone to take money for relief work to the mission there. Richard could not leave Bucharest and no one else could take the responsibility. I had to go.

'You mustn't!' exclaimed Anutza. 'These Russian soldiers are hungry for women. You walk in the streets and you find girls with their throats cut and no one does a thing!'

In normal times it wasn't a long journey. But the Red Army was seizing every train and car for their own use. At the stations there was unimaginable confusion and panic as swarms of hungry and displaced people tried to crowd into the few wagons available. After a long search I found a corner. For days we rumbled across the country to Budapest. I was the one woman in a train full of Russian soldiers.

When I arrived German troops were still engaged in house to house fighting. All was in ruins. There was no bus, no taxi, no transport of any kind. I walked everywhere past smoking ruins, unable to find any of the people I sought. The Germans had deported many who never returned. Others had been killed in the last days of street fighting. At last I found Pastor Johnson, leader of the Norwegian mission and Pastor Ungar, a Hebrew Christian who led the free church where Jews and other nationalities worshipped. They couldn't believe their eyes. I seemed like an angel sent by God, they said, coming from nowhere with help just as the famine was at its worst. As people emerged from the cellars food grew scarcer. There was nothing. A horse, killed in the fighting, was cut up for meat and eaten.

Many church buildings had been razed to the ground and hundreds of brethren were homeless. The help I brought was very welcome.

I met Prof. Langley, the Red Cross representative in Budapest, who never tired in his relief work. We ate a meal together before I departed. I said, 'May Christ reward you for what you have done.'

Langley replied: 'When I boarded a tram once and found I had no money for the fare, someone paid for me. And when I tried to thank him, he said, "Don't thank me, I'm repaying what somebody did for me yesterday when I was in the same situation." So it isn't Christ who has to reward me—but I who pay a debt towards him.'

From Budapest I went to Vienna. Normally, it's a four-hour journey. Now it took six days!

I found a train about to leave early one morning. People were clinging to the doors and sitting on the roof. It seemed impossible that anyone else could get aboard.

Then I heard my name called. Perched on top of a goods wagon were a group of girls, all Auschwitz refugees, who'd stayed with us in Bucharest. 'There's no room, but we'll make room!' they laughed. So from Tuesday until Sunday we sat on that roof and reached Vienna. This city too, was starving and badly damaged. I contacted friends and Christian leaders there after many adventures and returned only when the work was completed.

For weeks I was completely out of touch with home. Richard told me: 'We feared terribly for you. I saw you in visions, in day dreams.' When he opened a book, he saw before it my face. When a branch tapped the pane he awoke thinking I was back. 'I walked in the mountains,' he said, 'and called your name aloud. It seemed to me that I heard you answer.'

And I had heard, I had answered. I'd found myself searching those littered streets and calling, 'Richard! Richard!' We were so close.

The country was now run from Moscow. But the local Communists still played at democracy. 'We want friendship with everybody!' they said. 'Freedom of worship? Certainly. An all-party Cabinet with King Michael as constitutional monarch? Why not?' It was done simply to dupe the Western powers.

The mask was dropped when the Soviet Minister Vishinsky marched into the palace one morning and gave orders. The army and police must be disbanded. The King must appoint trusted Communists to key posts, or else ... We knew how in Russia the Church had been made a tool of the state. How long would it be before they got to work in Rumania?

I was arranging the church for Sunday service when Pastor Solheim came in, looking disturbed.

He said, 'Strange news. The Government is summoning what it calls a Congress of Cults. Every confession, every religion in fact, is asked to send a big delegation. And the conference is to be held in the Parliament building! Who ever heard of such a thing? What can they be planning now?'

Everyone had a guess or a rumour to tell. Many churchmen believed what the Government had said about 'full religious freedom'.

But Richard wondered, 'Is it not happening here as it happened in Russia? Lenin strongly defended the persecuted sects, until he came to power. Then tens of thousands of them died in concentration camps. First the church is lulled into acceptance. Then the blow falls.'

We conferred with Solheim. He was head of the Mission and he must decide.

'We'll go, and we'll speak out,' he said.

On the chosen morning we climbed Parliament Hill. There they all sat, crowded into the galleries and on the floor of the great hall, Moslem and Jew, Protestant and Orthodox, some 4,000 bishops, pastors and priests, rabbis and mullahs.

Red flags hung everywhere. Stalin was formally chosen as honorary president of the Congress. Up on the dais were all the top Communists: the puppet Premier, Petru Groza, the powerful Minister of the Interior, Theoharo Georgescu.

There was even a service in the Patriarchy beforehand. The Communist leaders crossed themselves. They kissed the ikons. They kissed the Patriarch's hand.

The speeches began. Groza, who was simply a quisling of Moscow, explained that the new Rumanian Government was in favour of Faith, any faith, and they would continue to pay the clergy. In fact, they planned to raise stipends. Warm applause greeted this news.

Priests and pastors replied. One after another, they said how happy they were about this appreciation of religion. The State could count on the Church if the Church could count on the State. A bishop remarked that streams of all political colours had joined the church in its history. Now Red would enter, and he was glad. Everyone was glad. All their gladness was broadcast to the world over the radio, direct from the hall.

It was absurd and horrible. Communism was dedicated to the destruction of religion. It had shown its true face in Russia. They spoke out of fear for their families, for their jobs, for their salaries. They could at least have kept silent, instead of filling the air with flattery and lies.

It was as if they spat in Christ's face. I could feel that Richard was boiling. So I told him what was already in his heart and said:

'Will you not wash this shame from the face of Christ?'

Richard knew what would happen: 'If I speak, you will lose a husband.'

At once I replied—it was not my courage, but given to me for the moment: 'I don't need a coward for a husband.'

He sent up his card. The Communists were delighted. A representative of the World Council of Churches and of foreign missions was going to make propaganda for them. Richard went up to speak and at once a great silence fell on the hall. It was as if the Spirit of the Lord was drawing near.

Richard said that when the children of God meet, the angels also gather there to hear about the wisdom of God. So it was the duty of all present not to praise earthly powers that come and go, but to glorify God the Creator and Christ the Saviour, who died for us on the Cross.

As he spoke the whole atmosphere in the hall began to change.

My heart filled with joy to think that this message was going out to the entire country.

Suddenly the Minister of Cults, Burducea, jumped to his feet. 'Your right to speak is withdrawn!' he shouted. He bawled orders from the dais to minions.

Richard ignored him and went on. The audience began to applaud. He was saying what they had all wanted to say.

Burducea bellowed, 'Cut that microphone!'

The congress shouted him down.

'Pastorul! Pastorul!' they chanted rythmically. 'The Pastor! The Pastor!' From 'a pastor', Richard had become 'The Pastor'.

The uproar lasted minutes. The shouting and clapping went on long after the microphone wires were severed and Richard had stepped down. That ended the Congress for the day. We made our way out through noise and confusion.

At home, Richard's mother had heard everything on the radio. When the broadcast was interrupted she imagined she would never see him again.

'I thought they'd arrested you both. What will happen now?' she asked, white-faced.

'Mother,' he replied, 'I have a powerful Saviour. He'll do what is best for me.'

No official move was made. But soon Communist hecklers were sent to break up our meetings. Recently we had opened a new and bigger church hall. Week after week rough-looking youths pushed their way in at the back to whistle, jeer and interrupt.

'We ought to be glad,' said Solheim. 'Better a rowdy audience that cares than a silent one that only pretends to listen!'

We worked out street-preaching tactics. Many souls were too shy to join us in church. This way we could reach them. We would meet in a group on a street corner to sing hymns. This was totally unknown in Rumania and a crowd always gathered. Then I'd deliver my message, which had to be short and sharp.

Outside the great Malaxa factory one afternoon there was a protest meeting against the Communist take-over. I spoke to workers gathered there about salvation. For some it was the last warning. Next day police opened fire on a crowd at the factory. Many workers were shot.

And once I spoke from the steps of the University. The crowd grew until it filled the square. I'd never had such an audience. People came running from side-streets. Traffic was jammed along one of Bucharest's biggest boulevards. There was no heckling. Just prolonged applause.

While I was telling Richard about my success, Anutza burst in.

'It's all over town that Ana Pauker made a speech outside the University. They say she's been sent back from Moscow to run Rumania for Stalin!'

Mrs. Pauker was a Communist schoolteacher who had gone to Russia. She became an officer in the Red Army. She was dark and Jewish, and when I began to speak in such a public place, the rumour spread that the notorious Ana Pauker—who had shot her husband Marcel with her own hand for 'deviation'—was back.

But no one could understand why Comrade Pauker was telling them to repent of their sins. We roared with laughter.

In 1947 the arrests began. Rigged elections, in which every fraudulent and violent device was used, put the Communists in full control. Leaders of the opposition, honest and dishonest police chiefs, and civil servants were liquidated in a wave of terror. Then came the turn of all the Catholic bishops and innumerable clergy, monks and nuns. On the night they were arrested religious broadcasts were made as usual to the West. Tens of thousands of ordinary people disappeared into jails and labour camps. Others joined freedom fighters in the mountains.

The Jews, who had been able to leave Rumania in the early confusion under the Russians, were now trapped. The borders were closed. By then thousands had fled, leaving all they possessed, preferring life as destitute refugees to 'freedom' under the Soviets.

Anutza had reason to believe she was on the list of Jews to be arrested—suspected of heaven knows what 'crime against the state'. Anyone who had had to do with foreigners was suspect—even the barbers who shaved them.

It was a sad farewell. We had become so close.

'Like David and Jonathan,' cried Anutza. 'Only I am Jonathan. Jonathan loved most!'

We embraced in tears. Anutza said, 'I'll work to get you both out of the country. We'll meet again in freedom.'

Richard was sick in bed that day. She knew that he was in great danger of arrest. She leant over the bed and kissed him, making some promise.

And she did work, we did meet. Only it took twenty years.

The terror spread. Secret police burst into homes and made long searches. Then you were taken off to 'make a statement'.

They said, 'Bring nothing, it'll be only for a few hours.'

Foreign newspapermen saw vans going through the streets labelled 'Meat', 'Fish', 'Bread', and so could report that the population was being provided for; they did not know the vans carried not food but prisoners.

Then we had our first warning. Richard was working in the mission when a plain-clothes man walked in.

'Inspector Riosanu,' he introduced himself. 'You're Wurmbrand? Then you're the man I hate most in life.'

Richard stared at him.

'We've never met before. What do you mean?'

'You remember about ten years ago you used to go out with a girl named Betty? A frizzy blonde who talked a lot?'

'Well, what about it?'

'Tell me why you didn't marry her?'

'I never thought of it.'

'No, but I did! Wurmbrand, if you'd only married her. You'd have made me a happy man.' And he meant it.

'But just to show there's no hard feelings,' said the magnanimous Inspector, 'I've come to give you a tip. There's a big fat file on you at secret police HQ. I've seen it. Someone's informed against you lately. Been talking to a lot of Russian friends, haven't you?'

Riosanu rasped his sandpapery hands together.

'But I thought we might come to an agreement.'

For a bribe, he would destroy the report.

I joined the discussion, and we agreed on a sum. Stuffing the money into his pocket, Riosanu said, 'You've got a bargain. The informer's name is ...'

'No!' I broke in, quickly. 'We don't want to know.'

I wished to feel no resentment against the man. Silly, perhaps. But in those days we couldn't know how many lives informers would destroy.

Riosanu shrugged. 'As you please,' he said. And he was gone.

Shortly after this, Richard was taken in for questioning. Nothing was said about 'subverting' the Red Army. We still had some influential friends, and through them we obtained Richard's release after three weeks. But we knew it was no more than a respite.

More and more of our friends and helpers were arrested.

I remember the day I first saw a man who'd been tortured by the Secret Police. He could hardly speak through purple and swollen lips. He'd been a kind, friendly man, with a word for everyone. Now in his eyes you saw only hatred and despair.

With bribes and threats, the Communists put certain church leaders to work for them. They threw suspicion of treachery on those who refused to become traitors. The most obstinate went earliest to prison.

One political obstacle remained. Our beloved young King Michael would not give in without a fight. Only in December 1947, after the United States and Britain recognized the Kremlin's puppet, Groza, was he forced to leave. Groza and Gheorghiu-Dej, a fraudulent lawyer and an ex-railwayman, were the rulers of the country. They ordered the king to abdicate. The palace was surrounded by troops. He had no choice. On that day, the 'Rumanian Popular Republic' was born.

I remembered a proverb: *The earth trembles when a servant becomes a king.*

It seemed a very small cough, and so much was waiting to be done. But in a week I was in bed with bronchitis. Hunger, shortages and the Budapest adventure brought me down with a thump. So I was on my back, feeling exhausted and ethereal, when an uninvited visitor called. A Russian woman doctor. Her face was a mask of tragedy.

Mrs. Vera Yakovlena knew us only slightly. She'd come from a town in the Ukraine where countless priests and churchpeople, including herself, had been deported to Siberian labour camps. From which few returned.

She wasn't interested in my illness. She had a message to impart.

'We worked to clear the woods, men and women together. We had equal rights: we could die of starvation or freeze to death.'

Mrs. Yakovlena touched my arm with a hand that bore thick white scars. And trembled with memory. 'Every day people died, collapsing from overwork in the snow.'

Her punishment when she was found witnessing for Christ was to stand for hours barefoot on ice. When she failed to fulfil her work quota, the guards struck her with their fists. She fell in the snow. And went without the watery broth which was allowed them when they returned to camp.

Weeping, she wandered out into the yard to be alone. And in her misery crossed into the forbidden area near the wire, where prisoners were shot at sight.

A harsh voice yelled, 'Hey! is your mother a believer?'

Frightened, Mrs. Yakovlena gasped, 'Why do you ask?' For in that moment she had been thinking of her mother.

The guard said, 'Because I've been watching you for ten minutes, but I haven't been able to shoot you. I can't move my arm. It's a healthy arm. I've moved it all day. So your mother must be praying for you.' His voice warmed. 'Run back. I'll look the other way.'

Mrs. Yakovlena saw the soldier later that day. He laughed and raised his arm. 'Now I can move it again.'

She survived ten years in this camp. Most of the others died. But she came back to tell how, in sorrow and need, God had shown his might. Now she was a doctor in the Soviet Army.

My head ached. Instead of pondering on the miracle, I could think of nothing but her sufferings. What did it mean? Why had she come to tell me such things?

As she stood up to leave, I struggled dimly with my weakness and asked her to stay the night. To wait at least until Richard returned. But already she was at the door. Briefly she paused to say: 'My husband was also taken by the GPH. He's been in prison twelve years now. I wonder if we'll ever meet again on this earth.' Then she was gone.

Twelve years? I couldn't understand. Much later I learned that this messenger from God meant to tell about the sufferings which I and my husband could expect. Ananias, the head of the Christian Church in Damascus, was also told two thousand years ago, 'Show to the new convert, Paul, the future Apostle, all the things which he will have to suffer for my sake.'

It wasn't too late to leave the country. Although it grew more difficult every day, thousands were still buying their way out. I knew that Richard didn't really want to go. But he said:

'Under Antonescu's rule we were never imprisoned for more than two or three weeks at a time. With the Communists, it can last for years. And they may take you, too. And Mihai—who will look after him, and the other children?'

Then another odd thing happened. A pastor we hadn't seen for a year came to the house. God had used Richard to convert him. He'd been an alcoholic, going from bar to bar, and Richard, meeting him one night, had gone with him, talking, arguing, persuading. When he awoke the next day from his drunkenness, he was a changed man.

Now he reminded us of this. And several times as we talked, he repeated: 'What struck me most in what you said then was a verse: "Escape for thy life; look not behind thee." The angel's words to Lot.'

When he left, Richard asked me: 'Don't you think that may have been a message from God? Why should he come to see us after so long, and repeat over and over, "Escape for thy life"? Wasn't it a warning that I must save my life by fleeing?'

I said, 'Escape for what life?' Then I went into the bedroom and opened the scripture where Jesus says: 'Whosoever will save his life shall lose it and whosoever will lose his life for my sake shall find it.'

I asked Richard, 'If you leave now, will you ever be able again to preach about this text?'

We didn't speak again that night about leaving.

But a few days later, Richard said, 'If we go to the West, won't we be able to do *more* for the church in Rumania? If we stay I'll follow the others into prison. It'll be the end of our life together. I'll be tortured, perhaps killed. And if you're imprisoned too, it's the end of the mission. The Solheims are foreigners. They won't be allowed to stay. Mihai will be brought up on the streets—a Communist. What good will it do to anyone?'

I said, 'I think we'll have to stay.'

Then came a last sign. We'd begun to hold meetings in private houses around Bucharest. They were safer than churches. And never had we had such blessed services, so many conversions. As if God, knowing what lay before us, gave greatest comfort before gravest trouble.

One night we met at the home of a rich man who had lost everything except his great house—soon that would go, too. We took it in turn to keep guard. A secret prayer meeting like this could have landed us all in jail.

Some fifty of us were gathered for an all-night vigil. Towards midnight, a woman kneeling with the rest cried aloud, 'And you, the one who thinks of leaving! Remember that the good shepherd did not desert his flock. He stayed to the last.'

She had no knowledge of Richard's problem. We all looked at her, puzzled, but she didn't speak again.

When dawn came we walked home through cold streets. It was January and fine grains of snow were falling. I said: 'We can't leave now.'

Richard agreed. We told everyone, 'We're here to stay.' They were very happy.

The woman who had this warning presage about Richard was at the station when he came back fourteen years later. She came to meet him with flowers. He remembered her, and said:

'I don't regret taking your advice. I'm thankful for it.'

Richard Vanishes

'Richard, what do you think hell is?'

We had spent an evening with friends, and inevitably talk had turned to the Communists. A politician we all knew, a good, upright man, had been arrested, and after a few weeks had hanged himself in his cell. What had he suffered to drive him to suicide? Someone had said: 'He must have gone through hell.'

'Hell is to sit alone in darkness remembering evil you have done,' Richard replied.

Within a few days he was in that hell himself.

On Sunday morning—February 29th, 1948—Richard walked alone to church. I followed and found Pastor Solheim in the small office, looking upset.

'Richard hasn't turned up,' he said. 'But he has so much on his mind. He must have remembered some urgent appointment and forgotten he has to come here.'

'But he promised he'd see me here in half an hour.'

'Perhaps he met a friend who wanted help,' said Solheim. 'He'll come.'

Pastor Solheim took the service. I telephoned friends, but he wasn't with any of them. Fear grew in my heart.

In the afternoon Richard was due to marry a young couple we knew.

'Now don't worry,' said Solheim. 'You never know with Richard. Remember the time we had that summer camp, and he went off to buy a newspaper in the morning and then telephoned at lunch-time to say he wouldn't be back for breakfast?'

I smiled at the thought. Richard had remembered some urgent business and got a lift into Bucharest. He must have done something like that again. Sunday lunch at our flat was usually a happy crowded occasion. It was not much of a meal. But we talked and sang, and for many who came it was the great event of the week.

Now we sat silently, waiting for Richard. But he didn't come. The night before we'd also had many guests. Richard was talking away happily. Suddenly he stopped. Someone said, 'Richard, you look sad—why?' He answered strangely, with a quotation from Ecclesiastes: 'I said of laughter, it is mad.' It was quite outside our discussion. It came from the depths of his heart. And now we did understand what madness it is to laugh. No one spoke.

Pastor Solheim had to perform the afternoon's wedding. We telephoned all the hospitals. I went around casualty wards, thinking he might have been in a street accident. No sign.

I admitted to myself at last what I must do. I must go to the Ministry of the Interior. He had been arrested.

And then began the hours and weeks and years of searching. Of trailing from office to office. Of pushing at any door that might open.

I learnt that important prisoners were kept in cells in the Interior Ministry's basements. So many women were seeking arrested husbands, sons and fathers that an 'information office' was opened to handle inquiries. The stairs were crowded with mothers and children. They stood hopelessly waiting to ask for news. A slogan decorated the otherwise bare wall:

WE WILL BE RUTHLESS TO THE CLASS ENEMY

Each in turn put her question. The officials pretended to examine lists of typed names. They peered into filing cabinets. But of all those missing men, no trace could they find.

A rumour spread that Richard had been taken to Moscow. (It had happened to Antonescu and others.) But I couldn't believe he'd gone from my life. Evening after evening, I made a meal and sat by the window. I thought, he'll come tonight. He's done nothing. He'll soon be free. The Communists cannot be worse than the fascists, who always let him go after a week or two.

He didn't come. I put my forehead against the pane and wept. I went to bed late, but couldn't sleep. In the morning, Pastor Solheim went with me to ask the help of the Swedish Ambassador, our ally in the past. Mr. Reuterswärd said he would speak at once to the Foreign Minister, Ana Pauker.

Mrs. Pauker's answer was ready: 'Our information is that Pastor Wurmbrand has absconded from the country with a suitcase full of dollars entrusted to him for famine relief work. They say he is in Denmark.'

The Ambassador brought the case up with the Prime Minister. Groza repeated Pauker's version, with a jovial promise: 'So Wurmbrand's supposed to be in our jails? If you can prove that, I'll release him!'

The Communists were so sure of themselves. Once in the Secret Police cells, a man ceased to exist.

No one else could intervene now. The only hope left—which thousands were trying—was bribery.

'You know Theohari Georgescu, the Cabinet Minister?' asked Klari Meir, a friend of my schooldays. 'His brother lives near us, and I've heard that he can open prison doors for the right sum. I'll talk to his wife for you.'

Mr. Georgescu was willing. So long as everything was kept absolutely secret. But the price of his favours was high.

I met him, as he wished, in a squalid hovel on the outskirts of town. He was a squat little man in a smart new suit.

'I'm Georgescu,' he said 'I arrange things. A word to my brother and it's as good as done. Guarantee? You have my word.'

We could find the sum he asked, though with great difficulty. It was handed over.

Nothing happened.

It was not the first nor the last time we were swindled in this way. There was nothing we could do. I'd met thieves and criminals in plenty, but these professional tricksters were in a class of their own. Some were high-ranking officials. Few were Communist in anything but name.

'Who knows what's coming?' said a high Party man who'd come to our flat by night. 'Perhaps the British and the Americans.'

With this in mind for the future (and a cash reward for the present) he tried to help. He would do what he could, so long as it did not endanger his job.

A third Communist official was reached through a woman friend who'd known him as a student. They had secret meetings, as if they were lovers, to disguise negotiations.

Nothing came of it all.

After some months of wasted effort a stranger came one evening to the door. The man was unshaven and reeked of plum brandy. He insisted that we talk alone.

'I've met your husband,' he said. And my heart turned over.

'I'm a warder—don't ask what prison. But I take him his food, and he said you'd pay me well for a bit of news.'

'It depends ... how much?' I said. We'd had so many failures.

'I'm risking my neck, you know.'

The sum he named was huge. He would not bargain.

Pastor Solheim was as doubtful as I. He told the warder: 'Bring me a few words in Wurmbrand's writing.'

He gave him a bar of chocolate from the famine relief stores.

'Take this to Wurmbrand and bring back a message with his signature.'

Two days later the man returned. He removed his cap. He felt in the lining. And handed me the wrapper from the chocolate bar. I read:

'My dearest wife—I thank you for your sweetness. I'm well—Richard.'

It was his handwriting. Bold and clear, determined and yet troubled. No possibility of mistaking the tempestuous serenity of those lines.

'He's all right,' said the warder. 'Some can't take it, in solitary. Don't like their own company.' He breathed brandy. 'He sends you his love.'

We agreed to pay the money if he would continue to carry messages. Finally he said: 'All right. But people have got twelve years for this. You know, it's not just the cash.'

He risked his freedom out of a divided love: he loved the money, loved the drink it bought. And he also loved Richard. Sometimes he slipped him extra bread. He continued to bring us verbal messages.

'What do you do with this money we pay you?' I asked.

'Get drunk!' he laughed. But the Lord had touched his heart, if not yet about drinking.

Solheim and his dear wife Cilgia, friends in time of trouble, dropped everything and worked only to keep my courage up and rescue Richard. Pastor Solheim came with me to the Swedish Embassy where we were at once received by the Ambassador. When he saw the scrap of paper with Richard's writing he quickly drafted a note to the Premier: —

'You promised to release Pastor Wurmbrand if we could prove that he is in a Rumanian prison. I now have that proof in my hands.'

Groza passed the note on to Ana Pauker at the Foreign Ministry. His joke had misfired. She sent for Mr. von Reuterswärd and stormed at him. If she said that Wurmbrand had fled to Denmark, then so he had. She would not be insulted by the envoy of a minor power who was poking his nose into a purely domestic matter. She was not a liar!

The Ambassador was declared *persona non grata*. His superiors questioned the wisdom of his intervention. Richard was a Rumanian national, even if he did work for a foreign mission. Von Reuterswärd replied that his conscience obliged him to help a man whom he knew to be innocent. He'd been lied to by a Minister of State, and it was his duty to protest. The Ambassador was a man of God and Governments do not always take kindly to such men. He was recalled to Stockholm and retired from the diplomatic service.

Soon after this, Groza was hoisted to the even emptier position of President of the Grand National Assembly. Once he met Pastorel, the famous Rumanian satirist, and taxed him with putting out malicious jokes about him.

'I'm entitled to respect—I'm the President.'

Pastorel: 'That's a joke I've never made.'

In bitter jokes, the heart finds its revenge. This is what inspires the tragic jokes for which the Jews are known. Now you could be jailed for telling one: Pastorel was sent to prison for six years.

Next, Solheim—who thought of Richard as his other self and of Rumania as his second homeland—was obliged to leave the country. He had identified himself with us and his mission-station, as all good missionaries do. He could help no more. But we still had loyal friends, although to be friendly with us was to put oneself in danger.

The wife of a political prisoner could get no ration card. They were only for 'workers'. The wife of a political prisoner could not work. Why? Because she had no ration card, and therefore did not exist.

I didn't argue that the highest authorities in the land denied that Richard was in prison.

'How am I to live? And my son?'

'That's your business.'

Mihai had become again my only child. Before Richard's arrest we had lost the orphaned children who had come to us from the Nazi massacres in Eastern Rumania. Hearing that the Russians had decided to repopulate, with refugees, the two Eastern provinces (Bessarabia and Bucovina) which they had annexed, we realized that sooner or later the children would be taken from us. Hundreds of Jewish orphans faced this plight. How much better if we could get them to Palestine, where the new State of Israel was about to be born! In agony of mind, we decided to let our boys and girls go. It seemed so much better than waiting for an unknown fate to catch them under the Soviets.

They joined a little army of refugees aboard the Turkish steamer *Bulbul*. Weeks passed. No news came of their arrival. Each day Richard looked more haggard. An international search began, spreading from the Black Sea to the Eastern Mediterranean. Gradually, hope faded. It was thought that the *Bulbul* had hit a wartime mine and gone down with all aboard. But to this day, no one knows. The ship set out. It did not arrive. There were no survivors.

The pain was terrible. We had loved them as our own. When

we finally accepted the truth that they were lost, I didn't want to see or speak to anyone. Rare are the men who can comfort men. All my beliefs, in the Resurrection, in everlasting life, were put to a hard test. I had to understand that it is not among the dead that you must seek your lost children, but among the living. Many times I thought I could never overcome this pain; but the Lord gave me strength to go on. Then one day, the word of God slipped quietly into my heart, saying, 'My peace I give unto you.' I understood anew the word Patience which is repeated so often in the New Testament. In the Greek this word —*hypomone*—means 'To remain under': to accept, to bear the pain as given from God. It will bear much fruit. God gives as well as takes away, and he put around me many new young people. It remained only not to forget: to have a pitiful heart after all that I had learned.

In my grief I had to comfort Mihai. How bitterly he wept. I held him in my arms and told him a story which I'd often heard on Richard's lips. It comes from the Talmud, a book of great human wisdom.

It is said that during the absence of a famous rabbi from his house his two sons died, both of them of uncommon beauty and enlightened in the Law. His wife bore them to her bedchamber and spread a white covering over their bodies. In the evening the rabbi came home.

'Where are my sons?' he asked. 'I repeatedly looked round the School, and I did not see them there.' She brought him a cup. He praised the Lord at the going out of the Sabbath, drank, and asked again: 'Where are my sons?'

'They will not be afar off,' she said, and placed food before him that he might eat.

When he had said grace after the meal she addressed him: 'With your permission, I wish to ask you a question.'

'Ask it then,' he replied.

'A few days ago a person entrusted to me some jewels, and now he demands them back; should I return them?'

'What?' said the rabbi. 'Would you hesitate to return to everyone his own?'

'No,' she replied. 'Yet I thought it best not restore them without first acquainting you.'

She then led him to the room, and took the white covering from the dead bodies. 'My sons! my sons!' loudly lamented the father. 'My sons, the light of my eyes!' The mother turned away and wept bitterly.

At length she took her husband by the hand and said, 'Did

you not teach me that we must not be reluctant to restore that which was entrusted to our keeping? The Lord gave and the Lord hath taken away; blessed be the name of the Lord.'

At this time, when so many tragedies were pressing down on us, I found great joy in one of the greatest events in history. The State of Israel came into being in 1948, fulfilling the Bible's prophecies about the return of the Jewish people to their homeland.

'I will gather them from all the countries whither I scattered them in my wrath,' says God to the prophet Jeremiah. The return was part of a plan which God laid down, when he blessed the father of Jews, Abraham, and all the world partook of that blessing. Now I saw God's plan coming true, to remain so for ever. When the prophets pledged that God would gather his people from the corners of the earth, they did not know how many nations and continents the Jews would be scattered among. People were eager now to interpret the great events they were witnessing. Men who had not looked at a Bible for years began to search the Scriptures as if they had just been published. Ezekiel, Jeremiah, Amos were pored over, in the hunt for clues as to the next step.

A great new exodus began from Rumania. The Nazis had massacred half a million Rumanian Jews. Those who were left had had more than enough of the Communists, who had once seemed liberators. Jews in the Eastern provinces seized by Russia were being gathered from the street for labour in Soviet mines. The one difference this time was that the Soviets took Rumanians as well as Jews. They were driven off in trucks without a word to their families. Few ever returned.

A young man from my home in Bucovina told me, 'My brother spent four months hidden in a hole behind a cupboard to avoid deportation. I got out with only the clothes on my back. I told a Soviet bureaucrat that he could have my flat with all its contents and every penny I had in return for a passport. I got it and left. So much for Communism—it's simply thieving of everything by everyone from everyone.'

That was how it was: people gave all they had to get out.

Not long after the birth of the State of Israel, Ana Pauker signed a pact with the new state. It allowed Jews to leave the Communist paradise, for hard cash. The Rumanian People's Republic was in need of foreign currency. It sold Jews for so much per head, depending upon how much brain was in the head. Scientists, doctors and professors cost most.

Every night crowds waited outside the visa office. Old people and young, grandparents with babies wrapped in blankets slept on the pavement. The story was told of the stranger who saw a line of Jews that stretched from the police station to Parliament Square. 'What is this queue for?' he asked. 'Oranges.' 'But in that shop across the street they're selling oranges with no queue.' 'Ah, but we wish to eat them from the tree.'

The Government wanted to keep 'Operation Israel' secret. Special trains left from out-of-the-way stations and obscure sidings. None went from Bucharest Central. Only after dark, from remote suburbs. But each one was packed.

Night after night, we went to see off friends with tears in our eyes.

'Next year in Jerusalem!' The cry has echoed from ghettos and synagogues for centuries. To know that this time it was true brought such joy to my heart.

In the Book of Exodus it says that 'a mixed multitude' left Egypt with the Jews. And this proved again true. Many fled from Communisim with forged exit visas, pretending to be Jews. A multitude of strangers found a refuge with the departing crowds.

A high-ranking police officer told me, 'If you give me money and help in getting a visa, as a Jew, to leave the country, I can get your husband out of jail.' A friend I trusted said that this policeman could do what he promised. The offer gave me new hope. I told Mihai.

He was by that time ten years old. Tall for his age, and with sharp cheekbones and questioning eyes. At school he was learning to be the son of a 'social outcast'. It was a hard lesson. Mihai adored his father. It was not easy to explain why he should be taken from us and locked in prison. Sometimes I trembled for Mihai's faith. When I told him about the new hope, he was excited. Next morning, his elation had gone. He said:

'Mummy, I had a dream. I saw our neighbour holding out his hat and begging two birds to come into it. They fluttered around —and then they flew away.'

He said it meant that nothing would come of our scheme. A few days later we heard that the policeman who had offered to help us was himself under arrest. Mihai has had many premonitions in dreams.

Every day more people vanished. Once a number of well-known prisoners were released. They came home in ambulances and showed their bruises and scars and told of the tortures they had suffered. When the required impression had been made, all were re-arrested.

I wept to think that Richard might be at that moment bearing torture. I feared that he might break, and betray his friends.

He had promised that he would die rather than do so, but who can say how much a man can bear? St. Peter promised that he would not deny Christ.

If Richard died I knew we would meet in the next life. We had agreed to wait for each other at one of the twelve gates of Heaven. We had decided that our rendezvous would be at the Benjamin Gate. Jesus made an appointment like this with his disciples, to meet them after his death, in Galilee. And He kept it.

My Arrest

One evening in August I came home late. Mihai was staying with friends in the country so I was free to go my rounds. We women did pastoral work for the church in secret, under the guise of nurses or charwomen. And the hours were long. It was almost 11 p.m. when I finished cleaning the house and caring for the six children of a man whose wife was in hospital. He'd had land and money, but both had been confiscated by the Communists.

I came home through streets that were being decorated with Red flags for the annual celebration of the Red Army's arrival. I was too tired to eat and planned to go straight to bed.

But I found my cousin, who was staying with us while waiting to leave for Israel, very alarmed. A suspicious visitor had called.

'He said he came from the Living Space Office,' my relative told me. 'Talked about putting more people in the flat. But I'm sure what he really wanted to know was how many exits you have apart from the front door.'

I knew then what to expect. A police raid. I wasn't surprised. Just too exhausted, almost, to care. Mihai was in God's good hands. That was what mattered. I went to sleep, commending my husband, my son and all my loved ones to God's care.

At 5 a.m. they hammered on the door. My cousin opened. I heard shouting. Boots clattering on the stairs.

'What's your name?'

'Hitler,' stuttered my cousin, who did indeed have that distressing name.

'What! Arrest him!'

My poor cousin tried to explain. His mother had married an Orthodox Jew with beard and curls called Haskel Hitler, who refused to change his name, despite the terrible complications it produced. But the farce ended. They realized he had no connection with his namesake. They pushed him aside and shoved their way into the bedroom.

I was sharing it with a woman guest, a dear sister in the faith. We sat up in bed, clutching the clothes round us.

'Sabina Wurmbrand?' shouted a bull-necked man in charge, who never stopped shouting as long as he was in the flat. 'We know you're hiding arms here. Show us where they are—now!'

Before I could argue they were pulling out trunks, opening cupboards, emptying drawers on the floor. A shelf of books crashed down. My friend sprang from the bed to retrieve them.

'Never mind that! Get your clothes on.'

We had to dress in front of six men. They trampled over our things. From time to time they shouted out, as if to encourage each other to keep up the meaningless search.

'So you won't tell us where the arms are hidden!'

'We'll tear this place apart!'

I said, 'The only weapon we have in this house is here.' And picked up the Bible from under their feet.

Bull-neck roared, 'You're coming with us to make a full statement about those arms!'

I laid the Bible on the table and said, 'Please allow us a few moments to pray. Then I'll go with you.'

They stood gaping while my friend and I prayed together. I embraced my cousin and his mother.

'Next year in Jerusalem!'

Their eyes were full of tears.

'*Leshana haba be-Jerushalaim!*' they answered.

As they led me out, the last thing I did was to snatch up a little parcel from the sideboard. It contained a pair of stockings and underwear. A day or two before a girl from our church had made me the gift. I'd put it aside, unopened, never guessing that it would be the most important thing I took with me to prison.

I was pushed into the back of an Oldsmobile. Blacked-out motor-cycle goggles went over my eyes so that I wouldn't know where we were going. The drive was brief. Minutes later I was lifted out and swept across the pavement. My feet hardly touched the stairs as I was dragged upwards like a bound sheep. I bruised my shins as they hustled me round a corner. The goggles came off. There was a push in the small of the back. A door slammed behind me.

I was in a long bare room crowded with women. They sat on benches, on the floor. The door kept opening to admit more. I saw the wife of a liberal politician. A society woman whose features I'd seen in the newspapers. An actress in a thin low-cut dress. A lady-in-waiting from the Palace.

We were the dangerous, the 'socially rotten' elements of Rumania.

By evening several hundred women were crammed into the

room. The round-up was on national scale for the anniversary of August 23rd Freedom Day, the Communists called it. The day of the capitulation before Russia.

We huddled together under a single ceiling bulb. No food or drink came.

Each woman was cocooned in her own fears.

How long would it last? What would happen to our children? Mihai had lost his dear father. Now his mother was taken from him. Our home and everything it held would be confiscated. He'd be thrown on the kindness of friends, who were themselves in danger. As I prayed for him, a woman leapt up and beat on the door with her fists. She screamed:

'My children! My children!'

Others cried out for husbands, lovers, sons. A woman beside me collapsed in hysterics. Another was sick. The single toilet overflowed. The door opened only to admit more women, who shouted indignantly at the guards: 'But I've done nothing!'

The actress confided, 'I'll be released. You'll see!'

They thought their innocence would save them! As if this were not 1950, and a Communist State.

All of them had been told, 'You're wanted by the police to make a statement.' Some passed ten years making their statements.

Next morning we heard brass bands. The Freedom Day parade (attendance compulsory) was on. The windows were painted over. But if the parade was passing below we must be in the police lock-up in Bucharest's main street, which was called Victory Street.

Thousands of boots tramped by. Slogans were rythmically chanted:

'AUGUST 23rd HAS BROUGHT US FREEDOM.'

One was a rhyming jingle:

'DEATH TO THE THIEVES AND TRAITORS IN PRISON!'

'Shame!' murmured the socially-rotten elements.

The new national anthem was roared out in march time:

'BROKEN CHAINS REMAIN BEHIND US ...'

Never in the history of Rumania had so many people been in chains.

How the hours dragged, with nothing to do but wait. The day and the night I passed in that room were timeless, a taste of hell which never ends.

At last guards brought black bread and watery soup in heavy metal cans.

Next day a sergeant began calling out names. Were they letting us out?

My name was on the first list. Again the blacked-out goggles. I was put in a van and taken to what I learnt later was Secret Police headquarters, on Rahova Street.

Before pushing me into a small cell, a woman guard asked those already inside: 'Any of you know this woman?'

Nobody did. I was allowed to join them. The policy was never to put friends together. You were permitted no comfort. You were to be alone. During the interrogation stage you never stayed long enough in one cell to make a friend you could trust. Each new arrival could be an informer, planted to spy on prisoners.

Apart from a young medical student, my companions were peasant women, arrested at random. Terror was being used to enforce collectivization on the land. Fierce battles had been fought with officials sent to seize farm property. An unknown number of peasants were executed at drumhead trials, and nearly 100,000 had been given jail sentences.

Days later I was moved into solitary confinement. My cell contained only an iron cot. No bucket—the first thing a prisoner looks for. How I mourned the missing bucket. It meant more than food or warmth or light. Stomach upsets caused by the food, 'interrogation fright' on hearing your name called meant nothing to the guards. You were let out at 5 a.m., 3 p.m. and at 10 p.m.

High in the wall was a small window, secured from outside with an iron grill. The cell was damp and chill, even in August. How glad I was of my light summer coat and those woollen stockings.

How long before they called me? What would they ask? I remembered past troubles with the police: waiting for Richard in the cafe across the road from the station; the fear that he'd never leave. He'd said, 'Hell is to sit in darkness remembering past sins.' I had so many, and now they were vivid before my eyes.

The warder who brought food—boiled oats—was an older man. They were better than the young ones. Often he said a sympathetic word.

'Thicker today!' he murmured, winking at the gruel. Plainly he was one of those who still thought the Americans might come and turn the situation on its head.

Once he offered to smuggle out a letter. But I suspected it might be used to trap friends who received it.

He whispered a hoarse story of how he had asked an officer: 'Why are there so many people in jail?' 'Mind your business, or there'll be one more,' said the officer.

The warder grinned delightedly. 'And what happened? Next day they arrested *him*! Nobody knows why. Never saw him again! Ah, them that judge today, tomorrow will be judged!'

At night I lay trying to block my ears against the crash of steel doors, the scrape of studded boots, the guards' obscenities.

Doors were unlocked near me. Each time I thought: mine next. But it was several claustrophobic days before they came.

The cell door opened.

'Turn your back!'

Goggles snapped over my eyes. I felt black panic as they pulled me by the arms along passages. Left, right, left right. Round corners. Were they going to shoot me? To die without warning in the darkness!

We stopped. The goggles came off. I stood blinded by sunshine in a big room. Guided by the warder, I sat in a real chair and steadied myself with a hand on a real desk. A big oak desk stained with ink. Behind it sat two men wearing the blue-tabbed uniforms of the Secret Police. A heavy middle-aged major cultivating a moustache. A young fair-haired lieutenant who had been present at the raid on my flat. The lieutenant stared at me with a curious knowingness. He had clear blue eyes. His blond good looks reminded me of someone. Unaccountably, he smiled.

I shivered. Then I realized: he looked like the boy I'd loved so many years before in Paris. The resemblance was extraordinary.

I expected to hear that some charge had been made against me. But the major said, with weary patience: 'You know, Mrs. Wurmbrand what your offence against the state has been. Now you will write for us a detailed statement about it.'

'But what should I write? I don't know why you've brought me here.'

'You know very well,' he said. On a side table were pen and paper. I wrote a few lines saying that I had no idea why I'd been arrested. He glanced at them, nodded, and asked for the next prisoner.

All the way back to the cell the guard shouted and pushed me, blindfolded, into walls. When the door shut behind me I saw his eye through the small spyhole.

'Now you'll sit and think until you write what the officer told you! Or you'll get the treatment!'

Torture. Bullying, mockery, humiliation. Mental torture to soften you up for interrogation. Tape-recorded voices screaming. A firing-squad volley on loudspeakers in the corridors. The torture of being a mother parted from her child.

Physical torture. I'd seen the results of what they did in these cells.

The problem of what to tell interrogators was not new. We'd

faced it in Nazi times. Some believed that you must not lie—
even to save others. They acted on the belief. But love is higher
than truth. I don't tell a thief where money is kept in the house.
A doctor is right to deceive a madman who has a gun, so that
he may be disarmed. Communist hatred is unreasoning madness. We have a duty to mislead those whose sole aim is to
destroy.

The major and his assistant were waiting for me next day.
He had a string of questions on a pad which he ticked off in
turn. Their aim was to extract information that could be used
against Richard.

I remember one thing the major said: 'Every man has his weak
point.' And the lieutenant turned his sculptured blonde head
and gave his knowing smile.

They would be trying to find Richard's weaknesses. His interrogation would be ruthless. The major was a long time coming to
the point. He made a little speech about the blessings of Communism. He assured me that they were my friends. Pastor Wurmbrand's friends, too. They wished to release him, but needed
some information first. He asked what Richard had said on this
or that occasion to colleagues.

I replied that we discussed religion, never politics.

The major smiled, very sincerely, and said, 'Mrs. Wurmbrand,
the Bible is full of politics. Prophets who rebelled and complained
against Egyptian rule. Jesus spoke out against the ruling class of
his day. If your husband is a Christian he must have clear
views about the Government.'

'My husband doesn't interest himself in politics.'

'Yet he had an audience with King Michael before the king
left the country. Why?'

'It was not secret. The king gave audiences to many people.'

'How long did this audience last?'

'About two hours.'

'And in all that time there was no reference to politics?'

'As I say, my husband isn't interested in politics.'

'Well, what *did* he talk about?'

'About the Gospel.'

'And what did the king say?'

'He was in favour of it.'

The lieutenant gave a little snort of laughter and quickly put
his hand to his mouth. From the look in the major's eye, I thought
he was due for a resounding reprimand later.

The major's smile became more sincere than ever.

'Now, Mrs. Wurmbrand. You're a very intelligent woman. I

can't understand your attitude. You and your husband are Jews.
We Communists saved you from the Nazis. You should be grateful.
You should be on our side!'

His eyes narrowed. He spoke more slowly.

'Your husband is accused of counter-revolutionary activities.
He could be shot. His colleagues have spoken. They support the
charge against him.'

My heart turned over. He was lying, of course. And watching
for my reaction. I tried to look blank. He continued:

'They may just be trying to save themselves. Perhaps *they* are
the real counter-revolutionaries. We can't judge, unless you tell
us everything that people working with the mission used to say.
Everything. Speak out, denounce the real counter-revolutionaries
and your husband will be free tomorrow.'

The major turned and smiled at his aide, inviting him to share
in the happy vision. His pupil said encouragingly: 'You could
go home to your family.'

How sweet that thought was. I put it away, and said: 'I
know nothing.'

Back in the cell at night, nursing bruises won from the guard,
I felt my feet against the end of the cot and thought: 'Poor
Richard, his feet will be hanging over the end.' He was so tall.

What were they doing to him now? At one moment I was
ready to say anything to be safe with him again; the next, I
trembled. I wanted him to live and I wanted him to resist, and
the two wishes struggled within me.

The major looked tired, his eyes were slightly bleary, but in
them there was also a glint of triumph. He drummed his fingers
impatiently on the desk-top. The questioning this time centred
on the Nazis. What Germans did I know? What were our connections with them? Was I aware that people were being shot
for harbouring Nazis? Why had I hidden officers in my home?

I could truthfully say that I had not hidden Nazis. To me they
had been simply men. They were in need, and we tried to help
them whatever their beliefs, as we'd helped persecuted Jews
and gypsies earlier.

'You deny the charge then. Well, we have a surprise for you.'

He pressed a buzzer under his desk. Guards brought in a man
who I recognized at once: Stefanescu had been with us in 1945.
He knew everything that we had done for the Germans.

He shuffled forward. Nervous eyes flickered from the major
to his aide, to me. He swallowed, and his eyes closed, shutting
out the world.

'Now, Stefanescu,' said the major, lighting a cheroot. 'Tell us how the Wurmbrands kept Nazis in their home. You know this woman, of course?'

'No.'

'What!'

'I've never seen her.

'You're lying!'

'No, sir.'

Stefanescu closed his eyes again.

The major shouted and ranted. He put his face an inch from Stefanescu's and bawled at the top of his lungs.

Dazed Stefanescu kept on repeating that he didn't know me.

Yet he knew me well. And he had no good intentions towards me. God had blinded him for that moment.

Finally, the major impatiently told the guards to take him away. He looked at me with speculative eyes, stubbing out the cheroot. After all, he seemed to be thinking, it's absurd: a Jewess, who loses all her family in Nazi pogroms, hiding Nazis in her cellar. Risking her husband's life as well as her own. He switched to asking me about our work in the Red Army.

I managed to dodge the dangerous questions.

Lying awake in the cell later I remembered the big gangly Red Army boys who'd once filled the flat. With what wonderful simplicity they had heard the word of God. One had danced around the room with joy when Richard told him that on the third day Christ had risen from the dead.

The day's events encouraged me. I had a strong feeling of the divine presence in my solitary cell. God had given me the strength and wit to fend off questions about printing Russian Gospels and receiving relief funds. Perhaps the worst was over.

A piece of chalky plaster had worked loose from the wall. I picked it up and drew on the dark blanket a big cross, in thankfulness.

The new interrogator was a big sweating man with a bald head. I stood a long time before the ink-stained desk while he read documents in a brown file.

The blond lieutenant was making notes from a thick text-book. Now and again he looked up at me, slyly. As if he knew something I didn't know. The look on his handsome face was amused and excited like a child in a cinema who knows that something splendidly nasty is going to happen in the next minute.

The bald interrogator's arms were covered in thick hair. At last he began. The questions were all personal. My family, friends, trips abroad. Days as a student in Paris. He was warm and friendly. Smooth.

'And now,' he said, in the nondescript official voice of one giving instructions about filling up a form, 'we want you to write down your sexual history.'

I was slow to understand. He explained patiently.

'Your sexual history. You have one, I suppose? Your first experience. The first boy you went with. How he fondled you. How you returned his kisses. What happened next. Did he possess you on the spot, and which spot? Or was that left to the next one who came along? Tell us about *his* embraces. Compare the two. Or three. Continue with your other lovers. We want a complete account, blow by blow, so to speak.'

The polite calm tone was like a slap in the face.

The lieutenant was looking at me. His tongue passed over his lips until it found a small red sore at the side of his mouth.

'Write it all down. We want every detail. I'm sure there are plenty.'

I tried to keep calm.

'You have no right to ask such a thing. You may accuse me of being a counter-revolutionary or what you like, but this isn't a court of morals.'

The hairy fingers tapped the desk-top.

'This is whatever we choose to make it. The story is spread that you are some kind of saint. We think otherwise. We *know* otherwise. Now we mean to show in your true colours.'

He stared at me, unblinking.

'As a whore,' said the lieutenant.

'I shan't do as you ask, of course.'

'We'll see about that!'

The bald interrogator blazed, firing obscene questions at me. A stream of four-letter words poured out of his mouth. He punctuated questions by slapping a meaty palm on the desk.

I was soaked in sweat. My head swam. I thought I might faint. I kept refusing to write.

After an hour he stopped. The lieutenant by then had gone back to his book. They'd done all this before, it was a bore.

'Time is on our side,' said the bald interrogator.

He had saved up a last twist of the knife.

'Your husband has already confessed to being a traitor and a spy. You're on your way to the rubbish heap.' He came round from behind the desk and breathed in my face. 'But you won't leave this place without telling us the facts about your sex life.'

He glowered at me for a long moment.

I was trembling, convulsively.

Back to the cell, along sour-smelling corridors. The goggles came off a moment before they pushed me inside, and for the first time I saw the number above the door.

Seven.

I was in Cell 7. The holy number. Number of the days of creation. The seven-branched candlestick.

I lay on the cot and sobbed. After a while I grew calmer. My body lay there in the darkness, but my spirit rose and passed the bounds of prison.

I remembered the words, 'We are crucified with Christ.' If a time came when I had to say, 'It is finished,' I wanted to give only last words of love to parents and friends and the thief near me, like Jesus. God was with me in my affliction.

'Get up!'

Mielu, the red-faced head warder, was in the doorway. I rose and faced the wall.

'It's not a hotel here. If everyone lay around putting on fat they'd be fighting to get in. You're going to learn what prison's for.'

Mielu means in Rumanian 'Lamb' but he was not a lamb. Besides the regular morning inspection he prowled corridors making snap checks.

'Turn to face me. Anything to report?'

'Can I have a spoon to eat the soup?'

'If you want to speak to me keep your mouth shut.'

He cackled at his own joke. It had made him well-known in Rumanian prisons. They said he'd sold bootlaces in cafes before the war. He owed his present position to efficiency as an informer. He had to prove his importance to everyone, on every occasion.

At midday a greasy soup arrived. You had to drink it all. That was the rule. Hunger-strikers were forcibly fed. Two guards held you while a third poured it into your mouth. When this happened you got a soup that was slightly richer than usual: Egg-yolk and sugar was added to keep the 'patient's' strength up. It contained, they said, as much nutrition as three days' of the normal brew. So people refused to eat in the hope of being forcibly fed!

I smiled, remembering how fastidious Richard had been about his food when we first married. How glad he'd be to return to home-cooking now!

Both of us knew by heart passages from the second book of Moses, Exodus. It tells how the children of Israel came out of slavery in Egypt. God delivered them.

Every night in Cell 7 I recited these verses. I knew that Richard, somewhere, was doing the same. God would deliver us.

'Ready to answer my questions now?' Hairy-fingers came close, giving off a smell of alcohol and tobacco. 'Are we to be edified by the sex-life of a saint?'

The blond lieutenant glanced at his older colleague, looking a little shocked at this coarse opening.

He had his textbook and notepad again. I suppose he was one of the new 'proletarian leaders'. A bright lad off the factory floor. Trying to pass exams and win promotion while the interrogation mill ground on around him.

The bald interrogator ran through his routine of obscene questions for twenty minutes. I kept repeating that he had no right to ask such things. Then he paused and lit a cigarette. I imagined the lieutenant would take over. But when the older man walked out the young officer went on studying.

I stared at him, trembling a little. My eyes wouldn't focus properly and my knees felt as if they might give out. I hadn't slept.

How he reminded me of the boy in Paris, long ago. Where was he now? Both were handsome. But how many things a beautiful face can hide. Now and again he looked up from his book and gave that knowing smile. As if he knew the answers to all his coarse colleague's questions.

I stood for three hours. It was a fairly common practice. To avoid wasting their free time, they called a prisoner and let her stand there while they studied. They signed a receipt when the prisoner arrived, another when she left. That officially accounted for their time.

The older man returned and grilled me for another hour. Who I'd slept with, what I did with them.

I was very tired. Exhaustion came in black waves. But I found the strength to say: 'I will not tell you what you want.' I could give him one piece of information, though—the worst 'sexual history' will not prevent a person becoming a great saint if God wills it. Mary Magdalene was a harlot once. But she will be revered when we have been long forgotten.

The interrogator grunted an obscenity. 'Take her away,' he said.

The blond lieutenant yawned and stretched as I was led out.

Days later I moved back to a communal cell. It was like an icebox. Winter was approaching now. My summer coat and wool stockings were the envy of the cell. I was rich!

I tried to share my riches. The coat served others as a blanket, a dressing-gown, as gala wear for interrogations. I offered the stockings to a girl wearing only a thin cotton dress. Tears ran unchecked down her white face.

The four other women in this cell, to my astonishment, were wearing full evening dress. Only it was not very full. Low-cut, sleeveless gowns of white satin that trail on the filthy cement floor are not ideal prison dress.

'We'd been to see a film at the American Embassy,' one of them told me. 'It was about polar bears. On the way home in a taxi we were stopped and pulled out into the street. They took us to Secret Police headquarters. "We know everything. You're American spies!" they said.'

Interrogated for days on end, starved and kept without sleep, they denied the charges. Now they were awaiting trial. The elegant dresses were reduced to rags. Strips had been torn from them for handkerchiefs and towels and other needs.

Each woman in turn handled my coat with delighted cries. It might have been a mink stole.

'Would you like to wear it at your next interrogation?'

'Oh, that *is* kind. I feel so naked with bare shoulders before those beasts. It'll give me courage.'

The door opened sharply and all our hearts jumped.

'You,' said the guard. They could never pronounce my name Like many other Jewish names, Wurmbrand is of German origin, and the 'W' sound baffled them.

'Put the goggles on.'

The blind-march along the smelly corridors began.

I entered a room full of men's voices. A silence fell. I could feel them staring at me. It was eerie. Hearing nothing, blindfold, aware of the eyes on me. What now?

'Take the goggles off!'

Bright lights dazzled me. The new, long interrogation room had no windows. It seemed to be underground. Behind a long table sat ten uniformed officers, including the three I'd already met. They stared at me.

'Do you know what has happened to your husband?'

'But don't you know?' I said. 'You should be telling me!'

'Sit down,' said the major with the moustache. 'If you co-operate and answer all our questions, we may allow you to see him.'

I really believed they might. We'd committed no crime. Perhaps he'd been tried, acquitted. How naïve I was in those days.

They had batches of photographs spread out on the desk. Men and women. A sergeant held them up, one by one.

'Who's this?'

'Who's this?'

'You know this man?'

'You know this man?'

Of the lot, I recognized one man. I tried to keep my eyes blank, and go on steadily saying no.

He was a dear friend. A Russian soldier, baptized in our home. It was a police full-face and profile shot, not a good one. But how he had changed! Where was he now? I kept on saying: No. No. No. Shaking my head.

They shouted and bullied. Questions. Questions. Some I couldn't answer. Some I wouldn't. It was a long session and I became confused by the noise and blinding light. My head whirled.

'We have methods of making you talk which you won't like. Don't try to be clever with us. It wastes our time. It wastes your life.'

The repetition, the insistence were maddening. My nerves were stretched to breaking point.

It was hours before they sent me back to the cell. I lay on the straw mattress and sobbed wildly, noisily.

'You're not allowed to cry.'

The guard stood in the doorway.

But I could not stop. My tears affected the others. They began to weep, too.

The guard, wooden-faced, turned and closed the door.

I sobbed for two hours. Then I picked myself up and tried to think. The questioning led from subject to subject and person to person. Anyone I named would be arrested and grilled in turn. I must name no names. I didn't think I could bear many more sessions like that.

But the next cross-examination was played with new tactics. The bald interrogator was alone, and smiling.

'Mrs. Wurmbrand, you're only thirty-six years old. The best years of a woman's life are before you. Why are you so obstinate? Why do you refuse to co-operate with us? You could go free tomorrow if you'd only give us the names of these traitors ...'

I didn't answer.

'Let's talk sense. Every man has his price, every woman too. D'you know the story of the man in the nightclub who asked the waiter: "How much is that blonde at the bar." "She charges 100 francs." "And that brunette." "Very special. 500 francs." "Well, how about that girl in the corner with a man." "Oh no sir, she's married to him, you couldn't have her for less than 1,000!" .

He roared at his own joke, and wiped his face with a handkerchief.

'You're an honest woman. You can raise your price. Judas was a fool to sell his boss for thirty pieces of silver. He could have held out for 300. Tell us what you want? Freedom for you and your husband? A good parish for him? We'd look after your family. You could be very valuable to us. Well?'

When he had finished talking there was a silence in the room. At last I broke it.

'Thanks, but I've sold myself already. The Son of God was tortured and gave his life for me. Through him I can reach heaven. Can you offer a higher price than that?'

The bald man suddenly looked very tired. His voice was hoarse, frustrated. He clenched his hairy fist and I thought he might hit me. The hand went back. But he smoothed his pate and only sighed deeply.

October 23rd was our wedding anniversary. But remembering the happiness of that day made me more miserable.

Winter had come. Mihai always caught cold so easily. He slept the sleep of the young, full of small movements, and often tossed the coverlets to the floor. Who would put them back?

Sometimes Mihai was wilful. Once we'd gone for a picnic, and he'd drunk from a stagnant stream although I told him not to. He had a bad throat for weeks. Then he'd climbed a tree and fallen out. He nearly died that time. Who would stop him taking risks now? There was his Aunt Suzanne, whom he loved. But she had her own troubles. A hundred doubts and anxieties pierced me every day.

In November, the prison director came personally to the cell. A small group of women were told to be ready to leave in ten minutes. No questions were allowed. Fearfully, we gathered our poor bits and pieces. We expected either to be freed or shot.

In fact, I had been sentenced to forced labour. A board simply decided, in my absence, that I should serve twenty-four months. When that time ran out a new sentence would be imposed. I was one of many thousands of prisoners classed as 'administrative'. We went without benefit of trial to the slave camps. At that time we did not know we had been sentenced.

They were an essential part of the economy now. The camps had gone up all over the country. 'Saboteurs' who failed to fulfil worknorms, gypsies, criminals, priests, prostitutes, wealthy bourgeois—the whole gamut of people who failed to fit into the Communist world went there for re-education. The camps were huge, with a permanent population of 200,000. Men, women and children. Their ages ranged from twelve years to seventy and over. By such methods 'socialist reconstruction' went forward in all the satellite countries.

The State did what it liked and published what it liked. No word appeared in the newspaper about trials and sentences.

Only congratulations to the Government in creating jobs for all. What marvels it was doing. So unlike the West, where millions were unemployed.

Prominent people in the West pointed to Rumania as an example of a country which had satisfactorily solved its unemployment problems.

Before partaking in this satisfactory solution, I was moved to a transit prison, Jilava, the most feared jail in the country.

Jilava

When the truck dipped suddenly and went down a ramp all the women squealed. The light cut out. There was a hollow clang of steel. We stopped, waiting in uneasy silence for orders.

'Take the goggles off!'

It was a big underground basement without windows. Walls shiny with damp. Greasy stone floors. Uniformed women guards milled about. A squat muscular figure with ginger hair wagged a finger and warned:

'I'm Sergeant Aspra*, hard by name and hard by nature. Don't you forget it.'

She sat down with a colleague, as attractive as herself, behind a trestle table. A clerk was entering names in a ledger.

'All superfluous articles of clothing,' declaimed raucous Aspra, 'are deposited on joining this establishment. So get out of your clothes.'

They took away my summer coat. But left the thin dress, the stockings, now full of holes. An inventory was made. Hours later we tramped along dark passages, vaulted and arched. A smell of decay hung on the humid air. Behind steel grilles stood security troops in khaki forage caps.

I wasn't wholly a stranger to Jilava. It was a fort built in the last century. The cells were deep underground. I'd come here when mass arrests started, with a girl who thought a friend was among the inmates. They ran a finger through the files and said they had no trace of him.

I made the same eight-mile journey from Bucharest after Richard disappeared. I filled in long forms and waited long hours, to be told that nothing was known about him.

Once two fifteen-year-old schoolgirls had shared our cell in the interrogation centre. They had joined a secret patriotic group. 'God help you if you ever get to know what it's like at Jilava in Cell Four,' whispered the elder girl.

Sergeant Aspra unlocked a heavy door crossed with iron bars.

'This lot for Cell 4!'

*Aspra—in Romanian, 'harsh'.

It was the middle of the morning, but the cell was almost dark. A weak electric bulb hung from the ceiling. Two long tiers of wooden bunks lined the sides of a high vaulted room. A narrow corridor ran down the middle. At the far end was a small window, painted over and barred.

Dozens of eyes stared down at me.

'I'm Viorica, your room-chief,' said a voice. A hand waved. 'Give her the end place.'

At the darkest end of the cell stood one lavatory bucket, beside an open drain. The bunk given to me was directly above it. The bucket was shared by fifty women, most of them with bowel trouble from the foul food.

It was airless and suffocatingly hot on the top tier. Sweating women lay half-naked. Wherever you turned your eyes you saw thin arms and crooked legs, fallen chests and sores. It seemed a medieval charnel house.

On some bodies there were marks and scars of torture.

Women lay on the concrete near the door, hoping to breath a little air.

'They're fools!' said a girl near me. 'The damp from the floor is more deadly.'

Jilava is a Romanian word meaning 'damp'. The fort was surrounded by a moat. There, dangling from what looked like a small gibbet was a length of railway line. When it was struck with an iron bar at 5 a.m. we rose. A queue formed for the bucket. The cell filled with talk and argument. Canteens clattered as they were filled with water for washing.

On my first morning in Jilava I heard someone singing a hymn. 'There go the nuns!'

My heart lifted. 'Nuns, here in Jilava?' I asked.

'Yes, and if Aspra hears them carolling she'll tie their hands behind their backs again. She did it for three hours last time.'

A pale girl of about eighteen stopped chewing a crust and said: 'That's nothing! In my last prison, Mislea, they tied the religious women up and put gas masks on their faces. It was horrible!'

Other nuns were held in adjoining cells. Through walls twelve feet thick women could still communciate, at great risk, by placing a tin mug against the stone to listen for tapping. The sound was amplified and could be plainly heard. But one had to watch constantly for guards, who put their eye to the spyhole.

Messages were passed in a kind of prison morse. We learnt that 200 women lived in the four cells of our wing. And up to 3,000 men elsewhere. In a fortress intended for 600!

People learn what it means to be on this earth with nothing to do when they enter prison. Not to wash, or sew, or work. Women talked with longing about cooking and cleaning. How they would like to bake a cake for their children, then go round the house with a duster, and clean the windows, and scrub the tables. We had nothing even to look at. Time did not pass. It stood still.

'When I think how I used to complain about being overworked,' said my neighbour. 'I must have been mad!'

A mother understands when the children leave home what a joy working for them was, what wretchedness it is to have nothing to do.

We stood in line at 11 a.m. for soup. Each woman received a slice of black bread. Calmed by the thought of food to come, they waited quietly.

The moment the steaming keg was out of the cell, quarrels flared. Women fought over a piece of bread which they thought was bigger than its neighbours. It began always in the same way, 'You bitch, you know it was my turn for first today.' Insults were screamed. The cell rang with a hideous caterwauling.

The door burst open. Guards rushed in, striking out with sticks. Aspra bellowed: 'We're too good to you, you *** If this goes on, you'll starve tomorrow!'

Spilled soup lay in pools on the floor. Sobbing came from dark bunks. When the guards had gone, with a crash of the door, uproar broke loose. Fifty women shouted the rights and wrongs, until Aspra came in again, trumpeting. 'There'll be no more food today, or tomorrow either!'

When they'd gone, recriminations were hissed and muttered.

The girl next to me touched my arm.

'You poor thing. You didn't eat.'

'Never mind, it wasn't very appetizing.'

'It's the rotten carrots. The State vegetable trust dumped 300 tons here. Nobody would buy them even for pigs. We've been swallowing it for weeks. Look—my skin is quite yellow. We call it "Carrotitis"!'

Her name was Elena, she said.

'A big masterful woman peered at me.'

'And who are you? Why are you here?' she demanded. 'You haven't said a word since you arrived.'

I told them my name, and that I was a pastor's wife.

'Religious, eh? Know any Bible stories?' asked a grey-haired peasant woman.

'Yes, tell us something,' came other voices. 'It's so boring here.'
But the masculine woman became still more hostile.

'You'll turn this place into a vicarage.'

And she walked off, stiff with rage.

'Don't mind Elsa Gavriloiu,' said Elena. 'She's an old Party
member. Ever so grateful for the chance she's been given to
study her ideological errors in Jilava re-educational institute!'

The other ladies laughed and were briefly comforted, until
they remembered that for the next thirty-six hours there would
be no food.

To cheer them up, I told the story of Joseph and his brethren,
which shows how the wheel of life can turn when everything
looks hopeless. While their faces were alight with interest I told
them some of the story's many meanings.

'You remember that Joseph's father gave him a coat of many
colours. In it were dark threads as well as bright ones. Both belong to life. Though his envious brothers sold him as a slave,
Joseph lived to become overseer of a great household in Egypt.

'Again the wheel turned, and he was thrown into prison. Yet
he rose to be ruler over all Egypt and saved the country from
famine. When his brothers, not recognizing him, came seeking
corn, they feared that this great lord of Egypt might steal their
asses. That's how it is often with us. We worry over little things,
and lose sight of the deep meaning which might be hidden in
them. Some sorrows are only great because we look at them from
a narrow human perspective. We cannot see to the end. Joseph in
the end was Egypt's first minister and the rescuer of the brothers
who had sold him.'

While a handful of women listened, the rest of the cell hummed
and squawked like an aviary.

I caught a glance from gingery Viorica.

'Be careful,' whispered the peasant woman. 'If Aspra hears
you talking of God in here, there'll be trouble.'

Next morning Viorica appeared in the lane between bunks.

'I know who you are!' she pointed a finger at me. 'Hours I've
been puzzling my head. Now I know.'

I thought she'd heard about my small sermon and meant to
deliver justice.

'I knew your name was familiar. I said to myself, where have
I heard that name . . .'

The others stared. I sat on the top tier like something in a
side-show.

'Yes,' said stringy Viorica, triumphantly. 'She's a preacher. The
wife of that Pastor Wurmbrand!'

The room chief proudly explained that her uncle had charge of an Orthodox church in Bucharest. He had heard Richard's speech at the Congress of Cults.

'The only one in 4,000 to stand up and speak like a man of God, when all the others cheered the Communists,' said Viorica. 'You know they sacked the Minister of Cults afterwards?'

She turned to me.

'I've been to your church. I thought the service was lovely.'

So I was the heroine of the hour. I came down from my purgatorial perch above the bucket. Viorica found me a better bunk ten feet away, which had become vacant. There she paid me a state visit.

'It's no joke being room chief,' she said. 'Another day like yesterday, dear, and I shall go mad.'

Viorica's powers were great. She recommended to Sergeant Aspra who should do the coveted laundry jobs. How humbly women begged to be allowed to wash the guards' dirty underwear. It was hard work, but infinitely preferable to sitting in the darkness and stench of Cell 4, doing nothing.

I received my first dishful of *tertch*—maize boiled in water—and looked round for something to eat it with.

'She wants a spoon!' jeered Mrs. Gavriloiu. 'Lap it up!'

I tried to eat the thin, damp-smelling gruel from the shallow tin dish. But it dribbled down my chin. To lap seemed too animal, and I gave away my morning *tertch*.

But the saving thought came, Why not wish to be humbled? Our Lord was, to the utmost. I remembered Gideon, the Biblical hero who went to fight the enemies of Israel. God told him to take as soldiers only those who lapped the water of the river with their tongues 'as a dog lappeth'—that is, those who were prepared to accept the last humiliations.

When the next meal came I lapped my food.

Later, Elena showed me how a piece of wood could be splintered off and with a fragment of broken glass carved into something resembling a spoon.

A woman from Mislea jail told how an extra ration had been given there to nursing mothers and pregnant women. 'But then it stopped.'

'What happened?'

'Half the women immediately said they were pregnant, the others were jealous and caused scenes.'

None of us was fat enough to pass as pregnant, though some were becoming swollen with hunger. Only later did we decide that starvation was official policy. It made us listless and so less troublesome. Then, when they wanted people for the labour camps the thought of better food made us keen to 'volunteer'.

Usually we gathered around the nuns' bunks.

'Put your experience with the ladies's guild to work—keep us from squabbling,' said Mrs. Stupineanu, Elena's closest ally.

A tall stately woman, she had been left a widow of some means. Until Communism came. Then, having lost everything, she survived by selling candles and sweeping out the church of which she'd once been a generous patron. She told a strange story.

One morning in church, as she stood beside her table of candles, she saw a stranger. He crossed himself, not from right to left like the Orthodox worshipper, but from left to right, in Catholic style. He bought a candle but seemed to know little Rumanian. It emerged that he was a seminarist from France, travelling in Europe. How distressed he was at what he'd seen of the persecution of the church!

Mrs. Stupineanu exercised her French, telling him more. Why, in that very church, before that very altar, police thugs had obscenely tortured the priest!

Next day Mrs. Stepineanu was arrested. The Frenchman was a Communist agent. The widow was offered the alternatives of keeping the Secret Police informed about churchgoers—who they were, what they said—or going to jail.

'I've been in Jilava a year now,' she said. At forty-six, her hair was white.

There were two Catholic sisters who glowed with calm goodness. Uncomplaining, they looked after the older women. They washed sore bodies. They sang hymns. They brought comfort where none was looked for.

'But are you allowed to sing?' I asked, at our first meeting.

'We are allowed to sing, and they are allowed to beat us,' Sister Veronica replied.

Sister Sophia, the younger of the two, showed livid bruises on her arms and neck.

'We sang very softly,' she said. 'But someone informed on us. They ran in kicking and beating and slapping. Afterwards Sergeant Aspra banned all talking. But how can you keep fifty women quiet!'

Sophia had played the organ in churches and led us in hymns. Others knew songs written for the Army of the Lord, a Salvation Army-type movement rooted in the peasantry.

Most women were of the Orthodox denomination. The illiterate countrywomen greatly feared dying without the priest's last rites. They believed that they became ghosts, unable to enter heaven. Nuns repeated the words of the funeral service, and although the women were not sure that this would work, it seemed better than nothing.

'Lord, give rest among the saints to thy servant who has fallen asleep,' the nuns chanted. 'Give her rest among green pastures.'

Green pastures. We were under the earth. Over our cells grass grew. Cows pastured there. How happy they must be in the sun with plenty to eat!

The nuns in Jilava included Mother Superiors, novices, lay sisters who did social work. Girls of eighteen, women of sixty. When the Government abolished the Greek Catholic church, monks, priests and nuns who refused to merge with the Orthodox church (which was under Communist control) were imprisoned. There they joined their Roman Catholic brethren.

Sergeant Aspra's deputy was Corporal Georgescu, a dull slow girl with a flat face and a still flatter voice. She mustered prisoners for exercise.

'When I say get outside, no one is to be last. All out together!'

Fifty women cannot use one door simultaneously. But nor could you argue with Georgescu.

'When I give an order, you obey,' she droned. Behind her back women giggled, imitating the nasal tones, until they grew quite hysterical with laughter. But they scuttled out quickly when she began to shout. It was always the old and infirm who received her blows, since they were the last in the rush.

'Don't you know what pity is!?' I cried. 'It's written that those who show no pity will have none from God in the end.'

'No, I don't know,' she crowed. 'And I don't want to know.'

But even Georgescu had a weak spot. Although she never gave permission for medical treatment as long as I was in Cell 4, she would allow women suffering from toothache to visit the dentist.

She'd suffered, too, from toothache. She knew what it was.

How wooden these women guards were!

I was used to people who loved, hated, reacted in some personal way. But these girls in uniform had been turned into puppets. If the order was to beat, they beat you. We might have been carpets. And if the order was to go slow, they ignored us. They had passed through security police schools where blind obedience was taught. Most were peasants, who had never owned anything so smart as their new uniforms, nor possessed such expensive toys as their revolvers. They ruled Rumania, and Rumania was their world.

Their demonstrations of the dictatorship of the proletariat in action were directed chiefly at teachers, professors' wives and other people of culture. It was not simply the resentment of the unlettered. They were indoctrinated with the idea that 'bourgeois intellectuals' menaced the progress of world Communism. They still believed in the Party and its promises.

To look at Sanda you would have thought her one of the saner people in the cell. She was young and clear-eyed. Tall, with long dark hair. She'd taken a science degree only a month before her arrest, she told me. Her light voice seemed to skim along over the surface of things. You never knew where it would settle next. She had been arrested because of her brother, who was with Colonel Arsenescu's freedom fighters in the mountains. Some of her remarks at university had been reported to the police.

At times, as we talked, a frightening blankness would glaze her eyes. The voice would die out in mid-sentence. I'd seen this before in prisoners and it alarmed me.

One evening, bunks around Sanda's bed were vacated.

A woman clambered up to join me on the second tier.

'Please let me sit with you,' she begged. 'Sanda's been so strange. I think she's going to have another of her turns.'

I went to look at the girl. Tears were flowing unchecked down her face. Her long fingers twisted a strand of hair, nervously.

Suddenly she cried out: 'I don't know, I don't remember, I've never seen him before ...'

Viorica ran down the gangway.

'It's too bad!' she whined. 'Why don't they take her out? As if I didn't have enough on my hands.'

Women crossed themselves in panic.

Sanda was breathing hard: her face reddened. Then, with a shrill yelp, like an animal with its leg in a trap, she leapt from the bunk. Arms flailing. Black hair flying. Striking out at anyone in her path. Seizing a pile of mess tins from the sill she hurled them at Viorica's head. They missed and smashed against the door.

Heads vanished under blankets. Screams, noisy weeping filled the air.

Two strong girls wrestled with Sandra. They struggled back and forth in the narrow lane. Viorica shouted useless advice.

'Grab her, trip her! O God, O God!'

A legion of invisible devils seemed to have poured in.

It was Sister Veronica in the end who had the presence of mind to throw a blanket over Sanda's head from behind. They tumbled on the floor. The two girls held Sanda down. Her writhings ceased.

She was still. They lifted her into a bunk, unconscious, clothes torn and wet with sweat.

Then my flesh began to crawl.

From the far side of the cell came a man's voice.

The cold, controlled voice of an interrogator. Asking questions. The same questions. Over and over again.

Trembling, I went to the other end of the cell. A pale young girl cowered in a bunk, knees up to her chest, rigid with fear.

She began, in her own voice, to give replies: 'I don't know. I wasn't there.'

Then screams: 'Please don't hit me! No please. PLEASE. AhhhhhhH!'

Her eyes were open. She was reliving, in a trance of fright, her interrogation in a secret police cell. With eerie and mechanical exactness she reproduced the interrogator's deep voice, and answered with a breathless litany of 'don't knows'. And made choking, coughing noises as if with pain from some kind of torture.

It was only the start.

For an hour the cell was filled with the appalling cacophony of cries and sobs. One woman after another succumbed. An evil force seemed to surround us in the fetid darkness. The single bulb cast mad shadows on the vaulted ceiling.

At first I felt numb with shock.

Then, like an iron that reddens in the fire I felt something swelling in my breast, and found myself living again my interrogation. The nights of fear, the wondering what they were doing with Richard, what was happening to Mihai.

I fought off madness with prayer. Not acting consciously, but letting the words well up in a stream. The nuns were doing the same.

As if it were the one safe place in hell, women crowded round our bunks. Prisoners squeezed in beside me, clasping my hands; they seemed to be fleeing from a nightmare pogrom.

The guards had experienced these tragic scenes before. They kept out.

Sanda, who had set the match to the fuse, lay sleeping, hearing nothing.

The sound of sobbing began to fade. In an hour only exhausted snuffles from the dark broke the silence. The sense of fear dissolved.

For a long time I lay awake, praying silently: 'Lord, if you have given me some influence among these women, give me also wisdom of heart to win their souls for you.'

Outside in the long corridor the steps of a guard retreated, becoming fainter, and somewhere in the recesses of the prison a great door shut with a hollow boom. I thought I could hear, in another cell, a woman coughing. Tiny, faint jungle noises echoed in the vast warren of Jilava as 3,000 souls tried to sleep and forget.

Next morning I came face to face with Elsa Gavriloiu, the old Party member. She was rumoured to be a former Secret Police officer, who had fallen from grace. Many victims of Party purges were now entering the prisons.

Elsa stuck out her large jaw at me.

'Start that preaching in here again and I'll hammer on the door until the guard comes.'

I said, 'Elsa, do you still believe in the Party?'

'Certainly. I haven't changed my beliefs. My arrest was all a mistake.'

'Nor has my arrest altered my faith. In fact, it's stronger. I want to tell people what a friend they have in Jesus.'

'You'll get the whole cell punished. I don't intend to suffer for you and your God. Anyway, he hasn't helped you much.'

'This God you so dislike,' I wondered. 'What sort of being is he? If you say "I don't like Jack" you know what type of character Jack has. What is your idea of God?'

'Ha!' She relished the chance for a textbook reply. God was the fanatic who wouldn't let science tell the truth. The patron of the exploiters of the proletariat. With the money they squeezed they built churches to Him. He blesses weapons of destruction on both sides.

I said, 'What you call God is certainly very unlovable. The God I love is another. He shared the poverty of the workers. He was brought up among the oppressed. He fed the hungry and healed the sick. He teaches love. He died for us . . .'

'Love!' Her voice cracked. 'What good is that? To me, anyway. I tell you, I'm all hate! If you knew how I loathed those treacherous comrades who put me here. I wish them in hell! I gave my whole life to the Party, and this is what they do to me.' She bowed her head. There was a hint of a tear in her eye. It didn't seem that there was anything I could do at that moment.

'Praying? Forgive them, Father?' She hissed the words. 'I don't accept forgiveness, it's lies.' She began to weep.

'It's all the same,' she sobbed. 'If the Yanks come, I'll be hanged. If the Communists stay, I'm stuck in jail. Forgiveness!'

The tears ran. After a while she sat up and wiped her grey face with an edge of her skirt. Then she began to look at me with a speculative glance.

'Sabina Wurmbrand, you're sly. I tell you to stop preaching and in five minutes you're preaching to me.'

But Mrs. Gavriloiu didn't threaten to call the guards this time.

Now I was known to everyone in Cell 4. Women came for French and German lessons.

'All Mrs. Wurmbrand's lessons start with the words "Dieu" or "Gott",' laughed Fanny Marinescu, my best pupil.

Some came to me because it passed the time. Others thought it would be useful when they were freed. With Bucharest full of Allied troops, interpreters would be in demand.

Fanny's husband and her mother were both in prison. She was twenty-five years old, quiet and shy, with cropped hair and large round eyes.

We spoke first in the courtyard, after the morning count. Sergeant Aspra and her aides were bawling the odds like bookies.

'Look, a blade of grass,' she whispered. 'Fancy it growing down here.

'How powerful life is!' She put the grass to her lips.

We became close friends. Our French lessons were conducted by writing on the soles of shoes greased with soap. Nothing was supplied in Jilava. Neither paper, nor clothes, nor linen, nor parcels from home. But periodically DDT was dusted about. If you spread it on the soapy sole you could write fairly plainly on it with a splinter.

Sometimes we had to stop the lesson, because she was in pain. 'I don't know what it is,' she'd gasp. 'It comes in waves.'

But to see a doctor was virtually impossible. At long intervals a medical orderly might appear. Sick women mobbed her, shouting, begging for aid and drugs. The orderly allowed three or four 'urgent cases'—ones that made most trouble— to go to the infirmary.

Treatment took two forms; sulphur pills for diarrhoea; aspirins for anything else.

Then Fanny Marinescu collapsed. She was carried out on a blanket. In a few days she was back: a doctor had diagnosed intestinal tuberculosis.

'They promise that I'll be given an operation,' she whispered, trying to smile wanly.

Weeks later Fanny was moved to a prison hospital where she died.

The disease had revealed itself to be not tuberculosis, but cancer.

Later, I met Fanny Marinescu's mother in a labour camp, and had to break the news of the tragedy.

Across the gangway, in the bunk opposite mine, was Mrs. Ioanid. Her son was in the mountains with Colonel Arsenecu's *maquis*. Her two daughters were also in jail—one in Mislea, the other with us in Jilava, but in an adjoining cell.

The mother saw her daughter walking in the exercise yard. She had scratched a tiny peep-hole in the painted-out window. Anyone caught near it was immediately punished. But sixty-year-old Mrs. Ioanid was prepared to take any risk for this glimpse of her youngest child. As she gazed tears ran down her face.

Sometimes she clambered painfully up to my bunk and talked of her husband and children. She asked about Richard, who was known to many prisoners by name. How did we first meet? Was he always a pastor? A Jew converted to Christianity? Wasn't that rather rare?

'It's a long story,' I said. 'And sad and bad at times, as well as happy.'

I hadn't until now allowed myself to go far back in memory. But Mrs. Ioanid listened so quietly, sitting in the drab light, her lined face in shadow, that I seemed almost to be talking to myself.

From time to time she would murmur, 'Yes?' or make a small exclamation of surprise at what, I had to agree, was a strange story. It began with our first meeting. Richard was twenty-seven and I was four years younger.

My Conversion

I turned into a street in Bucharest where the Wurmbrands lived.
An uncle of mine was a regular caller there and I accompanied
him for the first time. I looked up at the house. There was a young
man, standing on the balcony and wearing such an angry expression that I almost turned back. Seeing my uncle, he waved
and came down. When the greetings and introductions were
over he told me bluntly why he had been looking so cross.

'My mother is nagging me to get married. She has the very
girl—an heiress with a family business, two houses and a million dowry.'

'It sounds very nice.'

'Yes, I don't mind having the business and the inheritance.'
He laughed. 'It's the girl I don't like! But mother says it's the
best way if I want us all to be rich. And I came out on the balcony
and saw you.'

He added, jokingly, 'The thought came into my mind that if
I could have a girl like you I wouldn't care about the million.'

I didn't go back to Paris. I took a job in Bucharest, and we
met every evening. Richard and I found we had everything in
common. Both of us had been poor as children, both of us were
Jews who'd put aside our religion.

Richard was an up-and-coming business man, using his keen
wits to make good money for the first time. He enjoyed spending
it and we went together to night clubs and theatres and didn't
think too much about tomorrow. Yet something made him say
one evening: 'I'm not an easy person. You would suffer a lot with
me.'

But we were too deeply in love to think of anything else.

We had a religious wedding. A wineglass was smashed on the
floor in the traditional way. It was meant to remind us of Jerusalem trodden under the feet of the Gentiles.

Happiness lasted less than a year. Then Richard developed
an annoying cough. He came back from the doctor white-faced.
It was a tuberculosis: there was a patch on one lung. He must go
into a sanatorium at once.

At that time T.B. was a lingering disease which often proved fatal. I felt as if Richard had been sentenced to death. It seemed the worst tragedy of my life, a cruel and horrible trick which was being played on me at my moment of greatest happiness.

When Richard left for the mountain sanatorium, I went to live with his mother. She was kind but many nights I cried myself to sleep.

Every fortnight I went by train to visit him. The place was beautiful. Calm, with great views across hills and valleys covered with green woods. Richard, after a time, seemed almost content there. He said: 'For the first time in my life, I'm resting.'

He seemed thankful, and grew better. But a strange change was coming over him.

'I've been thinking about the past. All the people I've harmed. My mother. And many girls you don't know about. I've thought only about myself.'

'Don't grieve about it,' I said. 'I've also lived such a life. This is youth.'

One day I found him reading a book given to him by a woman patient in the sanatorium.

'It's about the Brothers Ratisbonne,' he said. 'They founded an order to convert Jews. Others have been praying for me while I wasted my life.'

He talked about Jesus Christ. It was the greatest shock he could have given me. In Orthodox Jewish families like mine it was forbidden at that time to mention Christ's name. We had to look away when we passed a church. I'd outgrown my strict Jewish upbringing, I thought. But that Richard should even think about such things upset me terribly.

I knew all the history of Christian persecution of my people. How Jews were forcibly baptized, and how they had killed their own children and then themselves, in thousands, rather than change their religion. How they were forced to listen to Catholic Masses, and stopped their ears with wax to avoid hearing what they considered blasphemy.

And what we saw around us was not encouraging. The Orthodox church was strongly anti-semitic. So was the Lutheran. The biggest anti-semite body in the country was called the 'National Christian Defence League'. Its chief activity seemed to consist in beating Jewish students and smashing Jewish shops.

So I couldn't see what, in past or present, might persuade Richard to turn Christian. No one had ever explained to me what it was really about.

Richard grew slowly better. I tried to talk to him about the good times we'd have when he got back to Bucharest. He tried to tell me about his discovery of the New Testament, which told the life of Christ. Before, we hadn't thought of having children. Now Richard was talking about how we should bring them up.

He convalesced in a mountain village. And an uncanny thing happened there. An old man, a carpenter, passed the time of day with us. When he heard that Richard was a Jew, his eyes lit up with excitement. Putting a rough hand on his arm he made this little speech: 'I asked God to grant me one favour at the end of my life. Because Christ was a Jew, I wanted to bring a Jew to him. And since there are none here, and I cannot leave the village God must send me one. And here you are, in answer to my prayer!'

Richard was deeply moved, but my heart sank. Before we left, the carpenter gave him a worn Bible, saying, 'My wife and I have prayed for hours over this, asking for your conversion.'

Richard read and read in it.

I didn't know what to do. I was utterly dismayed. Few outsiders can guess how strong a hold anti-Christian feelings may have on a Jewish heart. Besides the historical reasons, there were nearly always personal ones. As a child I had to walk home from school past a corner where two bigger girls lay in wait to pull my hair 'because you're a dirty little Jewess'. And they were Christians. It was a game, of a kind. And then, when I grew up, the Nazi persecution of Jews in Germany began.

Richard told me that Jesus himself was a victim of injustice, but I couldn't bear to hear that forbidden name on his lips.

'I don't need him,' I said. 'You don't need him. It isn't natural. We're *Jewish*—it's another way of life!'

And when he spoke of being baptized, I quite lost my head. 'I'd rather die than see you become a Christian. It isn't natural!'

I said that if he had to have religion he could practise his own Jewish faith. And for a time he did. He went to the synagogue, but even there he talked about Christ. Then he persuaded me, frightened but also a little curious, to look inside a church.

It was full of pictures of the saints, and he showed me that half of them were Jews, as were Jesus and his holy Mother Mary. The commandments taught to every child were those of the Jewish Book of Moses. The psalms were the Jewish psalms of King David. The Old Testament was full of arguments and prophecies about Christ.

'The fact is,' said Richard as he led me around the strange, vaulted building, 'that the Christian religion is simply our Jewish faith opened to all the nations of the earth.'

Who made it possible that Jewish values, morals and wisdom

should prevail throughout the world? Should reach to so many hundreds of millions over two thousand years? Only Christ could have done it. Because of his work the Holy Book of the Jews had been translated from Hebrew into a thousand languages and dialects. And now the Bible was read by ignorant peasants and by the greatest scientists—Pasteur, Einstein . . .

So with patient arguments over many nights, Richard wore down my objections. I read the New Testament. I admired and loved the Saviour. But I felt in sympathy with Gandhi when he said: 'From Christianity give me Christ and you can keep all the rest.' I wanted nothing to do with his followers who had wronged my people.

Richard wouldn't have this. 'You can't accept Jesus without accepting his disciples. He would not leave them to come to you. And you can't accept the disciples without calling even Judas a friend, as Jesus did.'

In time, my intellectual objections were overcome, but I knew that the emotional ones were still there. They grew not weaker but stronger: for while my mind whispered: 'He's right', my heart, my whole upbringing were in revolt. For weeks more this internal struggle raged within me.

One evening Richard walked in from a prayer meeting at the Anglican Church Mission to the Jews. He took my hands in his and said he had 'surrendered his heart to Christ'. Soon he would be baptized.

I'd thought of myself as a tough, resilient character. But the news was more than I could bear. I shut myself alone in my room for hours. And I decided that on the day he was baptized I would kill myself.

When it came, and I was left alone, I locked my door and threw myself down on the floor, wracked with dry sobs. A terrible emptiness, a windy desert, stretched away inside me. In my desperation, I cried aloud: 'Jesus, I can't come to you, I don't want Richard to be yours, I can't bear any more!'

I shocked myself with the force of my own cry. I lay there for a long time, sobbing.

And then, slowly, I grew calmer.

Something had changed within me. Life began to flow back.

When Richard returned from baptism, which had been done in another town, I went with flowers to meet him at the station. He was so happy. And we sat up until late at night, discussing all that had happened. I saw now that I had been quietly moving towards this change with a silent force I hadn't understood, although all the while I'd thought my mind was in charge.

But if I'd given way, I wasn't yet prepared to call myself a

Christian. I was young. I wanted to go to parties and dances and cinemas. Not to sit listening to sermons in churches.

To humour me, sometimes Richard would agree. At a party we went to one Sunday evening I suddenly realized that I was not enjoying myself in the least. The noise and the drink and the smoke and the jokes grew worse. And everything about the conversation was either boring or disgusting. My thoughts were no longer there. I said to Richard, 'Can't we leave?'

To my surprise, he said it would be rude to go so early. Reading my mind, he kept me there on one pretext or another. Until I felt sick of the whole thing. Until I felt almost physically unclean.

Very late, as we were going home, I said impulsively, 'Richard, I'd like to be baptized at once!'

He smiled.

'You've waited a long time. Let's wait now until tomorrow.'

He took me next day to meet his new friends from the Anglican Mission, Pastor Adency, a saintly man, and Pastor Ellison, who also seemed to me to belong to another world. Both had given up everything for their ministry and from them I learnt a Christianity that meant sacrifice and self-renunciation.

I was overflowing with such happiness that I had to share it. On the day after my baptism I hurried to work and told a friend, a Jewish girl, never doubting that she'd be won over too. (I'd forgotten already what I'd been through myself!) But the more I said about my change of heart, the less she wished to hear.

'So now I've lost you!' she said, and turned away, weeping. We'd been very close.

It was only the first lesson.

After my conversion I had a child. We hadn't wanted children in the past, fearing that they'd interfere with our gay life. Our son Mihai was born in 1939. Already the darkest clouds were gathered over Rumania. We were in Hitler's orbit, and we knew that Jews must soon be uprooted. So everything in reason pointed against having a child. But we had Mihai. How glad we are today to have him!

Richard's mother was almost as proud as we were. On the first day she hurried to tell all the relations: 'The very image of Richard, and so intelligent!'

Richard told me, 'He's dark like you, and very beautiful. But he only cries; when will he say something clever?'

We were so happy.

* * *

By the time I had finished my story, the evening was almost

gone. Around the cell, quarrels and arguments were taking their inevitable course. Arms and gesturing hands cast an embroidery of shadows on the ceiling and the cell hummed like an angry hive, as women settled slowly in for the night.

Promises

Men's voices sounded in the corridor. Boots stamped smartly.
The great door swung open.

'Stand up!'

A posse of guards filed through the door. After them came
nine officers. They stood in a semicircle just inside the cell. Braid
glittered on their clean, well-pressed uniforms. Facing them,
the ragged band of women with long, greasy hair. No one spoke.
The officers stared at us in disgust, and one held a handkerchief
to his nose. Then they filed out again, with no word said. The
door crashed shut.

We had been inspected for the first and last time in Jilava.

Uproar! Everyone had a theory as to what it meant, for in prison
it means something if there are three beans rather than two in
the soup.

'Don't ask me how I know, dear,' Viorica told her friends.
'But the Americans have delivered an ultimatum to Moscow! I
heard it yesterday, but I didn't believe it then. Now, this is for
your ears only!'

The 'secret' was around the cell in a flash. Chattering women
in every bunk played endless variations on the theme. They
saw themselves free and acclaimed as national heroines. The
Americans were coming! If they hadn't already arrived.

It kept us happy until the door was again flung open.

'Come and get it! Carrot soup, my ladies!'

The stench of the steaming keg had preceded its arrival. But
many older women didn't stir. They were by now too weak.
This lethal diet—although we couldn't guess it then—was part of
our preparation for the labour camps. It certainly exposed the
weak ones. The 'inspection', too, was a preliminary to the move.
Our fate had been decided without reference to America.

'It's slave labour, of course,' a young teacher told us. 'But at
the Canal you get a pound and a half of bread a day. And macaroni!'

What bliss! Jilava overflowed with rumours. Every newcomer had something to add about the Canal's wonders. The

huge project, which would cost billions, had long been talked about. The Canal was to run for forty miles across the bare plains of southern Rumania, to link the Danube with the Black Sea.

Millions of tons of rock had to be blasted. Special factories were built to make the cement. Plant was hired from Russia at exorbitant fees. An army of engineers, clerks, administrators was already at work. An entire new government department had been set up, and all Rumania's economy centred on the Canal.

In the labour camps which had gone up along the route it was said that one might even receive parcels.

'Whatever you like from home!'

'Chocolate!'

Chocolate was everyone's dream.

Warm clothes were freely available, and medical attention, at the Canal.

But better than all this: at the Canal you could see your children and your husband—not merely for a brief visit, but for the whole day.

We believed all this. We thought about little else.

'But not everyone will have the right to go,' warned Viorica. 'As the political officer said to me just the other day, "in a Socialist society work is a privilege that's not for bandits".'

Overcrowding in Jilava grew worse. Cell 4 had space for thirty people. By Christmas 1950 there were eighty. You couldn't move without treading on bodies lying in the aisle. How the air stank!

We were overjoyed to be taken out, one morning, for a bath. But this happiness, like all prison delights, was short-lived. Along dark corridors we hurried, pushed and pummelled by male warders. The sudden exercise was too much for women who had lain on their backs for months, and some collapsed.

'Five minutes! Five minutes!' bellowed a young lieutenant with a gypsy face. 'Undress, shower and get out here again. And no talking! Or you'll all be punished.'

Immediately a woman screeched. And turned on the woman behind her.

'You trod on my sore heel!'

A murmured apology came.

'Perhaps you don't know who I am?'

But we all knew that: she was one of the worst informers in the cell. Calmly, although still breathless from the race along the passages, the offending woman—who was nearly seventy—replied:

'My dear, I scarcely know who I am myself. How could I know who you are?'

A frenzied shrilling rent the air. The lieutenant blew fiercely on a whistle. Red with anger, he shouted:

'No showers! Back to your cells! Move!'

And along the dark corridors, smelling of urine, guards struck out. And swore.

Back in Cell 4, we heard shouting from next door. Some were demanding revenge on the informer. Others wanted to punish the frail old lady who, it appeared, was the wife of a former National Party Leader, one of the country's greatest democrats. Poor Mrs. Mihalache! She played only an accidental role in this farce.

The truth came later—the showers didn't work. The plumbing had broken down. Yet the order had come from above: baths! How to wash so many women without water? The head warder solved the problem by arranging for the informer to create a disturbance.

Mrs. Mihalache's poignant answer spread through the jail. How could we know who we were? Our families, belongings, identities had been taken away. But does a caterpillar know that it will turn into a butterfly? Perhaps in Cell 4, cocooned in suffering, future saints were being made.

Corporal Georgescu arrived next morning with a sheet of paper in her hand. 'Everyone on this list must be ready to move at once!'

Expectant silence.

'May we know who's on the list?' Mrs. Gavriloiu dared.

'Don't give *me* orders!' She grasped Mrs. Gavriloiu's dress threateningly. 'Here!' she pushed the list at her. 'Go on, read it to them. You all make me sick!'

Georgescu read with difficulty, and the list was handwritten.

The names were read out and the group left the cell. No reason was given for their departure. Few now believed they could be going home. But nothing could be worse than Jilava!

We watched them go enviously. Taking pity, women who were leaving gave away precious odds and ends.

'Would you like this handkerchief, Sabina? I'm afraid it's not too clean.' Mrs. Ioanid offered the article that had served her as towel, table napkin and much else.

Sister Veronica, the nun, gave me a long, pleated black underskirt. 'Take it, take it!' she begged. 'I have another one and there must be ten degrees of frost outside.'

I took it. The skirt trailed on the ground, but my legs were warm. Sister Veronica kissed me cheerfully and hurried off, perhaps to her death.

And I went on waiting, day by day, for my name to be called.

I remember January 6th, 1951 I'd been lying in my bunk with my head full of memories, for it was Mihai's birthday. Richard had decided before the birth that we'd have a boy, and even when he'd arrive. One evening he said, 'Enough is enough. If he doesn't appear by 9 p.m. I'll call a taxi and take you to the hospital.' 'But I have no pangs.' 'I'll decide in this family when you have pangs!' So he did take me to hospital and when he came next morning he had a son to look at.

After a difficult birth, I was in the post-operation ward. 'How about another,' he said. 'I'd like two. But quicker this time.' And I'd smiled and said, 'Sorry—it can't be done.' But how happy we'd been. Now Mihai was eleven.

That day my name was on the list.

I was out of Cell 4 by 8 a.m. and waiting in the corridor. My light summer coat was returned. Georgescu and the guards were quite comically polite to the line of waiting women. They knew no more than we did about our fate. And perhaps we'd meet again in altered circumstances. The Americans might yet come!

All day we hung about, bitterly cold. Women from other cells joined us. At last we climbed into trucks which drove to Ghencea, a transit camp near Bucharest.

I saw barrack huts where men and women sat working. We were led across iron-hard earth, under the winter stars. What heaven! After so many months underground in Jilava, I could look up and see the moon sailing through little clouds. Friend of lovers! How often she'd obliged by hiding her face in the old days, when Richard kissed me in the street!

Ghencea was an old German army barracks, a great barbed-wire enclosed space of dilapidated wooden huts with outside lavatories. Discipline was lax. You could walk through a door and talk to people from the other huts unhindered. For a moment, unhappiness was washed from our minds. Through the clear, frosty air came cries of greeting.

'Release?!' cried a lanky girl with dark eyes, on hearing the hopeful talk of new arrivals. 'What an idea! This is the departure point for the Canal. You'll be packed off there in a few days.'

Now there was more news of the Canal. How labour camps and new towns were springing up along the route. A new deep sea harbour was being built at Tasaul. The whole Karasu Valley must be drained.

On the third day I was brought before the commandant, Captain Zaharia Ion, who had been a Party member since the Twenties.

His emaciated body moved loosely in the carapace of its grand-
iose uniform. I must have looked startled. He smiled from a skull-
like head.

'Do you know why I look like this?' he demanded. 'Because I
starved in jail under the bourgeoisie! People like you!'

I said I was sorry if he had been unjustly imprisoned. 'But I
don't belong to the bourgoisie.' He looked at me thoughtfully.

'I'll make you an offer.'

Instead of going to work on the Canal I could stay as a privileged detainee in comparative comfort at Ghencea. All I need
do was report to him in confidence on the prisoners from time to
time.

'Thank you,' I said. 'But in the Bible you can read of two
traitors, one who betrayed King David and one who betrayed
Jesus. Both hanged themselves. I don't want such an end, so I
won't become an informer.'

'Then you won't see freedom again!'

As for Captain Zaharia Ion, none of his 'bourgeois' persecutors
was as merciless as his Communist comrades proved to be, for
they arrested him on false charges later and he died in prison.
Now he has been officially 'rehabilitated'. Will this comfort the
soul in whose existence neither he nor his brutal masters believed?

In a shunting yard near Bucharest we boarded a train at last
for the Canal. The long, black 'duba' (prison wagon) was crowded
not only with 'politicals' but with thieves, street-walkers and gypsies. We were pushed through the sliding doors by ill-tempered
guards. We sat in half-darkness waiting to move. Light filtered
through small, barred windows, high up. At last we began to
creak slowly south.

Once I glimpsed a shining stretch of water. River banks of
thick green grass. I remembered the river Prut which ran near
my home town. In the woods we picked wild strawberries to eat
with sugar and cream.

It was many hours later that the train stopped and we tumbled
out, tired and aching. CERNAVODA, read a sign on the platform. The name of a small town by the Danube. The camp was
miles away. We began to march through the black, wintry night.
At last we passed through gates strung with barbed-wire, under
tall watch-towers. Searchlights played over rows of identical huts.

PART TWO

The Canal

As our group entered one of the huts at the end of the line a shout of greeting went up from the crowd gathered inside.

'Valiea! Good old Valiea!'

She ran forward to be embraced.

Valiea was a gypsy of a girl of about twenty-six, and an accomplished thief. Many gypsies stole, but Valiea's exploits were famous. She was taken under the wing of the gypsy leader, an older woman with a lovely hooked nose and torrents of jet-black hair. They found her a bed, gave her food, chattered together like starlings.

I knew no one and no one knew me. Or looked at me. It was late on Saturday evening, and they were sprawling about after the day's work. I looked around for a place, but there were already too many prisoners for the few beds. So I sat down on the floor, and at once a woman on the next bed began to tell me about her daughter. She didn't know if the girl had also been arrested, or if she'd been thrown out on the street.

'But the great thing here is that we can hope for a *vorbitor* (official permit for visits from relatives). We can even ask them to bring clothes!'

This news, the thought that I might see Mihai, kept me awake all night. I turned it over and over in my head. Towards dawn I dozed. And woke up with heart pounding. There was a scuttling and squeaking in the dark.

'Beast!' gasped the woman beside me. 'It jumped on my bed!'

Now I recognized that acrid, animal smell. Rats!

An educated voice a little further on said mildly, 'Really, the rats have more reason to consider us a nuisance than we them. They've been here longer. By some generations.'

Another said, cheerfully, 'You should save some bread for them at night. Keeps them from biting.'

On Sunday morning, after a night on the floorboards, I hoped for rest and a chance to wash and repair our clothes. It was a vain hope.

The whole female section of the camp was ruled by a woman prisoner with a long criminal record. Biddable Rina had been chosen by the camp commandant for her hatred of politicals. While the criminal prisoners lounged about, the politicals were down on their knees scrubbing and scraping the floor.

'All new arrivals will gather outside for a visit to the bath-house,' she cried.

We lined up and were marched away over the frozen mud under an escort of armed guards.

Among the educated women and well brought-up young girls were a handful of prostitutes. They squeaked and shrieked and, in the way of obscenity, gave as good as they got.

The guards laughed, and stamped their boots. Rina had wrapped her head in a coloured scarf, from which her small nose emerged like a pig's snout as, cackling, she urged them on.

The world spun round. The wet concrete floor came up to hit me. The strain of the journey, the hunger and shame made me faint. I was carried back to the hut and placed on a bed.

Now a strange thing happened. I was thrown a jacket and skirt of sacklike material in dirty grey and white stripes. My stockings were full of holes. But I still wore the long, pleated skirt given me by the nun in Jilava. With my black hair and Jewish looks, I must have had an outlandish appearance.

The politicals looked me over and decided I was not one of them. So reasoned the gypsies, I was one of *them*.

I said, 'I assure you I'm not. I can't speak your language.'

The hook-nosed old woman looked wise, and patted my arm. 'We know, dear. *We* know.' They were convinced that, for some reason of my own, I was trying to hide my race. From that time on in Cernavoda, I was an adopted gypsy.

Wherever they are, gypsies live a life apart. But in Eastern Europe, Rumania was their favourite country. They roamed about in their caravans, the men wearing their hair long and well-oiled, the women in ankle-length skirts and rich petticoats. They were strikingly beautiful and many of them stole anything they put their hands on.

The Communists sent thousands of them to prisons or to the labour camps, where they continued to steal. It was impossible to hang up an old piece of clothing or a rag. Anything, everything vanished under those capacious petticoats.

Almost alone among political prisoners at the Canal, I lost nothing.

Richard and I helped the gypsies when they poured from Nazi camps at the end of the war. Now I had my reward.

They said I'd be re-united with my husband and child and travel over many seas and lands to find happiness. I didn't expect to wait fifteen years, though.

They did a good business out of fortune-telling. Women would give their bread away for the sake of hearing that they would be released soon, that their families would prosper. The gypsies had no cards, but they foretold the future by a still older means which may go back to their time under Tamerlane and Genghis Khan. They threw grains of corn on the floor and found hopeful wonders in the pattern they made.

Being nomads, gypsies settled anywhere. Even in prison, they were like a great family. Later, when we were allowed to send postcards to relatives, I acted as their scribe—none of them could read or write—and every message had to begin: 'To all the gypsy folk, greetings!'

Sometimes furious quarrels flared among them—it is no legend that sometimes gypsy women use their babies as clubs to beat each other and do not stop until both children are dead. At other times they would dance and sing wildly to forget where they were.

In time I came to know everyone in the hut, including the street girls. Some had beautiful natures, and when they heard the call of Jesus did their best to rise above the mud into which they had been thrown by life.

Next day, early in the morning, we left the camp. A cold wind blew across the plain from the Black Sea. The guards chafed their hands as we waited to move off, surly and resentful at parting from their warm bunks. If we stirred, they worked off their feelings with blows and swearing.

At the gates, under the iron watch-towers, the leading guard shouted: 'Taking out 2,000 criminals and counter-revolutionaries!' Or whatever was the number for the day.

The bitter wind blew in our faces and tore at our clothing. The column, it seemed, was endless. I looked forward and saw only ranks of prisoners with armed guards stamping at their sides. Sometimes I dared to look back (which was forbidden) and saw the column stretching away into the distance like one single, enormous beast, an entity with a life of its own. A blind, hopeless beast, the sum of all those bodies and arms and legs, with no purpose but to toil until it dropped. I thought of the slaves in ancient times. Of my forefathers in Egypt who laboured on the Pharaonic works.

We were building an embankment, men and women together. I had to keep filling a wheelbarrow with earth. Each time the barrow was full a male prisoner had to push it 200 yards, then run with it up a sharp incline to the parapet of the dam. He tipped out the earth and ran back for more. The men's task was harder than ours, but after the first few barrow-loads I staggered whenever I tried to lift the heavy shovel of earth over the side.

Each gang had a 'brigade-chief' with several helpers to check how much work you could do. The 'norm' required could be anything up to eight cubic metres a day. If, after tremendous efforts, we fulfilled the norm it was raised next day by so many barrow-loads. If we failed to fulfil it we were punished.

The 'brigadiers' were trusted prisoners. They had special rations—even some pay. And never did a stroke of work themselves. They ruled with powers of life and death. Rina wielded hers to the full.

Talking, and all other forms of human contact were forbidden, but I risked saying a few cheerful words to my companion as I filled the barrow, and quoted the Bible. He looked at me startled—a middle-aged man who looked like a peasant. Then he seized his wheelbarrow and trundled away. Another man came, another barrow. And another. And another.

Then a fourth man said, 'Count Rakosi thanks you for your beautiful words and he wants to know who you are.'

The 'peasant' was a Hungarian aristocrat from Transylvania, a Rumanian province thickly populated with Hungarians which had been under Habsburg rule for centuries. I was so surprised that I left my spade for a moment in the earth.

'Come on! Wake up!' It was Rina's voice from twenty yards off. 'Do you want a night in the carcer?'

I began to dig with frenzied strength. The man lifted his barrow and scuttled away.

'Carcer' was a word to freeze the blood. A box six feet high and two and a half feet wide, it was a common punishment in Canal camps. There, after a day's work, you had to stand without moving the whole night. Next day you went back to work again, with a good chance if tired of being ordered back to the carcer that night for not working quickly enough.

We were given a pound of bread at midday, with some soup

and oats. It was an improvement on Jilava, but a mockery of our hopes. And on this we had to work on until the end of the day.

Looking around at our emaciated crew, I thought it was no wonder that I hadn't recognized a Count. It was hard to tell one man from the next. All were in patched and ragged clothes. All wore the same expression, in which a kind of blank longing was replaced only by fear.

Yet some had been university dons and some editors; some priests, or business men, or high civil servants. Impossible now to tell them from the thieves, pimps and pickpockets who worked beside them.

We toiled on for another four hours. Light failed, and the great column formed up for the return to camp. On the way several prisoners collapsed. One fell beside me: without a word, two of the stronger men picked him up, placed his arms around their shoulders and moved on. An old woman was borne pick-a-back, her stiff legs stood out in stockings full of holes. There was a disturbance up ahead. A man had fallen and couldn't be revived. He was dragged to the side of the road. And hoisted on to the shoulders of three grumbling shapes in the growing dusk. The wind never stopped blowing.

At the gates, the leading guard shouted again: 'Returning 2,000 bandits.'

It was dark. In the West, the sky still glowed with a reddish tint.

'Bracing breeze!' one of the guards called, cheerfully, wrapped in his greatcoat.

I was chilled to the marrow. My hands and feet were blistered. Every muscle ached and my head felt as if it was someone else's property. Tomorrow, I'd have a streaming cold.

And now we had to wait, a dark herd huddling in the wind, as the head of the column squeezed through the gates. Other columns from different work-points had converged on the entrance, causing a long delay.

When at last we got inside the hut, a squabble broke out. One of the street girls discovered that something she'd hidden beneath her mattress was gone.

'Thieving gypsies,' she cried. 'I may be a whore, but at least I keep my hands off other people's things!'

Which brought a reply from Tania, a gypsy girl, who added: 'I might have stolen, but at least I never slept with anyone but my own man.'

Lisa, a Moldavian, shrieked, 'Who's that? Your brother?' And

cackled at her sad joke. Gypsies often had to sleep in one room:
man, wife, mother, mother-in-law, sister-in-law; sometimes in the
same bed.

But Lisa was herself a murderer. She'd killed her woman-
chasing husband with a shotgun, out of jealousy.

'Don't teach me how to behave!' Tania cried. 'I can give back
what I take if I want. You who've taken a man's life, can you
give it back?'

I tried to shut my ears to this high moral argument. After
further rowdy exchanges, Tania stalked back to the thieves' corner. The others received her with cheers, which she acknowledged
with a grin.

Tall and pretty, with glistening black hair, Tania was highly
respected by her colleagues. And feared, too. The adventures
she recounted with such gusto had earned her the name Black-
Hand Tania. Anyone who offended her ran the risk of being expelled from the circle. Anyone who cheated her ran the risk of
a night in the carcer, for Tania was not above tipping off the
guards about some real or invented crime to punish an enemy.
Yet her loyalty to friends was absolute and touching. And she
was so proud of her skills. Her riotous account of half-emptying
a dress shop had the younger girls in fits of laughter. She picked
out the sharpest among them for private tuition, and showed
keen character judgement.

The girls had an almost mystical admiration for her ability.
They reported that Tania was 'always reading books and stuff'
outside prison, and had once broken into a house when the owners
were out and found herself in a library. She began reading and
became engrossed, but after a time fell asleep in an armchair
with a volume in her hand. The owners discovered her there
when they returned from the theatre. Tania herself didn't
admit to being literate, considering it bad for her reputation.

One learnt to distinguish quickly between thieves, prostitutes,
gangsters' 'molls' and so on. Years spent in a specific sin had left
deep imprints on their souls. By their tricks of speech and behaviour you knew immediately, with no questions asked, what
you were dealing with. But Tania was an independent. She was
not without nobility.

To me she would say jokingly, 'Don't believe that we thieves
are without morals. On moral grounds I am decidedly against
any theft committed by another gang than mine.'

I tried, cautiously, to knock at the door of her heart. I wanted
to understand her better. I asked if, as so many were leaving
Rumania, Jews and refugees from Communism, she wouldn't
also like to get out.

'To hell with that!' She looked at me scornfully. 'All I'm waiting for is to get out of this dump and be together with my boy
friend. They couldn't catch *him*! I'm going to show these so-
and-so Communists what we can do.' Without any restraint she
tattled on about this paragon's underworld adventure, his looks
and other abilities.

What about her parents?

'Oh, my *parents*!' As if she spoke of some worn-out pieces of
furniture. 'They're a useless pair. My mother had looks as a girl,
so she had men, too. Then she had me. Exit Dad! Whoever he
was. She ended up with a dirty old drunk who used to wallop
her every night. And lots of other kids.'

Tania pepper-and-salted her talk with so many obscenities
that after a time you ceased to hear them. It was like becoming
used to a speech defect. I pitied her. I longed to touch just one
string of her soul and start an echo there. I hated to see her cor-
rupting others with no trace of regret.

And the great lover, it turned out, was her brother-in-law. The
prostitute's gibe had been near the mark. She'd had to share a
room with six others, and a bed with her sister and the husband.
So it happened. She was twelve at the time. And had been taught
to steal from the age of five.

Another day, she burst out:

'Yes, I know—"thou shalt not steal". That's what the police
said when they beat me up, the so-and-sos. I told them, *you*
are the so-and-so thieves. You've pinched all the land, all the
houses, the whole so-and-so country. Are you telling *me* what to
do? Sitting on your fat so-and-sos in plushy offices. You ought
to try sleeping summer and winter under the bridges in Bucharest
and then come and tell me not to steal.' She laughed harshly.
'Oh, they lammed into me. I lost all my front teeth. I've got this
new plate now.' She took it out to show me.

Her eyes flashed. A few of her admirers who'd gathered around
nodded sympathy.

'Tania, you're wonderful. I'd never have the nerve,' said Joana,
a fluffy young girl who'd been doxy to a Bucharest gangster.
He'd ditched her when the police came and was now safe in
Paris.

The other girls looked at me for approval. I said:

'Tania, you have great courage. With your energy and sharp-
ness, you could do a lot better for yourself. Just because your
parents were duds, it doesn't mean that you have to be. Lots of
great men and women had useless parents, or grew up as
orphans. If you directed your mind in the right way, perhaps
you could reach greatness, too.'

'Me, famous! Doing what?' She suggested some profane possibilities. 'Don't get me wrong. I LIKE stealing. It's my life, it's what I'm born to do!'

I ventured an example. 'One very great man began life as a swindler, a racketeer. He was called Matthew. But when he met the Lord, he was so moved, so enchanted with his goodness, that he left everything he had and became Matthew the Disciple. A thief became a saint, forgiven and loved throughout the world to this day. A martyr of the church, the author of the gospel read in the whole world.'

'Disciple, saint, martyr! Where does she find all these words?' Tania mocked.

The gulf between criminal and political prisoners (all those arrested for religious motives were considered politicals) was not often bridged. It was always the convicted women who got the jobs as norm-checkers or room-chiefs, making life hell for any member of the former middle or upper classes. The thieves addressed them sarcastically as 'Madam' and found a hundred small ways to take their revenge. The politicals neither wanted nor tried to make contact with their neighbours. Standing half-way between the two groups— a gypsy-Jewish-Christian talking with love to the worst criminals in the hut and reproaching sin in ladies of high rank—I naturally earned black looks from several sides.

Cernavoda was full of famous names. A breezy society column could have been composed about their doings. In the third person, perhaps. 'Queuing for the toilet this morning, Bystander noticed Countess X chatting with former lady-in-waiting, Baroness Y, over the latest kitchen rumour that all graves of socially opprobrious personalities are to be opened and gold and jewellery removed for the benefit of the State.'

What strange meetings we saw!

One working party consisted of fascist women. Their chief was Mrs. Codreanu, wife of the Iron Guard leader who had helped to push Rumania into alliance with the Nazis. He had boasted in a book that he'd never shaken hands with a Jew, or entered a Jewish shop.

Now Mrs. Codreanu slaved for the Communists alongside Jewish women. But the prejudice was unchanged.

'That criminal Churchill!' she raged. 'A Zionist, a Jewish stooge! And Roosevelt, surely a Jew himself! It's because of them we're here today.'

The guards were ruthless to these women. Fellow-prisoners attacked them. But they had courage. Because I tried to show them understanding and love, one of them approached me:

'My friends and I have decided that when all Rumania's Jews are wiped out, dear, you and your family will be spared.'

She was surprised that I didn't receive the news with enthusiasm.

Wives of other politicians and women who'd been involved in politics themselves held long discussions on how the world should be run. One said to me, 'I've been awake all night thinking out a plan for the future—do you want to hear it?'

I wasn't given any alternative.

'First, there must be a complete military reform. All the uniforms must be royal blue with big shakoes . . .'

I said: 'Thank you very much—there's no need to develop the plan further. If all the uniforms are royal blue, that'll be just enough.'

But sometimes people who seemed foolish or downright wicked had lessons to teach. An Orthodox sister in our hut swore, told spicy stories and stole like a gypsy.

I asked, 'But think, how will you be saved?'

She laughed. 'A monk taught me how to be saved. I keep two commandments without fail. I never judge another. And I always forgive those who sin against me. So God will be obliged to forgive me, too.'

Not the best theology; but I was glad to hear it, for she really had the virtues she claimed.

In 1951 more and more Communist women began appearing in the camps and prisons. At Cernavoda I met Marioara Dragoescu, who'd been imprisoned by the old regime as a leading revolutionary. Now she was sent to forced labour by her comrades as a 'counter-revolutionary'.

But she would go on fighting for the Communist ideal. The Great Marxist Society was around the corner. In Mislea, the big women's prison, she had nursed her two-month child—then it had been taken from her and put in a State orphanage. She didn't know if she'd ever see it again.

She'd commiserated with George Cristescu, one of the Party founders, who'd served his first prison sentence for Socialism in 1907. He'd also been the first Secretary-General of the Communist Party. Now, at seventy-two, he worked alongside us in the fields from sunrise to sunset, in snow, rain and wind.

Sometimes I filled his barrow with earth. He'd hitched himself to it like a beast. It was easier to pull than to push up the slopes. I remembered something Richard said shortly before his arrest and repeated it to him: 'Under a tyranny, prison is the most honourable place to be.'

A smile lit his face. A guard shouted at him and he hurried off, yoked to his load. Next day when we were out together, I whispered: 'I'm sorry to get you into trouble with my speaking.'

'No, speak! It's like music to hear something different after so long. I've hungered to hear a gentle voice as I hunger for colour after so much grey.'

Later he told me of his disillusion. 'This Communism they practise is not the ideal I fought and suffered for. I felt it would be dishonest on my part not to protest.'

Those of us who had faith realized for the first time how rich we were. The youngest Christians and the weakest had more resources to call upon than the wealthiest old ladies and the most brilliant intellectuals.

People with good brains, education, wit, when deprived of their books and concerts, often seemed to dry up like indoor plants exposed to the winds. Heart and mind were empty.

Mrs. Nailescu, the professor's wife from Cluj, said one day: 'How happy you must be to be able to think and keep your mind busy and pray! I can't. I try to remember a poem, and in comes the guard shouting. At once my mind goes back to this everlasting camp. I can't concentrate. I can't discipline myself.'

'Society' women were often the most pitiful. Life was harder for them than for anyone. They'd lost most, in the material sense; and they had fewest inner resources to fill the gap. A rubble of old games of bridge, hats, hotels, first-nights, lost weekends and lovers rattled about in their heads like junk in the back seat of a car. Their nerves gave way first, as did their soft white hands.

After work, women came to religious prisoners and asked, begged even, to be told something of what we remembered from the Bible. The words gave hope, comfort, life.

We had no Bible. We ourselves hungered for it more than bread. How I wished I'd learnt more of it by heart! But we repeated daily those passages we knew. And at night also, when we held vigils for prayer. Other Christians, like me, had deliberately committed long passages to memory, knowing that soon their turn would come for arrest. They brought riches to prison. While others quarrelled and fought, we lay on our mattresses and used the Bible for prayer and meditation, and repeated its verses to ourselves through the long nights. We learnt what newcomers brought and taught them what we knew. So an unwritten Bible circulated through all Rumania's prisons.

Meditation goes deeper and deeper. In the first stage, what meditates is not your true self, but what you had mistakingly supposed to be yourself—that is, a conglomerate of what you know from newspapers, books and the cinema. What is You in yourself is very small. In the second stage you must put aside more and more what is not You, what is borrowed, so as to reach the final reality in You. Once you have become Yourself again, it becomes relatively easy to communicate with a person whom you love. At a certain moment, as with a writer when an idea becomes a picture in his mind, you *see* the one on whom you meditate. Jesus said: 'Blessed are the pure in heart for they shall see God,' but not only God.

I conversed often with Richard, especially during the years he spent in solitary confinement. He transmitted messages to me. I had a deep inner certainty that we were in contact, that he was present. I was quite sure that he received my thoughts too. These moments recurred through all the fourteen years of his imprisonment, and for long after I was free. I have a note in my Bible, dated in pencil, 1953, some months after my release: *Richard came to see me today; he bent over me as I was reading.*

I always feared that he, too, might have been sent to one of the slave camps. How could he stand up to such work? Just writing and preaching used to consume all his strength. When a woman told me he was dead, I didn't believe her.

I'd asked everyone at the Canal if they'd had word of Richard, always frightened of the wrong answer, but no one knew anything. Then, three women arrived from Vacaresti, a prison where many of the sick were taken. Every new arrival was like the coming of the postman. We asked the usual questions, hoping for news of our relatives in jail. None had heard of Richard.

A few days later a woman from this group came to me.

'Every time you speak of God I remember Vacaresti,' she said. 'I was only there a short time, but we had a preacher there, too.'

Vacaresti was a converted monastery. Walls between the monks' rooms had been knocked down to make bigger cells. But a few small alcoves remained where special prisoners could be isolated.

'We were waiting on the landing to use the bathroom,' said the woman, 'when a man was heard talking from behind a locked door. He was saying, "Love Jesus and trust in God's kindness." We were so surprised. Everyone in the prison asked who he was. But it was kept secret, of course.'

Now she had met me, she was sure it was Richard. He seemed very ill. After some days he stopped preaching. She heard that he had died.

How many tears, in secrecy, streamed down my face. How the pain tore at my heart. But through this grief, hope grew. I continued to pray, and asked the Lord to add years of life and health to the man who served him faithfully even in the isolation cell.

I was worried that even Mihai might be arrested and sent to the Canal. He was twelve, and boys no older were there. Every day I saw a boy called Marin Motza, of the same age, with his fourteen-year-old sister. Their father was a former Iron Guard leader. He had mixed anti-semitism with a deep orthodox faith. When during the Spanish Civil War anarchists desecrated the churches, he said, 'They are shooting in the face of Christ. I can bear no more.' And he went to Spain and died there fighting on the side of the future dictator, Franco.

What contradictions there are in the human heart! He left a wonderful Christian testament. In this he said: 'When Christ promised that the gates of hell should not prevail against his church, he counted on the church fighting. This assurance doesn't stand if Christians do not do their duty.' How true a thought!

Now his wife and children were imprisoned simply because they had belonged to him. Mrs. Motza had an *idée fixe*: 'My son Marin will be king of Rumania when Communism is overthrown, since the exiled King Michael will never come back.'

The whole Iron Guard movement was full of inner contradictions. Its founder, Codreanu, killed and patronized the killings of men who hadn't even committed the crime of being Jews. But among his last words were: 'It does not count how a man dies; only how he resurrects.' He was strangled by his adversaries.

At Cernavoda camp we were given postcards and told we might write to invite our families to visit us on a certain Sunday. I suspected a trick: weren't we being duped into naming some friend who would then be watched and followed by the Secret Police? So I spent days asking myself: who can I write to? And will they be still there to receive my card? So many had been arrested.

Everyone around me was writing postcards. Each asking herself if there was someone at home to answer. If there was a home. There would be sons who had lost their faith or been arrested, husbands in prison or living with other women. I saw so many tragedies ahead.

But when the great day arrived, no tragedies were revealed; for though our relatives came we were not permitted to meet them.

I woke on Sunday long before reveille was sounded at 5 a.m. The light was on (it was forbidden to switch it off) and outside it looked still like the middle of the night. There was ice on the panes. I longed for morning to come.

And at last it did. I ran out hoping to see the visitors waiting in the compound by the gates. It was a long way off, separated from the camp itself by three fences of barbed wire and an outer zone—no-man's-land that you could not enter.

There I saw my son. Taller, slimmer, in poor clothes. I recognized the man at his side as the pastor of our church. (Since then tragic events have created a gap between him and us, but we remember and are thankful for the great help he and his wife gave in difficult times and if he hates us now we never cease to love him.)

I waved and waved, but they could not see me among all the other women lining the wire. I hurried back to the hut to tell the lady who had the bed next to mine.

She looked at me. At my stained and ragged dress, my odd shoes, the remains of my light summer coat, the piece of string that was my belt.

'You'll frighten the poor child if he sees you like that,' she said. 'Borrow my blouse—at least it's in one piece.'

Tania offered a long, bright gypsy skirt. Valia draped a white headscarf around my hair. Stockings, even a grubby handkerchief, were loaned to me. While we were admiring my new elegance a row broke out in the room.

Rina was in the middle of it, crowing triumphantly. We were to be punished. So many people had failed to fulfill their work norms over the past week that the visit was cancelled.

They had travelled all night from Bucharest, had spent the savings they needed so desperately, for nothing. We could not speak. We could not even receive the clothes and food they'd brought with them.

The group of visitors, about thirty, waited all day at the gates in the hope that the Commandant would change her mind. She didn't. We had no chance even to look at them or wave any more. Throughout the day, guards drove us away from the fence. Guns in the watch-towers were trained on us. From time to time a woman who'd been able to pass by the wire reported: 'They're still there!' But in the evening they were gone.

It seemed unlikely that I should ever see Mihai if they were going to insist on everyone fulfilling the work norms. A great number of prisoners had come from Jilava. Hunger and illness left them too weak to meet the ever-increasing demands made upon them.

But we could write again. There was another issue of postcards.

And several Sundays later, Mihai again made the journey to Cernavoda. This time there was no punishment. But the visits proceeded alphabetically, and my name always came last. The day might pass without my turn arriving.

Borrowed clothes went from woman to woman.

'How do I look?'

'Perfect!'

Most of them had been awake all night thinking what they would say, rehearsing the words over and over. But usually, when the moment came, they were too overcome to speak. And if you tried to ask about relatives or friends, the guards would stop you. Even the gifts of clothes, which we'd been told we could receive, were rejected on this or that pretext. The meetings gave to many more misery than joy. They hurried back to return the borrowed things, which were snatched up by the next person.

The others watched us sadly. Perhaps, on the next visiting day—in two more months—it would be their turn.

We were taken out to another barrack-hut near the gates. It was not, of course, the 'whole day with your families' we'd been promised at Jilava. It was fifteen minutes, standing in the same room, ten yards apart, with the guards listening to every word.

But when I saw my son, I forgot I was a prisoner and what I looked like and where I was, and simply with my eyes I embraced him. How thin he was, and serious! I gazed at him and he at me, and in a flash the fifteen minutes had passed. Our emotion wiped out time. We barely spoke. Not that it was possible to say anything intimate.

I remember that I called across the space that separated us: 'Mihai, believe in Jesus with all your heart!' Giving him the best counsel I could; knowing from my experience in prison among so many people, old and young, that only Christ can give the hope that lights the darkest place.

He'd been left like thousands of other boys and girls without a guide. The Communists would profit from that. As it happened in the parable of the prodigal son who wasted all he had and then turned for help to an elder who made him tend swine, men sent the young to live on ideas fit for pigs. I said, 'Believe in Jesus' knowing that Jesus alone has the words of eternal life and is the best guide for a motherless child.

He appeared to me very beautiful; every mother is convinced that her son is the most handsome. What was important in this encounter flowered later, as a tree from a small seed. How he had received my words I learnt only after my release.

I was pushed roughly on the shoulder and led out by the

guards. In our barrack-hut everyone crowded around, asking what Mihai had said, how he was. But I just shook my head. For hours I couldn't speak. I was somewhere else. I was not in prison.

In the evening there were many who had waited for someone who never came. Now they were weeping aloud as they lay on their straw mattresses.

The Carcer

At night, in every hut, a woman had to stay awake on guard duty. What you were supposed to be guarding was never explained (I imagine it was to prevent suicides), but you had to keep on your feet. Punishments for falling asleep were brutal.

A naked light bulb, dangling in the middle of the room, swung gently in the draught. Rows of women tossed and turned. Some snored loudly. Some cried out in nightmare. Every face showed marks of suffering and fear. How long were the hours. How desolately the wind howled outside. As if it had blown all these strangers here together: old, young; women of fashion, vagrants from under the city bridges. All they had in common was pain.

When I was a child I disliked night. Now I longed for it, as the one release from murderous work. Yet when dark came I couldn't sleep. I would rise and pray for the women in our hut, in our camp, for the millions of prisoners in the Communist world, and also for Christians who slept peacefully in the West, and those I imagined were praying for us.

Once, being in any case awake, I offered to take on a shift. It was Tania's. She had no trouble sleeping. But she refused, brusquely.

She said, 'Sleep yourself.' But meant it kindly.

Later, seeing me still awake, she came to sit on my bed. We talked in whispers. She told me one of her thieves' tales. She'd been in a prison which held 4,000 women. Among them was one who had been governor of that very jail under the old regime.

'She'd had a go at Communist prisoners during the war,' said Tania, 'and now she was inside herself, which was just where she belonged. It wasn't just that she cooked the books and pinched the food money. They all did that. But this one used to let out the smartest girls for a few days, then bring them in and take a cut of what they'd stolen.

When I tried to speak to her about God, Tania answered: 'Before you reach God, the saints kill you!'

It was a common saying in Rumania. There was no lack of

outward devotion to the saints, but few had any real idea who they were. I told her that the saints help and intercede for us and really can bring us to God. Saints kill nobody.

I said, 'Two worlds exist, the material and the spiritual—but only in the material do the laws of God and man say, "Don't steal". In the spiritual world, steal all you can is the rule. Steal whatever knowledge, manners, wit you can. In the material world, if you steal from me, I lose. But in the spiritual world I lose nothing. I am not against your being a thief. The trouble is that you don't know what to steal. Whatever you take today you'll lose, if not tomorrow, at death. But wisdom and knowledge of God, once taken from somebody, you have eternally.'

Perhaps the word did not fall in vain. Buried within us is a deep knowledge that 'Do not steal', with the exception above, is one of the fundamental rules of the universe. Something in us says, 'Don't desire another's property. And be discrete. Not only his possessions but his being is his sacred property.' God has ordained that people, like stars in the sky, shall be at a certain distance from one another. He has given us shyness, shame, pride, dignity, fear as a fence around one's individuality, and no one may jump this fence. Every man is like an atom which cannot be penetrated by force without disintegration, a release of destructive, revolutionary energies that may destroy the world.

Although so often hungry, Tania did not forget the birds. Each prisoner ate her small bread ration on her bed, carefully catching the crumbs. Every scrap was valuable: it was the only solid thing we had. But Tania took her hoarded crumbs and spread them out on the window-sill for the sparrows.

Once she said to a neighbour, 'Some Christian you are! You're all talk. You never give to the birds.'

To see girls like her giving away these precious crumbs caused me to believe that no man is wholly evil. Human nature when left to itself will show good will at least in such things as this: feeding birds when you are starving.

I was impressed to find in thieves a feature of character which is distinctive to the Tibetans, the people who, for thousands of years, has had the strongest sense of metaphysics. Sven Hedin tells the story that while we in Europe feed only domestic birds for the purpose of later feeding on them, the Tibetans put little cakes on the rocks for the wild birds. Sven Hedin himself, when he got lost, lived on these cakes. Is not wild life also a part of Brahman, the one great All?

In women murderers and in every kind of criminal prisoner you could find a small piece of disinterested goodness.

At Cernavoda we had to suffer indoctrination lectures every Sunday, when we hoped for rest. In the afternoon the room-chief marched us to the assembly hall, where a woman speaker addressed us. She began by telling us what she thought about God, which was not much, and she warned that anyone who spoke about Him would be punished.

'Outside, everyone is now Communist,' she explained. 'Only you persist in this religious folly, and we mean to educate you out of it. The Party is in power now and it knows best. You're not here in prison. I won't even hear the word! You are in an institution for re-education. You'll be building your own future happiness! Working for future generations! And by passing the norms of work laid down you may well hasten your own liberty as a rehabilitated citizen.'

Then came a propaganda concert. Among us were cabaret singers and small-time actresses, some from the German minority. They had to sing Communist songs mocking Germany, praising the Soviet victors. I felt the pain of their humiliation. Physical hurt passes and in a few hours may be forgotten. But humiliation, even when it seems trivial, sears the heart. Only now was I beginning to understand why Jesus spoke of being 'mocked and crucified'. I'd wondered before why mockery was worth mentioning in the same breath. Now I knew how it could hurt, and go on hurting.

A German woman was standing on the platform at the end of the hall. She was middle-aged, had once been plump and pretty. She clasped her hands pathetically as she sang, her voice cracking on high notes.

The officers in the front row hooted with laughter. What could be funnier than a faded fraulein making fun of herself? Tears ran down her cheeks as she quavered on.

Next came a woman, still quite young, who read a poem dripping with gratitude to the Soviets for saving us from the Nazis:

'Mother Russia, thank you
    for what you've done today!
'The glorious Red army
    has shown us all the way . . .' etc, etc.

This doggerel was loudly cheered by all present, the room-chiefs leading. Anyone showing a lack of enthusiasm was in for trouble. Informers were watching closely for socially-rotten reactions.

I couldn't condemn the women who took part in these charades. They were worn down with suffering. What was a misery to some of us was an hour's escape for others. And everyone was doing it: hadn't Rumania's most famous religious composer,

Aurel Baranga, turned his hand to writing Communist anthems? He was a prisoner at one of the Canal camps now.

Few resisted. And those who did were not unaffected by these indoctrination hours which went on every Sunday at almost every camp on the Canal. Some of the rubbish they threw at you was bound to stick.

I couldn't applaud at the meetings. Everyone said, 'Pretend, what does it matter? Is it worth a beating?' But when I heard God and fatherland slandered and saw beauty trampled in the dirt, I couldn't. There were always people standing at the back of the hall and I buried myself among them.

But I didn't escape. Someone reported me, and in the evening I was marched into the Commandant's office. Her eyes were unwinking under the peaked cap.

'I have information that you failed to clap during this afternoon's lecture and re-education class, Wurmbrand. All your behaviour here has shown you to be a counter-revolutionary force, unamenable to proper re-education.' She mouthed the ritual phrases, then licked her lips. 'We've tried to be good to you. Now other methods will be used.'

I wasn't allowed to return to the hut that night. I was marched to the guard-room and put into a carcer. It was a narrow cupboard built into the wall in which you could just stand. The iron door had a few holes to admit air and food was passed through a small slit at the bottom.

Carcers existed in every prison. They helped break down resistance before the extortion of a false confession. At the Canal it was the commonest punishment.

After a few hours, my feet were burning. The blood in my temples beat with slow, painful thuds. How many hours would they keep me here? How many years could I last in such conditions? I thought: this evil is spreading over the whole world; it will torment new millions; no one will escape. But this was the path of madness. I knew people had been driven insane in these boxes. They had let these thoughts of horror overcome them. But how to escape?

Richard had told me about the monks of Mount Athos, who repeat incessantly the 'prayer of the heart'. They say, with every heartbeat, 'Lord Jesus, Son of God, have pity on me.' I had used the prayer myself.

Then I remembered Richard had passed evenings explaining to me the numerical secrets of the Bible. Neither the Hebrews nor the Greeks had numbers as well as letters. The letters of the Bible are also numbers (a=one, b=two, and so on) and every number has a symbolic value. So I tried to count.

Drops of water were falling from somewhere on the roof of the box. It was a desolate sound. I counted them to make time pass.

One: there is one God

Two: there are two tables of the Law.

Three: is for the Trinity.

Four: Christ will gather his elect from the four corners of the earth.

Five: for the Five Books of Moses.

Six: the number of the beast in Revelation is 666.

Seven: is the holy number.

But the sound of dripping water went on, and when I reached fifteen, sixteen, the numbers meant nothing and I went back to the start: One, two, three, four.

I don't know how long I did this, but at a certain moment I simply began to cry aloud to avoid despair.

'One, two, three, four,' I cried, and again, 'One, two, three, four ... 'After a time the words became inarticulate. I didn't know what I said. My mind had moved into rest. It blacked out. Yet my spirit continued to say something to God.

I should explain this further, for it is one of the keys to survival in prison. With all the worry and misery you wished often to black out the mind. You sought desperately to escape, but you were hounded and obsessed by thoughts that could lead you into deeper mental trouble. Just as an injured leg is put into plaster to rest, so a tormented mind, a sick mind, a mind grieved by remorse needs rest if it is to be healthy.

It is known that there existed in the early church (and also in the Greek mysteries) a phenomenon known as *glossolalia*—speaking in unknown tongues. Religion could never find expression only in words. From the beginning it has been shown also in music, the dance and painting. Language is an imperfect tool: when I say, I love apple pie, I love my wife, I love God, I express three utterly different feelings with one word. And between love and hatred there are as many nuances of feeling that cannot be put into words as there are fractions between one and two. What a mother feels for her child cannot be fitted into words, and frequently she does not use them: she says calam-lumsy-toodleums, or whatever, and the child is very happy to hear it.

So there is this phenomenon of glossolalia, of unknown tongues, of unarticulated words. Out of the depths of the heart, in moments of ecstasy or terrible suffering, come sounds, come expressions of love towards God, towards fellow men, made up of words that exist in no dictionary. The mind blacks out: as the Bible puts it, 'He that speaketh in an unknown tongue speaks not unto men, but unto God.'

In the carcer, this blacking out of the mind, so as to allow unreasoning sounds to come out from the depths of the subconscious saved my sanity. After an hour or two my mind came back, rested. I found, too, that speaking in these unintelligible tongues has one great advantage. You never lie, you deceive no one.

One day soon after this we had an inspection from Colonel Albon, an official touring the Canal camps. It was short and sharp. He walked around Cernavoda, saying nothing, gave a contemptuous glance at the ranks of the grey and ghostly women and was about to leave when a gypsy girl ran up to him. It didn't take her long to say what was on her mind. She'd been secretly meeting a lieutenant in the Security Police and now she was pregnant.

The upshot of this was that Albon made a report to Bucharest, an inquiry was held, and much of what had been happening came out. So all the women were moved out of Cernavoda to a labour colony apart from the men a few miles further down the Canal. This was Camp 'Kilometre 4'.

Camp K4: Winter

We left camp early in the morning to work on the bank of the Danube. A bed of stones had to be laid in the water. From morning to evening we loaded heavy rocks aboard a barge. Then the barge was ferried out into the river and the rocks were dropped over the side. It was impossible to do this without making a huge splash and within minutes of starting work we were all drenched. The icy wind blowing across the plain of the Baragan froze our clothes stiff. It was like being encased in metal armour. My fingers were cracked and swollen from the cold, crushed by the heavy stones.

In the evening, when we returned to the hut, we could only go to bed in our wet clothes. There was nowhere to dry them, and if you did hang something up overnight it was sure to be stolen. Usually I slept with my damp dress under my head as a pillow and put it on, still damp, in the morning. It dried out on the way to work, just in time to get soaked again. How I longed for a little sun, shivering in the wind that rocked our barge. I was thin as a hurdle, and it seemed to blow right through me.

In the second week I was put to load stones into barrows. Other women wheeled them to the barges and flung them into the Danube. At least I stayed dry. But the stones were sharp and constantly tore the hands. My knuckles were raw, my nails broken and bloody. Sheer exhaustion somehow spared me pain. But I seemed to float a few inches above the ground, as in a dream.

Pick up a rock. Heave it, bent double, for 200 yards. Into the stockpile. Pick up a rock ... I wondered if I'd ever be able to straighten again.

In the afternoon, a car appeared on the horizon at the height of a guard's belt. The women glanced at it quickly, fearfully. No one spoke. Even the guards were afraid. The light flashed on its bonnet. A new, highly-polished car. It could mean only one thing. The Secret Police. Some prisoner was wanted for further questioning.

Every woman there was silently praying. Not back to the cells, the nights of torture!

At once the guards began to shout. The norm-checkers, always more slavishly vicious than their masters, scuttled about repeating their orders.

But for once, to our relief, no one was taken. Instead, a young woman was handed over to the guards. The wind flattened her cotton dress against her thin frame. Grey-faced, she stared at us in horror. We were caked in white stone-dust, the eyes big in our faces like death-masks at a carnival.

The guards gave her a push forward. I saw that she was barefoot. She began to work. It was pitiful to watch. She would drag a stone a few inches. Then her legs faltered and she fell on her knees, cutting them. She struggled up and moved it a few inches. The ghastly pallor of her face could only mean that she'd spent months, perhaps years in underground cells.

It was impossible to talk to her that afternoon. Somehow she survived the march back to camp. We passed under the watch-towers and the guard leading the column cried out, 'Reporting back with 350 bandits'.

Late in the evening, after I'd completed two hours of potato peeling in the kitchens, I got back to the hut to find the girl lying on her bed, which had been pushed in between mine and the next. The white dust stuck to her features, except where tears had carved channels through it. I brought some water and helped her to wash. She blinked her eyes and peered at me as if half-blind.

As she revived a little, others gathered around.

'Poor thing, she can hardly be thirty!'

'She's rather lovely, isn't she?'

'We must find her something for her feet.'

'And that dress—it's just a rag.'

One of the German actresses, Clara Strauss, rummaged in her bundle and produced a crushed old dress. From someone else came a pair of sandals. These treasures, so generously given, brought fresh tears to her eyes. And slowly she began to tell us a little of her story.

For two years she'd been in solitary confinement in the cells under the Ministry of the Interior. During this interrogation in Bucharest she had been kept without sleep for ten days, while the inquisitors worked on her in relays. Powerful lights and reflectors were turned on her face, night and day. Now she could only see objects within arm's reach.

But none of this mattered much, it seemed, beside the one great question.

'Is it true that we can see our children here? I have a boy and a girl, and I haven't seen them for two years, or heard of them. I left them with my mother, but she was nearly seventy and not well. Is there any way of getting news?'

Her demands were like begging-bowls held out to us. We tried to comfort her. I told her of my meeting with Mihai. But that was a mistake.

'You mean we'll be separated by the length of a room! But I can't see that far!'

She wept, and turned her face to the grey pillow.

In the following days, some of the women tried to discover the rest of her story. But she had retired behind a wall of reserve. Because she was so desperately weak, we gave her all the help we could in the quarry. It wasn't much. I made her eat a little of my bread, and chatted to her.

'Now we know why Christ at the last supper blessed the bread and then the cup. Usually, one says grace at the start of the whole meal and that's that. But here I've learnt that each thing has its own value. No one ever says here, "I had some bean soup", if there was a bit of bread with it. They say, "I had bean soup with bread". It's a treat on its own to thank God for.'

Suddenly she fell into my arms, sobbing.

After a time, she grew calmer.

'My mother, she's religious, like you. How I wish I could see her now! Or touch her. She had all the strength. She was the rock to which we clung. And I've been so stupid. If only I'd listened.'

She told me the rest of her story. It was a variation on a tragic theme which was becoming ever more commonplace: that of the Faithful Communist. In 1951 more and more Party members came into prison, arrested by former comrades. It was pitiful to see their confusion. Fascists could wallow in contempt and hate; they'd had their day of glory. Christians could love; theirs was to come. But the Communist women were lost. They'd trusted the Party like a God. Now it was like watching a massacre of the innocents. They suffered more than people like myself, who were ready for what was to come, who had seen what sort of regime was over us from the start.

Poor Helena Coliu! She'd been quite high in the Educational Department. Her husband was also a loyal Party man with a good post in the government. Helena worked selflessly for Communism. 'Proletarian spirit' was her watchword. The two children were brought up as faithful little members of the Communist Youth.

'I'd honestly have died for Communism,' she said. 'I believed that when the Party came to power it would turn Rumania into a paradise.'

Then she had a love affair with a sculptor.

'He was quite successful, if you judge by the number of busts of Stalin he was able to turn out in a week.'

But the sculptor grew bored, and left her. Helena, who had taken their affair seriously, felt bitter. In an unguarded moment she said to a friend, 'He's the sort of crank who'd help the partisans in the mountains. I wasted myself on a counter-revolutionary.'

The friend was also a fanatical Communist. She denounced the sculptor to the Secret Police, and he was savagely tortured. So tortured that he went mad.

Then Helena was herself arrested. She'd been sleeping with this man. She knew what his dealings were with the counter-revolutionaries. Now she was going to talk! Useless for her to say she'd made it up in a moment of temper, that she was a loyal Party member. Her two-year nightmare began.

At last she was brought to court. The sculptor was there, too, for a ten-minute hearing and a ten-year sentence. The man was completely broken. He neither looked at her nor spoke throughout the trial.

Worst of all, her husband was also present, with her two children. The Secret Police, of course, had not spared them. He had lost his good job. The children had been turned out of their school. They were cut in the street by their playmates.

'I dream about it every night. Even in the daytime I have hallucinations about Gregory. I see him as he was in court, grey in the face, and his eyes dead like a fish. Why did I have to do it! Why did we ever meet!'

I recalled again Richard's words: Hell is to sit alone in darkness remembering past sins. Old memories burnt like fire. You had no defence: no books, no radio, no distraction, no place to go when they came buzzing at you. Here self-deception ceased. Theories about new moral concepts didn't help. Here you knew that the new morality was the old lasciviousness. Helena's remorse was terrible. I knew what she was feeling.

Nearly every woman in prison felt similar burning remorse. Nearly everyone was religious in some degree. Outspoken atheists surprised themselves by calling on God. Everyone wished to have her prayer heard.

But their prayers were wrong. It was like praying that two and two should be something other than four. Accumulation of sins can only bring unhappiness and remorse. It was over sexual failings—adulteries, betrayals, abortions—that regret was most poignant. Women longed to talk about it and ease the pain. I remembered the words of David who had committed such a sin: 'Blessed is he ... whose sin is covered.' So covered by God that there is no need to uncover it before men.

In our hut was Mrs. Radu, wife of a well-known Bucharest business man. She had been a great figure in pre-war society, but her old friends would never have recognized now the gay Zenaida Radu whose hats and Paris frocks and jewels had been their envy.

The fashionable accent sounded strange, coming from that haggard face.

In the evening, as we sat on our straw mattresses, she saw me looking around at our extraordinary gathering of criminals, prostitutes, nuns, peasants and professors.

'What's your conclusion?' she asked, brushing back her greasy hair with a gesture which belonged to her 'smart set' days. 'You've seen it all—what do you think? For myself, I've only one thought left: if I could go free, I'd live happily on a crust for the rest of my life.'

Like many of her type, she had a deep sense of guilt for frittering her life away. Often she's spoken to me hesitatingly, hinting at some inner torment that she'd like to reveal. Coming to sit on my bed. Or staring at me from across the room. Always, I smiled back.

After several weeks, she told me her trouble. When the Communists took power she was left a widow with a small child. The parties were over, the money was gone, her beauty was going.

'All my lovely things were taken from me.' She sobbed at the memory. 'I had to work. My hands were *ruined*. All my old friends avoided me. And then—I had a chance to marry again.'

Again that gesture to quell her untidy hair.

'But men just do not want other men's children. I *knew* that my poor Jenny—and she was three at the time—was the obstacle. And I ...'

Sweat broke out on her forehead. It was a struggle to tell, and not to tell. I put my hand on her's. She began again quickly:

'I began to neglect her. I didn't feed her properly. It wasn't a conscious thing. At least ... she cried too much. I used to shout at her, "Shut up, little wretch!" She grew thinner and thinner. But I didn't care.'

It was as if she would die, bringing this out. She gripped my hand and twisted it as if she were in childbirth agony. And if she held anything back there would be no relief.

'I didn't care,' the dry voice repeated. 'I'd leave her alone and go out. To have fun! With him! I thought he was my salvation.'

'Then on cold winter nights after she fell asleep I'd open the window. The chances were that she might uncover herself and catch cold. Of course, I realize that now. At the time I told myself, "Fresh air is good for a child and I mustn't overfeed her." I didn't kill her. But I let her die of neglect.'

She whispered the last words of her confession. Not that anyone else was listening. Fifty voices were raised in the usual medley of complaints and quarrels and remembrances. Swearing. Singing bawdy songs.

'I've never told anyone. And I know already there can be no forgiveness for me.'

I tried to perusade her that this was not so. I said that in the original Greek of the gospel, Christ is Christos, which is almost identical with the word *chrestos*, meaning 'gracious'. We cannot think of him in any other way. Grace and forgiveness are in his very title.

She said, 'If ever I get out, I've only one wish, and that is to be good—because here I've seen in every way what it means not to be good.'

I replied, 'But no one's really good. Therefore the Apostle tells us that if we say we have no sins we are liars. But if we confess our sins then he, Jesus, is righteous to forgive.'

Zena finished her story. The prospective husband had turned out to be a philanderer. But she became his mistress and the small allowances he made kept her from factory work. This, combined with her 'bourgeois' past, was the only 'charge' against her. She'd been denounced by an envious neighbour as being of 'socially-rotten' origin and given a two-year 'administrative sentence' without trial.

During my journey through different camps and prisons I met many who had been arrested for absurd and fantastic reasons. At Camp K 4 was an old lady, universally known as Granny Apostol, whose crime was that she had once been kind to a lunatic.

The lunatic was an elderly metallurgist who'd made some small coins with the words 'NICOLAI, EMPEROR OF RUMANIA' stamped on them. He, of course, was Nicolai, and his chief pleasure was to give these coins to people. 'Keep this,' he would explain, 'because everyone who owns one will become my minister when I come to the throne.'

The Secret Police arrested this poor emperor and investigated all his friends and acquaintances. Whenever they found a coin, a man or a woman was tried. Sentences of fifteen and twenty years were handed out by rubber-stamp tribunals.

'How shameful!' cried Helena, the devoted Party worker. 'Couldn't you prove your innocence?'

'I could prove it all right. But who could I prove it to? God and the king are a long way off, as they said when I was a girl. It's still the same. What can you do with that lot? Ignorant, they are. Or frightened.'

Granny Apostol was a clever old thing, although she'd spent her life as a servant. She had a simplicity that saw through pretence to the reality of things.

It wasn't that our new rulers were ignorant, but that they were so conceited in their ignorance. Office-boys had become officers in the Secret Police. And this elevation of ignorance ran all the way through the Government to the top where Georghiu-Dej, the ex-railway worker, was establishing himself as Party boss. A joke went round at that time: Georghiu-Dej boasted to de Gaulle that he had liquidated illiteracy in Rumania. He asked, 'Do you still have illiterates?' The General answered, 'Yes, but not in the government.'

The officers at the Canal would not dream of conversing with ragged and dirty women. But if circumstances forced them to talk to us, we heard again and again the same parroted Party slogans. How many times I've been told, 'Humanity has produced four great geniuses: Marx, Engels, Lenin and Stalin.' If you could have asked about Plato or Bergson or Edison they would have had nothing to say, because they'd never heard of them.

The foolishness of those in power and the fright of the bewildered bureaucrats below them added to the long list of harmless and innocent people in prison.

There was the woman doctor who had casually remarked that she always used a thermometer made in the West. It was so much easier to read than the Russian model. Shortly after she arrived in prison for making this counter-revolutionary statement, she was joined by a nurse who was accused of 'non-denunciation' —failure to report the wicked words of her superior as a more 'loyal' nurse had done.

Another strange confrontation was between two ladies of pleasure. One had been, briefly, mistress to King Carol. And the other to the Communist Interior Minister, Georgescu. Both had made the mistake of boasting about their days of splendour. The royal companion was automatically contaminated by her contact with the Court. Georgescu's mistress had revealed too much about the luxury in which the new Minister lived, his fifty suits, his champagne and caviar parties. He had her arrested and sent to jail. Later he came to jail, too, imprisoned by his own comrades.

I met hundreds of people from religious sects who refused to conform. Christian Science ladies, Theosophists, Jehovah's Witnesses.

'It's Saturday,' little Annie Stanescu cried. 'It must be. They're beating the Seventh Day Adventists!'

Every Saturday the women from this sect were paraded and ordered to work. And every time they refused. They were savagely ill-treated, but nothing could move them. Orthodox and Catholic and Protestant believers would work on Sunday to avoid a beating, but the Adventists went on suffering week after week.

Scores of women came to jail because of an alleged apparition of the Virgin Mary. It occurred in one of Bucharest's main streets. Someone pointed to a church window and shouted, 'Look! The Virgin Mary!' And immediately hundreds began sighting the vision. Priests warned. The police made arrests. And still the crowds came.

The police thought they would resolve the question by smashing the window. Immediately, the Virgin Mary appeared in the next pane. So a whole series of windows were smashed. Then the Virgin moved up Victory Street and appeared in the windows of Police Headquarters!

It was when policemen themselves began seeing this vision (many of them had strong Orthodox backgrounds) that mass arrests began.

And so it went on. 'It's a great lottery,' said Clara, the German cabaret queen. 'Sometimes you draw a ticket marked "Prison" and sometimes one marked "Freedom".'

Zenaida Radu said: 'The ticket I want is marked "The West".' She turned to me: 'What do you say?'

I said: 'I drew my ticket long ago. On it is written, "Paradise".'

At 11 p.m. the door of the hut burst open. Half a dozen guards marched in, shouting at the top of their voices.

'Everybody up!'

'Commandant's inspection!'

Clang, Clang! Clang! on the steel rail.

Dazzled, frightened women jumped shivering from the grey blankets. We struggled and scrambled to gather all our things. Perhaps it was a move!

Our square-shouldered commandant walked in in full uniform, with cap and polished boots, as if she were taking a military march-past.

'Women! I want all those who can speak a foreign language to take a pace forward. And I mean a *foreign* language. Not Russian or Serbian. English, French—that sort of thing.'

A number of women stepped forward. Teachers, journalists, former ladies of the Court—a cross-section of bourgeois days. Our names were laboriously copied down. The guards became so cross in their efforts not to look foolish. This performance was always a misery. At last 'Double-V. Wurmbrand' was entered as a speaker of French and German and off they went. We had lost two hours' sleep, and for two more hours anguished arguments continued. What did it mean?

'Translators, that's what it is,' Clara affirmed.

'The Americans are coming!'

'And the French!'

'Lucky bitches,' said one of the prostitutes. 'Why should you have some cushy job just because you say you know a few words of frog?'

'And how about you, Clara Strauss, saying you speak French. We know you're a kraut!'

'Not speak French!' Clara gave her stagiest laugh. 'My darlings, my Phèdre was famous. *Oui, prince, je languis, je brule pour Thesée.*' Clasping her hand to her throat, she glared at Granny Apostol. '*Que dis-je? Il n'est point mort puisqu'il respire en vous. Toujours devant mes yeux . . .*'

'Oh, *please* let's get some *sleep!*'

But the criminal prisoners were bursting with malice and jealousy. And it was almost dawn when I fell into a sleep filled with restless dreams.

Yet, as we tramped to work across the plain that morning, my heart felt light. Could it be true? Work as a translator in some warm office, out of this eternal wind? Had some great international upheaval taken place? Our quarrying party was full of rumours.

I worked that day next to a tiny Jewish woman called Jessica. I'd noticed her about the camp many times. She had a calm, sweet smile which was like a promise of peace among so many anguished faces. Keeping an eye on the guards, I explained what had happened in our hut during the night.

'It happens in every hut,' she told me. 'And in every camp. Sometimes they come in and ask who is a foreigner. And the Germans and Jews hurry to give their non-Rumanian names, thinking they'll be allowed to emigrate. But there is no meaning in it at all. It is just to make you suffer.'

Before long I discovered she was right. It was simply another torment to exhaust the mind and sap the will. Many times the hut was dragged from bed after midnight for another instalment of this bitter farce. Once they came for lists of sportswomen. The rumour was that Rumania was short of competitors for the

Olympic games—anyone who could run or jump or swim might be taken for training! Most could hardly walk, yet this was accepted as an article of faith.

It made us more susceptible for re-education. A female choir had now been recruited and was learning Communist songs, starting with the *Internationale*:

'Raise up all the hungry of the earth . . .'
'And make a start with us!' carolled Annie Stanescu.

A play called 'The True Happiness' was also performed. It showed how true happiness consisted in building a Canal for Socialism. And had rhymes exposing the horrors of capitalist exploitation. And when we were told to weep for America's starving millions, I saw women actually in tears.

After villainous Uncle Sam's efforts to sabotage the Canal had been put to naught, an upstanding Young Communist sang in a soprano, like squeaking glass:

'How we love our father Stalin,
    Never will our joy in Party fade . . .'

The saddest part was the applause and cheering at the end. Some, at least, was genuine. Between tortured and torturer a love-hate relationship can arise. Guards who beat and mocked us were often called by endearing diminutives of their names.

'Before a house can be built, the swamp must be cleaned out, and all the vermin in it!' The younger guards, who'd been taught that we were all 'bandits', repeated these catch-phrases learnt in training-school. And we learnt to beware of blank-eyed girls in their early twenties. They could be more brutal than any man. So long as their indoctrination lasted.

But then they were posted to the Canal and for months and years they lived beside their prisoners in this desert place. They marched the long miles with us to the quarries. They stood over us as we laboured. And, although it was strictly forbidden, sometimes they talked with us.

They saw after a while that they were not dealing merely with 'vermin' and 'bandits' but very often with simple peasant women like those of their own family. It was the time of enforced collectivization, when land and beasts were being torn from their owners. As the guards came to learn that their own relatives were starving and being arrested, they began to doubt.

They lost their pride in the job. Then their faith in the Party. The assault on the church went hand in hand with the seizure of all the things they were attached to. This rising revulsion against the consequences of Communism brought about a wonderful change in some of our guards.

We had several schoolgirls at Camp K4, sent there because

they had joined patriotic student groups. Among them, fifteen-year-old Maria Tilea was a great beauty. Slave labour seemed only to improve Maria's looks. The skin became translucent, the dark eyes more vivid, the delicate bone structure more clearly marked. She had the self-confidence that came from a growing realization that she was liked and admired by everyone.

Nina, an apple-cheeked guard who had shown me some kindness in the past, was very attentive to this delicately-nurtured girl from another world.

'What a shame, poor girl. Why, she's just a child! They told me I'd be handling thieves and murderesses, but she's such a young lady!'

One day Nina asked Carine, one of my Christian friends: 'Are you one of the nuns?'

'No, I'm the wife of a pastor.'

'Ah, they told me about you. Giving your bread away and such. You'll make yourself ill. Here—you go to the toilet in a minute and put your hand up to the window ledge on the right.'

She went. She reached up and her hand met something wrapped in paper. A sandwich. It would have got Nina sent to a labour camp herself if her generosity had been discovered.

Carine and I had several talks with her. She told us how she had always gone to church as a child. And even when she had to join the Communist Youth she continued to attend—but walked miles to the next village where she wasn't known.

'Once on the way back I met one of the Youth leaders. She kept asking me where I'd been. "It's Sunday—you haven't been to church, have you?" I said I'd given up all that years ago. I wish I'd had the guts to tell her to mind her own business, but what was the use. I had a good cry when I got home. I felt like Peter denying Christ.'

She had cried, but to repent like Peter was something beyond Nina's strength. She let herself be parted from the church, drifted into the militia and became a camp guard. She swallowed the talk about building a better world (and wiping out the middle-class vermin in the process). She'd beaten and ill-treated prisoners to order. Now she saw what Communism had done in villages like her own. And she felt guilt.

Carine was not the only one she helped. I guessed by certain signs that she was befriending young Maria Tilea. The schoolgirl told me, months later when Nina was no longer with us, what she had done for her.

'My parents had still a little money left. And a few things were saved somehow when our property was taken over. I asked Nina if she'd take a message to them that I was well. When she went,

Daddy promised her money or a present if she brought me some things—aspirin, chocolate, a woollen pullover.'

It could have cost Nina her life. But she did it, smuggling the things into camp, refusing the bribe. The visit to Maria's home was a revelation to Nina. The pretty things, the restful house, the kindness of the Telias were all a new experience. Her belief in Communism was further shaken.

When first I began to talk to her, it was hard going. At that time she still parroted the gibes about religion they all picked up at the training-school. Her heart was closed. When I spoke of Christ she said: 'But we Communists are the best friends of Christ! If there is a heaven and Christ is judge, we'll be the most favoured of all. Your husband's a pastor; how many people do you think he's brought to Christ? A few score? A few hundreds? But we Communists take care that Christ gets every year thousands of customers who die with his name on their lips. We're filling his heaven. He ought to be grateful!'

I pointed out that this might mean more than she thought. The wicked man who made a sinner of Mary Magdalene also prepared her to be a saint. The one who instilled in Saul of Tarsus hatred of Christianity also laid the foundations for the future Paul. The Bible says where sin abounds, grace aboundeth even more. And I wondered if the Communists with their jokes about sending Christians to heaven don't attract the pity of heaven on them for their wickedness. This was a step to her conversion.

Nina became a Christian again, and this is something not easily concealed. A traitor like Kim Philby can work undiscovered for two decades because badness is all around and he may hide in it. Under every stone is another beetle. But goodness is a rare butterfly that strikes even insensitive eyes. No one can miss it, and some will want to kill it.

Some time in 1951 Nina vanished from Camp K4.

For long we didn't know what had become of her. Then three new arrivals turned out to be former guards from Canal camps who'd been sentenced for taking bribes from prisoners. Nina had been tried with them and given ten years.

Poor Maria was horribly upset.

'It's all my fault!' she wept.

I said, 'Don't take it so badly. It was what she wanted to do in her heart. She'll have greater joy as a prisoner than she ever had as a guard.'

We often talked about Nina. Carine said that she knew what lay ahead of her and she would come out at the end as a very strong Christian. Suffering would give her great authority to speak to others. But what if she died in prison? It would be for a good cause and God does not leave unrewarded even a cup of water given to one in suffering. He will reward her, too. Those who die for their faith leave behind the greatest legacy of influence for good.

The Danube

It snowed heavily during the night. As we formed up before the rows of huts, thick flakes continued to fall. The skeletal guard-towers had almost vanished behind the white veil. But the wind had dropped. Every sound was dull and dead.

From the distant kitchens steam was rising through a venti-lator. That promise of warmth was only an additional affliction. Few 'politicals' were ever granted kitchen work. The laundry ran it a close second. The daily quota there was tough—thirty sheets, thirty pillow-cases, plus shirts and underpants, all done by hand with scraps of low-grade soap. But at least it was inside.

That morning more than the usual number of women tried to report sick. Ana Cretzeanu, camp doctor and herself a prisoner, was not interested.

'Nothing wrong with you!' she said. 'Passed fit for work.'

How prisoners loathed that whining voice. Dr. Cretzeanu had sold herself for the right to stay indoors out of the snow and rain. She had powers of life and death in a sense that must have been new to the medical profession. She knew that in sending out certain women to work, she was condemning them to death. Some were so weak that they fainted on hearing that they must go out again to the quarries. But she had her orders from the medical board. The more women she allowed to go sick, the less was her own chance of survival or release.

In Hut 10 was another doctor prisoner who had kept her in-tegrity. The inmates used every subterfuge to keep her, if only for a few days, inside the camp. She was over sixty and unfit to march miles to the quarry, let alone work there. And she knew her medicine far better than Cretzeanu. But the camp command-ant was well satisfied with her choice of physician. The Hut 10 doctor had to push wheelbarrows.

An aspirin, a warm drink, any kind of pain-reliever was just a dream to us. Toothache had to be borne. The camp was rife with a variety of female diseases brought on by hard work. They were correctly diagnosed by teams of prisoner-doctors. Treat-ment was another matter.

As we tramped through the snow, Carine said, 'Let's not think about Cretzeanu. She's to be pitied. Whenever I hear her crying, "Fit for work!" I remember a friend of mine, a woman doctor, who deliberately joined the militia. For Christ's sake she put on that hateful uniform and played the convinced Communist only to help others. She did wonderful work for the sick before she was betrayed by an informer. She's in prison now.'

'Poor soul. She must have been a kind of saint.'

We stumbled on over the white plain under a dark sky. In the muffled silence the noise of hammering from the quarry sounded strangely desolate.

During the morning I crushed my fingers between two heavy blocks of stone. It was agony lifting each block into the truck. An elderly woman, a newcomer, noticed my trouble and tried to help me. She asked whether in prison I'd come across a girl called Fanny Marinescu.

'Yes,' I said. 'I knew her well. I used to teach her French in Jilava, and we became friends.'

'What happened to her?'

I said, 'She went to Heaven. She died of cancer, left too long untreated.'

Then the woman began to weep, and somehow I understood that she was Fanny's mother.

A guard posted himself next to us, and we couldn't talk. One didn't stop work because one's child had died. She stumbled blindly about, clutching the boulders, with tears running down her face. Our hearts and cut hands bled in equal measure.

It wasn't until next day that I could try to offer a few words of comfort. We were waiting at the midday break for the food to come.

'Fanny is in heaven now,' I said. 'She died in faith in the Redeemer, who is the giver of life everlasting.'

'In heaven! Easily said. If it was *your* daughter ...'

So I told her how I had lost my own family under the Nazis and my orphan children on the ship to Israel.

'Yet one need not lose peace and serenity. We are all transitory beings—but there is also an eternal existence with God. That is our comfort.'

We sat together, nursing our crushed fingers, waiting for the greasy soup. Our legs and arms trembled with exhaustion. She told me her name was Cornelia.

I said: 'Your daughter helped many prisoners through hours of depression, telling them about eternal life. I helped others.

And you help me to lift these stones. And in heaven is the great helper who cares for those whom we have lost.'

She seemed a little comforted.

One evening she came to my hut. Not many guards were about on cold nights and she had slipped across the yard unseen.

I felt someone sit down on the bed and touch my arm. I opened my eyes and sat up.

Cornelia smiled tremulously. 'Let me sit here a little. The devils don't seem to have so much power beside you.'

Every Christian reflects a little of the glory of the Lord. In times of suffering others might observe it.

'All our hut has been punished,' said Cornelia. 'I couldn't get out before. We've had to clean the floor every evening this week.'

She stroked her thin arms within the old cardigan, for warmth.

'But I didn't come here to complain. I want to tell you something I'll never tell anyone else as long as I live.'

The delicate face became transparent, the suffering was transfigured with joy.

'I fell asleep last night without undressing. And at once I was in a great field, as wide as the plain of Baragan where we work. But as far as the eye could see it was full of flowers. The air was filled with a piercing sweet fragrance. Like lily of the valley, and I felt that my daughter was there. Although it was so vast, it was also somehow homely. I'd never seen so many herbs and flowers in one place. There was a sound of wasps and bees. And clouds of butterflies, great masses of them, all glittering with colour, came towards me. I felt such tranquility of the spirit. All the beauty and majesty of the earth seemed to be gathered in one place.

'Standing alone in a corner I saw a woman who came towards me. She had eyes that looked gently into your very heart, and she put into my hands a bunch of white lily of the valley. Oh, the fragrance was sweet! It hasn't left me yet. From the centre of the field I heard the voice of a man, strong and sweet, saying clearly the words of Solomon's song: "As the lily among the thorns, so is my love among the daughters."

'And then I woke up and realized I was still at the Canal. And those fearful madmen the guards were waiting for me. But when they banged the rail at five I got up and went out to the quarries as if I'd been dancing in meadows to delight my Beloved one.'

'I still see the field of flowers and smell their fragrance and hear that voice. And the woman, I'll never forget her.'

The memory lived in her heart. She looked with new eyes on

the thousands of small kindnesses, beauties, signs and wonders
that are evidence of His presence.

Sometimes the stones of remembrance which we took from
the valley of suffering were beautiful.

Days later, the thaw came. I woke to the sound of water dripping from the hut eaves. The iron earth had changed to mud.
Blackened patches of snow still hugged the walls where drifts
had been, but the mild air was defeating them. How we'd all
longed, in these months, to be free of winter's grip!

Even the guards were feeling frisky. They shouted and barked
at us and each other like playful dogs. A light breeze blowing
from the south bore some undefined scent. Of the sea, perhaps.
Or spring.

I was working again on the ferry barges. Out we went into the
smooth, black waters of the Danube to heave our great stones
with huge splashes into the steam. Great hunks of dark ice
floated past. My hands and feet were numb, blue. Big gashes of
bland, blue sky appeared among the clouds of a new white-
ness.

Male guards always came with the column to and from camp.
They were the only men the women ever saw and ribald jokes
sometimes flew around their heads. Today there were more than
ever.

Annie Stanescu, a shrewish little prostitute, always led these
sessions.

'How you dare!' said Zenaida. 'That Peter has hands like a
gorilla. And all that black hair on the backs! I'm sure he's covered
in it, from head to foot. If one could see.'

'And there's women here that have!' Annie showed a mouthful
of gold teeth. A laugh went up.

'Ugh!' Zenaida was all refined horror.

'Though what they see in us to attract them,' wondered Zenaida,
'I cannot think. Can you picture a more unappetizing and sexless
band of creatures than ourselves? I'm sure we must all smell
dreadfully!'

Annie's retort to this brought screams of laughter from her
friends. Soiled words went to and fro. No shutting them out.

'Our little saint doesn't like nasty talk!' cried Annie. The guards,
loafing and smoking as we worked, looked at me, grinning.
'Thinks we're horrid!'

I kept silent. Which was, of course, reproof. But Annie, whose
loose chatter was rarely maliciously directed, had done me a
worse turn than she intended.

At the end of the day we lined up, worn and sore.

'Fall in! Fall in!' bellowed the guards. We marched, on this job, to an assembly point where trucks waited.

The muddy path ran along the riverside. I was aware that the eyes of the guard, the man Peter, were fixed on me. An ugly little grin narrowed his gaze. He nudged his companion, a dumb-looking youth with a flattened nose. Then he stuck out a boot so that I fell in the mud which had turned the path to slush.

The women guards roared with laughter.

A hand reached out and dragged me up. Slippery with mud, I struggled and cried out in Peter's grasp.

'What you need now, my lady,' he growled, 'is a wash.'

'Chuck her in the Danube!' screamed a woman's voice.

I felt the other man's paws on me. One caught my wrists and the other my ankles. I was jerked off my feet, swung once and flung through the air. I landed in the rocky shallows with a splash. The breath was knocked out of my body. I was stunned, but still conscious. Icy water poured over me, flowing fast so that it dragged me over the rocks. The current swirled around me. There were shouts from the bank, but I couldn't understand them. Every time I tried to get up the rushing water brought me down. I thrashed about in a futile way, wounding myself on the stones.

Two hands seized me beneath the arms. I was dragged through the shallows. The man who had hold of me tripped and fell backwards, sitting down in the water. Then I was lying flat on the bank.

Someone forced me to sit up, slapping my back. I felt hollow and sick. For the first time I was aware of a sharp pain in my side. Dizziness made me lie down again. When the sick feeling had passed I lay for a while hearing the river—was it the water of life which flows through Paradise? But then I looked up at the sky through black, wet, naked bushes. It was not heaven yet.

'She's all right. Get up!' A woman's voice. She stood looking down at me. 'Get moving, or you'll freeze.'

The young guard with the peasant face helped me to sit up. Hairy Peter was nowhere in sight. I tried to wring out the edges of my long skirt.

'Come on, come *on*!'

They pulled me up. I was shivering now, but with shock more than cold. The column was moving along a few hundred yards ahead. I limped after it, helped on by pushes from the woman guard.

When we joined the main party the women cast sympathetic glances towards me. We waited for the trucks.

Hairy Peter shouted, 'That's better. Nothing like a cold bath!'

My clothes were cold and clammy and my shoes squelched. I hugged myself and wondered about the pain in my side. It was growing worse. Once we were in the truck, every bump sent a red-hot stab of agony through me. The swaying truck made me feel very sick.

'That brute Peter!' Zenaida muttered her indignation: Our team boss, a criminal prisoner, was in the truck. They'd fished me out quickly once they'd had their laugh. After all, they had to report back to the guard-room with the same number of prisoners as had set out that morning. A slave-labourer less would have been a loss to the State.

Somehow we got back to the hut, where I wrung out my wet things. My side was badly swollen, and the skin had been scraped from my hands and legs. It was agony to raise my arms. Every few minutes during the night I tried to find a more comfortable position. But there was none.

In the morning I saw 'Doctor' Cretzeanu. A huge purple and yellow bruise like a map of Africa spread down one side of my body and it was impossible to raise my arm above waist level.

'Fit for work!' she pronounced.

I fell in with the others.

'What's the matter with *you*?'

The woman overseer was glaring. Perhaps I had swayed. I felt faint. I said, 'I can't go to work today. I'm in great pain. I think my ribs are broken.'

But Hairy Peter was watching out for me. He caught my wrist and pulled me out of the rank. 'What's wrong with her is that she didn't fulfil her norm yesterday. Get on with it!'

He spun me around and planted a large boot in my back. I wasn't so much kicked as heaved forward into the line of women.

So I went to work that day and every following day. I had broken two ribs (doctors established this after my release) but God healed them. We have seen in prison many miraculous healings.

Camp K4: Summer

The spring arrived. Patches of palest new green sprouted among the shabby grass that grew alongside the road to the stone-quarries. A little sweet grass in the tepid water called soup which came at midday was a great treat. But on that raw plain, though the rain fell and fell, good edible grass was rarer than bitter weed. Only the tougher forms of life survived, in that streaming wind, which took the soup from our spoons before they reached our mouths.

Eating grass was forbidden as was everything by which the politicals might better their condition. We pastured on it, like cattle, when the guards weren't looking. And we watched for informers, who spied on us even in this, believing promises that by doing so they would earn quicker release.

Frogs were also fair game, since their raw meat was considered quite a delicacy. They were surprisingly hard to catch. But sometimes an adventurous batrachian would hop into the quarry, where at once he paid the supreme penalty.

They lived in large numbers by the river. At night the sound of their voices carried for miles over the fields. I remembered that the Bible speaks of 'frog-like spirits'. I'd wondered often in the past about this comparison. Then came the Communists with their endless croaking of party slogans. 'Long live the Party, croak-croak! Long live the People's Republic, croak-croak-croak! Down with the warlike Imperialists, croak!' And I understood.

Snakes were less popular. The fat green grassy variety were devoured, but noise around the work sites frightened them off. A few were caught by those who worked to clear the stunted scrub and plant in its place marram grass to prevent soil erosion. Once a wild cat ran across the path with a grass snake in its mouth. A hail of stones and shovels were aimed at the startled creature. It fled without giving up its prey.

The longing for meat, or any protein, was the result of our soupy diet. Call it potato, bean or cabbage, none of it had any goodness. Vitamin deficiency diseases were common. Almost everyone suffered from bouts of diarrhoea. Scurvy occurred, and mysterious skin troubles. Cuts and bruises became infected and ulcers up to four inches in diameter formed on legs and feet. The poisons spread through the system and reduced us to utter exhaustion.

But we suffered less than the men. Special sections for priests and Iron Guardsmen at Peninsula camp were totally cut off from other prisoners. They worked longer hours and received less food. Staying alive depended on a prisoner's ingenuity. Or ruthlessness.

Anything that moved was eaten.

'Dog is quite good,' a priest who survived this camp assured me. 'But I cannot honestly recommend rat.'

At Cape Midia, the labour colony was composed chiefly of elderly men, many in their seventies. Harnessed like beasts to barrows of earth, often working barefoot, they could never fulfil the norms. But if a man once did, then the norms were raised. It was a policy of extermination.

Those who did not die, when they collapsed were often beaten to death. 'The graveyard at Peninsula,' we were told, 'is twice the size of the camp.'

The work norm is not a Communist invention. The Bible says that the Jews in Egypt were slaves who also had to fulfil a norm, which was constantly raised. At first they received straw to make bricks. Then they had to find it themselves. And they had to make the same number of bricks without straw supplies.

What distinguishes Pharaoh from the Reds is that he did not try and label his exploitation paradise on earth.

All our news was gleaned from new arrivals, of whom there was no lack. One evening the door of our crowded hut opened to admit another twenty women. They were all prostitutes, swept from the streets, dragged from their houses in police round-ups. This was the Communist way of 'liquidating the social problems of capitalism'; as usual the remedy was worse than the cure. The new batch had all come from the same prison and they were the most debased women we had yet encountered. Perhaps it was merely that they had suffered their own unrelieved company for too long.

Now with screams, punches and savage obscenities they cleared out a nest for themselves. A little group of nuns was ruthlessly bundled aside. They took refuge with the politicals on the other side of the room. Optimistically, the politicals tried to reason with the newcomers. The whores shrieked with laughter, imitating their accents. The common-law convicts looked on with sickly grins. As for the gypsies, the nuns' troubles left them indifferent, like most other intrusions into their own small world of chatter and squabbles and song.

Many of the prostitutes had open syphilitic sores on their lips. They would be using the same mugs and plates as us. Where they gathered the air seemed a degree more fetid. Sorrily, some had hearts which were as diseased as their bodies.

The shorn nuns huddled together under the reddish glow of a naked bulb, like a flock of bald young birds around their mother. Sister Mary was an elderly nun of ascetic looks and limpid spirit whose sore and sculpted face, sharp nose and round steel spectacles (preserved by some miracle of patient subterfuge) reminded me always of Pope Pius XII. Her beatific smile, delicate as a child's, was in itself a treasure.

'But if only she would stop lecturing about the flesh!' complained Zenaida. 'It isn't as if, poor soul, she has any herself to worry about.'

How hard she struggled to preserve her little flock in faith. And night after night the whores turned to rend them. Old Sister Mary told of St. Bernard of Clairvaux who, it seemed, had once in an inattentive moment, looked at a woman. Horrified at what he had done, he mortified the flesh by standing all night up to his neck in a freezing lake.

'What's 'e want to do that for?' The whores listened always with half an ear. 'The things people do to get a thrill!'

How they giggled and nudged and, occasionally, scratched.

The old nun warned her younger Sisters against even raising their eyes to the guards ... some were young and handsome ... they were in mortal danger ... even to harbour the thought was sin ... turn their eyes to the example of the saints ...

'Funny how some people have all the luck. I never met none of these saints. Though I'd seen it all. Such tricks people get up to. D'you remember the bishop?'

They remembered the bishop at length. The nuns blushed.

The woman called Victoria was, appearances proclaimed, a madam.

Sagging Victoria had somehow adapted her prison dress into something loose which positively frilled and frothed above the waist and fitted like bark below. Whether she had altered them or they had taken on her fearful personality was not clear.

'When I used to go for my weekly medical (prostitution was State-controlled) the police officer always picked me out of the line. Oh, I was quite something. Though you may laugh now. And that cop would take me along to the bishop's palace for the night. Old blackbeard! I 'ad to wear trousers like a boy.'

They rather approved, it was felt, of the roguish bishop. Who paid well, and confirmed everyone's opinion of the world.

'Chastity,' the old nun continued, smoothing one withered hand patiently against its neighbour, 'is like a mirror. Even a breath can spot its surface. Never let an evil thought mar your mind...'

She might have been carved from some hard durable wood. It was the durability that invited attack.

'You dunno much about your priests, do you?' One of the younger girls joined in the mocking game. 'Now I was taken along to do it with some of them. Oh, they knew all about women. *They* never thought much about their souls. A mirror indeed!'

'And St. Thomas received the gift of chastity so greatly that an angel promised that never would he lose it again, never would he be tempted. Notwithstanding, he avoided looking at a woman in case the occasion for sin arose.'

The whores were struck all of a heap with laughter. They shrieked and yelled and fell about in entanglements of flesh.

'Poor old guy! A nice promise! Not what he was praying for at all!' moaned Victoria, pressing one hand to her undisciplined stomach.

All shrieked again. Victoria wiped her eyes.

'Ah, we see through you!'

Whoever was being seen through, Sister Mary abandoned her lecture for something still more limpid. She said firmly:

'Let us say the rosary.'

Together they murmured, 'Hail Mary, full of grace...'

And all the whores together made the sign of the cross. They mocked everything holy. But ceremonial, the making of signs, unnerved them. Or brought them to the beginnings of respect.

It takes some time to say the rosary, and they let it end. But could not let well alone. It was as if Mary had stared them in the face.

A younger girl, with crimped gingery hair like wire, began again. But this time it was to blasphemous words about the Virgin.

But at this such a shouting and protesting broke out among the other occupants of the hut that the alarmed prostitutes clustered cawing around the gingery blasphemer to succour and protect.

'We've had more than enough of you!' shouted Annie Stanescu. And slapped the gingery one in the face. She told her what she was, where she came from, where she might yet go.

'Some women,' she further explained, 'are just low.'

The whores considered doubtfully the degree of their lowness, quite quelled for the moment by this fury and indignation. On learning that this little spitfire was of their own profession they looked nonplussed.

Annie was not one to let religion interfere with her 'work', nor was she on very familiar terms with the Gospel or God; but no one was going to insult the Virgin Mary in her presence. The Holy Virgin she understood and revered and would defend as her own mother.

Why is it that the Virgin inspires in so many, who are otherwise blind to God, this deep love?

The prostitutes took from life all moral standards; but nor could I agree with the nun's viewpoint, which simply contradicted life. There is potential good in evil.

I said that in Hebrew, the word *kedesha* has a root that means both prostitute and holy. Because holiness is to give yourself lovingly to anyone without distinction of race or creed; to give what is best in your soul.

St. Mary Magdalene was a *kedesha*. But she changed. And now instead of passing from the arms of one man to the next, she gave freely of what was good in her soul to everyone.

There is a real love that can help others. It means that you live and die in the struggle to help them become higher beings. And there is a base means of giving love; to be attached to a bit of flesh like a cow. Flesh decays and is eaten by worms; spiritual love is everlasting.

As for the bishop whom the prostitutes had ridiculed, I knew him. For all his weaknesses, he could say to the Communists who arrested him: 'I have not led a Christian life; I can die a Christian death.' The sinner these women mocked was now a saint in heaven. He had died under torture.

Two girls who arrived with this group were of a different class. They were known to the street women but spoke little to them, and they found beds in a far corner of the room.

They were sisters, dark intense girls with good manners and quiet voices. But prostitutes, said their companions, swept up like the others to serve 'administrative' sentences at the Canal.

An aura of sadness and mystery surrounded these sisters. No one knew much about their past. Though many poked and pried. Personal revelations were hoped for.

Victoria, while smoothing down her hair with water, or examining the development of her varicose veins, would say:

'Some girls just do not know how to mix. But we are all in the same boat, I say. If we cannot tell our troubles to our friends, then what are friends for, I should like to know?'

But Diana, who was nineteen years old, and seventeen-year-old Florea did not tell her, although Victoria, perhaps from force of professional habit, continued to be solicitous towards the girls.

Such ingratitude made Victoria angry. She would tread about with her puffy, dainty feet on other people's property and persons and thoughts. And laugh at smutty stories. And smoke, messily. I'd seen women fight over a guard's discarded cigarette-end; but Victoria, it seemed, had her own sources of supply.

So the sisters slaved and slept and might have remained a mystery to me if Diana had not heard my name spelt out by a guard. She asked at once if I knew Richard Wurmbrand. I said I was his wife.

'Oh!' she said. Then, quickly, 'What can you think of me?'

I asked her what she meant. She said her father was a lay preacher. He used to read to her from Richard's books, which he called his 'spiritual food'. He'd been sent to prison for his faith, leaving a sick wife and six children. Diana and Florea were the eldest. Both lost their factory jobs when their father went to jail. Soon the family faced starvation.

A youth called Silviu took her to the cinema one evening. He said he could get her a work permit. They went to a restaurant. After a meal with plenty of wine he made love to her.

Soon it happened again. Nothing more was said about work permits, but he gave her a money present. To help the family, she did not refuse it. And a week later he introduced a friend and left them together. When this man in turn tried to make love to her, she was angry. But he too produced badly needed money, and said he had only acted on Silviu's suggestion. She gave way.

Shame wore away under a stream of clients produced by Silviu. She grew accustomed to the life, even preferring it to factory drudgery.

I knew by the way she told the story that Diana was holding something back. She stopped and searched my face.

'I thought you'd be disgusted. Doesn't it upset you that I became a—prostitute?'

I said, 'You're not a prostitute, you're a prisoner. And nobody is a prostitute or a saint or even a cook or a carpenter all the time. Everyone is himself—the things you do are attributes of only a part of your being. They can change at any time. And I believe you've changed already in telling me about it.'

But Diana was not comforted. She sat on the narrow bed in

the bare hut, her hands clenched, her face taut with distress and guilt.

'If it was only me,' she burst out at last. 'It wouldn't be so bad. But I made my sister join me. Silviu suggested it, and said it wasn't fair that I should carry all the responsibility for the family. So in the end I introduced them and let him take her out.'

Soon, Florea, too, had been initiated. And the main difficulty was how to keep their secret from their eldest brother, a boy of fifteen, who adored them both. Like his father, he was religious, with a keenly sensitive temperament, but no knowledge of the world. 'He wouldn't like a fly to suffer,' as Diana put it.

But the sisters' new way of life, their late hours and the money in the house soon told neighbours what was happening, and they told the boy. The shock drove him mad. He ended in a mental home.

Not long afterwards, the father was released. When he discovered the truth, he said: 'I ask God for only one thing—that he will send me back to jail, so that I may not see.'

Now the tears were flowing unchecked down Diana's face.

'He had his way. He began giving children Gospel lessons and was denounced to the police. The informer told me later that he had done it to get the old man out of the way of our trade. It was Silviu.'

Before such a tragedy of betrayal, it was not easy to find words. I said at last:

'You feel shame over what you have done, and rightly. In a world of suffering, where even God is nailed to a cross, you can't allow his name, which you bear as a Christian, to be defiled. But this sense of pain and guilt will lead you to a shining righteousness. Remember, the soldiers not so much pierced Christ's side as "opened" it, that sinners might easily enter his heart and find forgiveness.'

She thought, and replied slowly. 'Shame, suffering. Yes, I've known them. But there is still something else to say. I didn't always hate the work I was doing. And now all the time bad thoughts come into my head. I can't keep them out. What shall I do? What *can* I do?'

Diana prayed for help, and it was given. They say that the more perfect a soul is, the more it feels pain. It was terrible to see how souls like hers asked in despair where they could find refuge now that this concupiscence had entered their hearts. Who is to judge Diana, one of many daughters of Christian martyrs? She sinned to get bread for her family. Perhaps the greater sin was that of Christians of the free world who did not trouble to send a piece of bread to save such as her.

The spring days began to lengthen. Wonderful gold and crimson sunsets filled the sky at evening in the West, beyond the Danube. It became a joy to march to work. Clouds of nettles and pearly cow-parsley sprang from the ditches, smelling moist and green. The earth grew black and oozy. Trees dared to put out shiny young leaves. One longed to touch, they were so small.

The balmy air affected us all. Light, leaves, grass, the sun, everything was changing. We couldn't help changing a little, too. New friendships blossomed.

Maria sat twisting her hair into a schoolgirl's pigtail as she sat in a patch of early morning sunlight.

The teacher, Paula Vieru, who liked to think herself cynical and hard, helped her and talked of books. Maria, eyes alight with interest, asked questions about this writer and that.

Zenaida and Clara were thick as thieves, swapping stories of gowns worn at pre-war opera nights. Of parties attended by royalty, and controversies over hats and hemlines.

Everyone became more willing to love, less ready to wound. But one of the norm-checkers surprised me with an accusation:

'Wurmbrand keeps herself to herself. Doesn't make friends.'

I said, 'Everyone here is my friend.'

The woman was angry.

'You and your clever talk.'

I wondered if it was true. I tried to help others. Some women reacted in a very exaggerated way, as if I had been sent directly from heaven. Others were puzzled, and suspected me of some darker motive. It was widely believed in Rumania that there was a Jewish plot to destroy Christianity by infiltrating it. I was Jewish—perhaps I belonged to the plot!

But I did have one friend who was truly close.

It was not speech that first linked us together, but silence. When even the nuns were sighing and complaining, she was silent. It said more than her neighbours' chatter. My eyes would sometimes rest on her as she sat, trying to repair clothes by night. She would look up and meet my gaze calmly. Or working at the quarries I would sense that she was close. There existed between us a thread.

She was in her early thirties. Small and dark, with black eyes that were deep and kind.

'I was quite sure you were a Christian.'

She smiled and looked at me with challenging eyes.

'I had wondered if you were perhaps one of us.'

I laughed and felt almost gay.

'Have you many years to serve?'

'No, only twelve.'

'Only. Then it doesn't worry you?'

'God can release us if he wills. And if he wishes me to stay here, I will stay.'

Mrs. Djamil was the wife of a hodja. She had worked for an organization called 'Help Crimea'. It had tried to help people who had suffered during the Nazi occupation of that area. Fascist connections! She and her husband were arested, then jailed.

The commandant of Camp K4 once asked her why she was there. She tried to explain. But the commandant had never heard of Crimea.

'You mean Korea, of course,' she said. 'You've been helping the South Koreans!'

Mrs. Djamil came from Ada-Kaleh, an island in the Danube, and she seemed undismayed at finding herself among so many Christians.

Catholics, Adventists, Jehovah Witnesses, Theosophists explained the errors of the Moslem faith, but Mrs. Djamil did not dispute.

'Mahomet is named *al amin*, "the Faithful", so I trust what he says,' she answered. She did not agree with the Lord's Prayer.

'To call God a Father brings too mild and human an idea to mind. For us God is the master.'

Even in our condition, she washed all she ate, and would not touch soup if there was a suspicion that it had been prepared with pork fat. Orthodox Jewesses followed this rule.

'Superstitious prejudice!' said Paula. 'Two thousand years ago perhaps there was a reason...'

But the devotion of these women to their religion won them respect. Prisoners asked them, not Paula, to share out the food equally.

With so many different sects and religions, we had our share of religious argument. But the virulence of former days was gone, in great part. A new understanding arose, at least among the women. Outside, we could not share the world without quarrelling. Here, we shared a hut, a lavatory bucket, everything. We were sisters.

The Baragan Plain

An error had been made in planning the Canal. The smaller irrigation projects would be flooded by the Danube's waters unless banks were built higher and root crops planted to prevent soil erosion. So we moved from the quarries to the fields, to dig and hoe at the height of summer.

The August sun blazed down over the vast plain of the Baragan. We rose at 5 a.m. and hurried out for muster. Hoes and spades (most of them worn out) were issued.

Then the long serpent-column set off, trailing a cloud of white dust like a pillar of fire.

I worked beside Janetta, the daughter of a former merchant. She was to become one of my closest friends and collaborators in the Underground Church. (She is now one of its leading personalities.) She would fulfil the norm for me and others who could not work well. We discovered that we'd been born on the same day. On birthdays, by way of a present, we would exchange some raw potato.

A great field of parsley stretched away before us to the horizon. It grew hotter as the day wore on. The trees quivered in the shimmering air. Not a cart, no living soul appeared.

Only the line of 500 struggling women, strung out across the earth.

Behind us the guards barked, wearily.

'Shut your mouths!'

'Work faster!'

'Hey! This isn't an ass braying. It's a guard giving orders. Move!'

They passed up the line, croaking.

Janetta said, 'How we used to long for summer!'

We worked dizzily in the scorching sun, in a waking dream of women hoeing on an empty plain. There was no scrap of shade.

I remembered the words of Job:

The servant earnestly desireth the shadow.

The schoolgirl Maria Tilea worked beside us, hacking with lean sunburnt arms at the dusty soil.

'We can't keep up with you!' gasped Janetta.

'Try my hoe! It's better.'

No, it'll just mean a different set of blisters.'

'You try, Mrs. Wurmbrand.'

So we argued, politely. The schoolgirl, the society woman and the pastor's wife.

The guards approached, shouting threats.

And passed on. Maria would have liked to hear of Janetta's gay life. The luncheons, the race meetings, the charity balls.

'I never think about all that now,' said Janetta. 'In solitary confinement I learnt that a kind smile is worth them all.'

We hoed another hundred yards. Sweat ran down our faces, mingling with dust and dirt. Valeria seemed to wear an antique tragic mask.

'In solitary,' she continued, 'I had a dream. I saw one of our Communist torturers taking a bath in my bath tub. And other officers were queuing at the door of the bath room to do the same. I shouted at the naked man "Out of here. It is not your place." He answered, "I believe that you Christians have a pool in your hearts like that in Bethesda. Men enter in it dirty and leave it cleansed." He left the tub. His naked body was now whiter than snow. And he had a lovely face. It was no more the man who had beaten me. Then others undressed and entered the tub. With this I awoke. I had had a revelation in my sleep. When any man enters a Christian's life, even by torturing him, he finds there a place where his image is cleared, beautified. We understand him. He might be a criminal for others. For us he becomes a forever beloved being.'

The story cheered us. And in that place it was a holy duty to keep up hope in others.

How slowly the hours passed in the big field. How the breath rasped in our throats and our tongues turned to felt. We hoed on, like pieces of machinery that can perform only one movement.

'Can you see it?'

A voice croaked, down the line.

'It must come soon.'

But the water-truck did not come.

Even the guards, who carried water-bottles, gazed anxiously towards the horizon. It was late. Hoarse from yelling and marching up the line, they relaxed.

We could stretch our backs. The relief!

'I'll faint if we don't drink soon.' Maria looked pale.

'Don't faint. They'll kick you.'

The sun climbed higher.

As we worked, I thought of Mihai. I saw his small figure,

thin-faced and tearful. Communism loves to steal youth, and they would steal him. What would they make of him, those men who didn't know what kindness is?

How many desperate prayers arose from mothers at that Canal!

I was brought back to reality by shouting down the line. A woman had fainted. The guards were beating her to make her stand. She flopped about in their arms like a fish.

Maria was afraid, and scratched faster at the dust.

'Maria look! The water-truck!'

A dark spot was moving down the road, far away.

The field buzzed with thirsty voices.

'Shut up! Get to work!' yelled the guards.

The truck was exposed to the sun all morning. The water would be far from refreshing by the time it reached us. We could see the old horse that pulled it, now.

We watched as if it were a mirage that might dissolve in the tremulous air.

'I'd like a dozen cool glasses of ice-water,' said Zenaida. 'A greasy pork chop and a mountain of fruit. Oranges, grapes ...'

Cries of 'Stop it!'

Prisoners were constantly dropping out to squat by the field's edge, under the eyes of guards. Dysentery was rife in camp, which was alive with flies and bluebottles. Many were affected. Their limbs were thin as sticks, and their skin grey with the trouble.

We had not eaten or drunk since dawn. Now it was past midday, on that furnace-plain. Eight hours.

A guard walked up the road towards the advancing truck. Then stopped, and turned back.

'It's the food truck,' Zenaida wailed. The women began to murmur, angrily.

The common-law prisoners, working near the road, flung down their tools. They began to shout.

The guards pulled out their guns.

A horde of shrieking women menaced them. One burst of automatic fire into that pack would kill scores. Maria buried her face in my shoulder.

For ten minutes the confrontation went on. The women refused to start work.

'Water!' they chanted. 'We want water!'

Guns were jammed into our ribs. We were herded into a group with the common-law prisoners. Ropes of arms and cold steel pressed back the furious mob. I caught Maria to me.

Now the food truck arrived on the spot. But the frightened driver, gaping at our rebellious swarms, was careless. The cart bounced over a rock, he pulled the wrong rein, the horse veered and for a moment the wagon tottered on its side. Guards yelled and tried to save it. The horse reared.

Over went the canisters.

Half a hundredweight of boiled macaroni tumbled soggily in the dust.

A howl of rage went up. Water, guards, the heat were forgotten.

The food, the precious food was down in the dust!

The women charged the cordon, broke it, and fell on the macaroni.

They snatched sticky handfuls and pushed it into their mouths. They pushed and shoved and fought.

Other women looked on in horror at the fearful show.

Janetta began to laugh, a terrible Homeric laughter, that shook her thin body.

'Luncheon is served!' she gasped. And put her hands to her head.

The guards were content. Danger was past.

An hour later, whistles shrilled and we went back to work. No water came that day.

In the afternoon two more truckloads of security militia arrived.

As I worked, veils of darkness moved before my eyes. My tongue seemed enormous. I remembered the last words of Jesus on the cross:

I thirst.

There is no water in hell.

I remembered the *pizzicato* at the start of 'I thirst' in Haydn's oratorio, *The Seven Last Words on the Cross*. He wished to convey an illusion of the crucified Christ, who seemed to feel on His lips drops of falling rain. I was envious, not having even the illusion.

At last, towards sunset, we formed up on the road for the march back. A mile short of the camp gates we passed some puddles of water in a swampy hollow.

Woman after woman fell on hands and knees to lap the muddy stagnant liquid.

A guard was posted at the spot to prevent them.

The next day an inquiry began in camp. Our 'rebellion' earned us some hours of extra punishment work on Sunday.

'This isn't a health resort!' said the commandant.

'Friends, the class struggle is reaching a climax!' Paula had captured our attention. 'There are only two classes left in Rumania: optimists and pessimists. Optimists think all Rumanians

will be transported to Siberia. Pessimists say they will have to
walk.'

But now few of us felt like laughing. Women collapsed
every day in the fields. At night, in the stifling heat of the hut,
they lay half-naked on their beds, in attitudes of utter exhaustion. We seemed scarcely to have lain down before the clanging
steel rail sounded reveille. A night's unbroken sleep was rare.

Once I was woken by Paula shaking my arm.

'They've beaten up Diana! Come quickly, she's badly hurt.'

The girl was lying, unconscious but breathing heavily, on the
bare floor. Blood ran from her nose, and a patch of her hair was
matted and sticky. Her lips were swollen. We loosened her clothes
and found her body cruelly bruised.

'What kind of game have they been playing, these guards!'

Paula was trembling. Diana moaned and stirred. Her eyes
opened.

'It's all right . . . I didn't let them, 'she whispered.

We made her drink. When she'd recovered a little, she explained
that two of the prostitutes had lured her from the hut to where
some guards were waiting. She was nineteen, pretty, and her
modesty provoked them. She would not submit. Finally, they
threw her into the nearest hut and ran off.

We spread both our blankets over her, for even in that stuffy
shed she was shivering. Paula and I sat beside her until daybreak,
talking in whispers.

'She has an intelligent face. She might have been a teacher.'

Paula was always looking for fellow spirits. She'd been a student
and then a teacher all her life.

'I dream about taking class,' she often said. 'I see rows of
faces waiting for me to speak. I see myself walk through the
pillared entrance, I hear all the sounds of school.'

She had written stories, which had earned her a place in the
Writers' Union. She marched in their ranks on August 23rd, in
the 'liberation day' celebrations. She knew some of Rumania's
famous authors: the poet Mihai Beniuc, novelists—approved
writers who turned out books glorifying Communism and deni-
grating the West. Agitprop saw to it that everything she wrote
contributed to 'furthering Socialism'. One produced straight propaganda, or one wrote about topics that were remote from the
contemporary world.

Paula agreed that hymns praising 'full-of-genius' Stalin were
silly. 'But all those battle-hymns addressed to God are not so
different!'

I said, 'The difference is that one praises the Creator of all living things, and the other lauds a sick creature who's killed millions.'

I asked why she'd been arrested.

'I made an unwise remark about falsifications in history textbooks. They were choosing people to re-write things as the Russians wanted.'

'All the muses are in chains.'

'Oh, but writers are very well-treated. We had special privileges and high pay and holiday centres . . .'

'But the high pay—which is only high for Rumania—is simply an insurance against your writing anything they dislike. Art and religion are equally persecuted. They survive only underground. . .'

So we argued the night away. The prisoners murmured and grimaced in their sleep. Names were muttered, or cried aloud; of children, fathers, lovers, friends. But most often, the word 'Mother!' Age and class had lost all meaning as they dreamt, and the soul in distress whispered from its depths the old cry.

It went deeper than a simple appeal to one's own parent. It was a cry for the eternal female tenderness and motherly care which exists for us in heaven. I remembered the vision of St. John the Evangelist, to whom the crucified Lord had entrusted his holy mother. It was given to him to see a great wonder in heaven—a woman clothed with the sun and with the moon under her feet.

I was brought before the deputy camp commandant, a red-faced woman with heavy broiled forearms and large, splendid teeth. Her uniform seemed to encumber her movements like chain-mail.

'You've been preaching about God to the prisoners. It must stop!' she warned.

I said that nothing could stop it. Furiously, she raised her fist to strike me.

Then stopped, and stared.

'What are you smiling about?' she demanded, her face quite blotchy with rage.

I said, 'If I am smiling, it is because of what I see in your eyes.'

'And what's that?'

'Myself. Anyone who comes close to another person can see themselves in her. I was impulsive, too. I used to rage and strike out. Until I learnt what it really means to love. That is to be one who can sacrifice self for truth. Since then, my hands do not clench into fists.'

Her hand dropped.

'If you look into my eyes, you'll see yourself as God could make you!'

She seemed turned to stone.

She said quietly, 'Go away.'

I have wondered often if Pilate did not look into Jesus' eyes and see the ruler he might have been in the 'king of the Jews' whom his own wife represented to him as innocent and just. The two names have come down the centuries bound together: 'Christ ... suffered under Pontius Pilate,' say Christians everywhere.

I continued to witness for Christ among the prisoners. The deputy commandant did not interfere.

As we hoed in the fields, Maria worked her way towards me along the row, changing places with her neighbour. Once the guard almost caught her. But at last she was beside me, offering help.

The guards spotted us whispering.

'Get to work!'

We hoed, vigorously. But that morning I was also feeling ill. Dizzy spells made me halt often, and each time I dared straighten my back, the guards would shout:

'You're for the carcer tonight!'

Waves of darkness washed over me. Maria's voice seemed to come from a great distance as she chattered, trying to make me forget how I felt.

I managed to stay on my feet until midday. I drank the cup of rank, watery soup and nibbled at the bread. But in the afternoon I collapsed.

The blazing sun seemed to spin round the sky. Then I saw Maria's face above me, her mouth moving, seeming to shout silently from a well of darkness.

Guards dragged me to my feet. Water was poured down my throat until I choked.

'She's all right.'

They swore at Maria: 'Don't stand gaping. Get to work!' Then straddled off, bobbing through the trembling air.

'You frightened me!' she said.

I had frightened myself. There is something specially frightening for a believer in fainting. You return to yourself, and realize that you have had a complete black-out. It makes you doubt the existence of the soul as a separate entity—a thought more frightening than the thought of death. Only in time could I convince myself that it meant no more than a dreamless sleep. Why should the soul always be self-conscious, always saying to itself,

'I am'? It is a poor existence if one must constantly tell oneself that one exists.

We went back to work, hacking at the tight-rooted weeds. The merciless sun sapped all our strength. I could barely hold the hoe.

Late in the afternoon, storm clouds piled up on the horizon. When whistles blew for the end of work, the sky was low and heavy. It hadn't rained for weeks, and we longed for it.

We were working far from camp, and battered lorries waited on the road to take us back. As we crowded in—unable to sit, but at least unable to fall—there was a flash of lightning, and the first warm drops touched our upturned faces.

Then the rain came, moving across the plain like a wall. In seconds we were drenched.

Maria cried, 'Lovely, lovely water!'

But the lovely water continued to descend as if tipped from a giant tub. Bellows of thunder split the sky. A bolt of lightning made the women scream.

The truck skidded and stopped. Its back wheels were sunk deep in liquid mud.

'Everyone out! Quickly!'

The guards conferred.

'Fetch wood,' they decided. But there was no wood.

In the torrential downpour, up to our knees in water, we women put our backs to the truck and heaved, while the men looked on.

The wheels spun, sending mud flying.

The truck stayed where it was. For an hour we worked in vain, until the sergeant ordered to us to march back to camp. Boots squelching, clothes clinging, we tramped through the rain.

The guards struck out at women who stumbled.

At last the ragged column of grey ghosts reached the gates.

'Reporting back with sixty-two bandits, Comrade Commander,' shouted the sergeant.

The damp bandits struggled to their huts. Some were at once put on kitchen fatigues. The rest tried to dry their clothes and fell asleep.

How queer the human mind is. Just before dropping off, there came into my head a joke Richard had told once. A man decided that to complain was futile: he decided that he would in future make the best of things. Just at that moment a wheel came off his cart. 'Never mind,' he said. 'Cabs have only two wheels. I have three. 'Im rich.' Then a second wheel came off. 'Why worry,' he said. 'A wheelbarrow has only one wheel. I have two.' A third wheel came off. 'Well, sleighs have no wheels at all, and they still get along,' he said. Then he lost the last wheel. 'I always wanted to be a sleigh-driver,' he exclaimed joyfully.

I fell asleep smiling.

Time stood still. Slavery was our whole life, the Canal our world. We were worn down into a hopeless acceptance of our lot. Even the news from outside never changed. Hunger, queues and oppression. And the eternal, 'The Americans are coming, they won't let you remain slaves.'

Despondency meant that work levels fell, and strange tricks were played in an attempt to raise them.

At a meeting, twenty women were picked out of the ranks, and told: 'You have been the hardest workers here. For this you will be released.'

The Commandant made a speech.

'So it's farewell and thanks, Comrades. Together we have struggled to build Communism and now the time has come to share the fruits of our labour! Now you are free! As a parting gift we give you an extra loaf of bread each!'

The twenty heroines leaned out of the back of the truck, waving Red flags and singing the International.

Again a deception. Ten miles down the Canal road, at the next labour colony, they stopped and were put back to work.

The effect on work norms at Camp K4 was electric. But this trick was performed in other camps, and soon we learnt the truth.

The Train

One morning directly after reveille the guards crashed in. 'Every-one to be ready to move within the hour!'

This wasn't a matter of two or three detachments. The whole camp was being alerted. Hundreds of women were preparing their bundles, rushing about like chickens, trying to embrace friends they might never see again. The guards added to the tension with their own unease. They knew no more than we.

The Americans had broken through the Iron Curtain! The Russians had occupied West Berlin! We were being taken to be shot!

'Not actually boots!' cried Zenaida's clear voice. Our first issue of footwear was in progress. They were being thrown out of a cart by the hut-leader without reference to size or aim. I won a pair three sizes too large.

When all was ready, the cases and bundles piled, the women lined up in ragged rows, the waiting began. What were we waiting for? No one knew. Where were we going? Everyone 'knew' something different. Prison life is one enormous wait, and this time we hung about until almost dark before boarding the trucks. We were driven to the marshalling yards.

No riots at K4. The sidings were deserted except for a few railwaymen. They'd seen it all before. The train was made up of goods wagons and a string of long, black prison carriages. Each of them was self-contained, with a heavy sliding door and a few small windows high up, covered by metal grilles. In appearance, a luggage van.

'Move! Everyone in!' The train guards specialized in this work. Sloppy-looking men on an 'easy number'. They let the K4 men shove us into the wagons, which took time. There was barely room to stand.

'We can't take anymore here!'

'My God, we'll suffocate!'

But more and more women were pushed in, until we were eighty-four in a carriage intended for forty. The big sliding door at last smashed shut and the bar was secured. The couplings clanged as the train jolted into life throwing us all together.

Our carriage contained some benches. One, it was revealed, concealed a W.C.—waterless, of course, and paperless, but noone thought of complaining about that. And it had a lid!

Women were settling down for the night, or quarrelling, or weeping—for what, they were not sure. The windy huts of Camp K4 had become home. And the unknown threatened. The rumour-merchants were predicting our mass execution. We were to be machine-gunned and thrown into the grave we ourselves had dug. And we would be better off that way, mumbled some of the simpler minds.

But no, assured a woman from Ploesti, in tones of authority: we were bound for Ghencea transit camp and an early release. She'd heard that Ana Pauker's clique had fallen from power and the Party line was being revised.

The wagon buzzed with surmise. That the horrid Ana should taste a little of her own poison! Few really believed it, but everyone seemed cheered.

A joke was told. 'What's the difference between a zebra and a Communist?' 'With zebras the lines are on the animal; with the Party the animals have to stay on the line.'

It was hard to find a space to sit, impossible to stretch out. We dozed in snatches and were woken often by the grinding of brakes, announcing yet another mysterious halt. Outside the narrow windows there was only darkness.

Slowly the autumn landscape was revealed. Cows grazed peacefully in the fields. The very sight of these homely beasts gave hope, after the long empty plains of the Baragan. And trees: leafless already, but holding their black branches to the sky as if in supplication. Then some peasants, free men and women, spreading dung over the dark earth. Three little girls waved and waved, never knowing that they had caused a hundred women to weep.

The train puffed and lurched across Rumania, always northwards. After an hour it stopped at a junction. We heard the sound of doors sliding back and bars rattling. Some buckets of water were handed in by the guards, while others stood by with machine-guns.

But the surly peasant youth in uniform was used to watering beasts and knew one did not answer their cries. And there was, anyway, no bread.

As the train moved on, speculation began again. The gypsies were babbling incomprehensibly among themselves, as always.

The peasant women from the collectives had already given way to remembering and mourning lost cattle and children.

Ony a few old acquaintances were in the carriage. Helena Coliu, the girl who still believed in Communism despite her beatings; Annie Stanescu, the cheerful little prostitute, and Maria Tilea were there. But no Zenaida, no Clara Strauss, no Granny Apostol, no Cornelia Marinescu. I didn't even know if they were on the train.

Amateur politicians near me were discussing the American elections. We knew they were to take place that winter. Truman had served his four years and Eisenhower—who had been Supreme Commander in Europe for so long—was going to save us all.

'Of course he'll be elected,' cried the well-informed lady from Ploesti. 'My information is that he'll ask special powers as President to free the captive countries of Eastern Europe.'

Sensation! And since the woman had passed through Ghencea transit camp only a month earlier she was believed beyond the dictates of her listeners' need for comfort.

I wanted to say that this same Eisenhower had handed hundreds of thousands of refugees from Communism at the end of the war to 'Uncle Joe', as Roosevelt called Stalin. Some committed suicide, some were hanged, some perished in Siberian camps. But I kept quiet. Why dispel illusions, when people needed them as a thirsty man needs water?

How slowly the train crept through the damp countryside. It groaned and grated over the points. It stopped and started. It stood for long hours in nameless sidings. Women took turns to crowd around the small windows, savouring the sight of farmhouses, of smouldering bonfires tended by silent peasants; tasting the first nip of frost in the autumn air.

The excitement of being on the move had worn off, the panic of being crammed into that rocking, lurching black tube turned to discomfort, and soon, with so many women ill, to misery. Despite numerous draughts, the wagon achieved a smelly airlessness.

There were many literary women there: writers, journalists, poets—published and otherwise—even some novelists. Gaunt, dark-haired Marina Capoianu, who'd taught English and French literature at Cluj, displayed an astonishing gift as a story-teller, recounting with a wealth of incident the classic novels she had once urged on unwilling pupils. At dramatic moments her strong, reach-to-the-back-of-the-classroom voice would boom out with Bill Sykes' curses on Nancy or Madame Bovary's passionate cries: 'Léon Léon! Till Thursday, till Thursday!'

One of the most popular of her stories was the melodramatic

'Portrait of Dorian Gray'. Wilde's novel of crime and punishment, told over three hours while we were stuck in a silent and deserted siding that evening, was a howling success. In the murder scene, she slapped a clenched fist repeatedly into the palm of her hand as Dorian Gray stabbed and stabbed again. Her audience almost burst into applause. (Oscar Wilde complained of the prison conditions of his time. If he'd seen these women, travelling like cattle, what would he have said?)

'Isn't it wonderful, education!' The peasants were astonished and amused. 'To be able to say all that without the book!' The intellectuals had been no less absorbed, but now began to run down poor Oscar for frivolity, or snobbishness and more febrile failings. In the argument, Janetta said that Wilde had put an allegorical meaning into a book of deep religious feeling. In Dorian Gray, the painter represents Christ, who paints his image in the heart of every man. But as Dorian's innocence is corrupted, the image of Christ becomes more and more distorted until Dorian can no longer bear to look at it. He puts it away from him, as all men do. Then one day the painter knocks at the door and asks to see the picture. But Dorian cannot bear that it should be seen. He made it what it is. So people do what Dorian Gray did: he killed the painter—Christ is killed—and in the moment he does, he kills the sense of his own life.

It is an allegory of Deicide, the greatest of crimes, but also that which at last brings pardon for all things, and renewal. The blood shed on Golgotha saved even Christ's murderers. Wilde's symbolism of the painter continues here: he knew that death would be his fate if he asked to see the painting; yet he came. By his sacrifice the picture of Dorian Gray was restored to its original beauty.

Now it was Marina's turn to look startled. 'Utterly far-fetched!' she cried. 'It's really an unconscious portrait of Wilde's own psychology. *He* was the fat, hideous, bloated portrait, and Dorian Gray represents his boyhood which he so longed for that he was prepared to kill his genius—represented by the painter—in order to restore it. Which, of course, is what he later did.'

Others eagerly interpreted the book in terms of the class struggle (that poor, cast-off waif and the downfall of the idle rich).

It was plainly a parable, said Mrs. Capoianu, ambiguous and many-sided like all good art. 'But not a very *English* book; quite Russian, in some ways.' So eighty women, trundling by train across Rumania, forgot fears of execution for a while and were entertained by Oscar Wilde.

At one stop the doors were wrenched open and a bag of

rations was thrown in. The loaves of black bread were newly-baked and smelled delicious; but had to be carefully portioned out among the groups. We gobbled it all down at once. At any moment we might arrive. Food saved up is food lost—it was the rule of prison life. For a moment the train-load of women forgot how their poor skins rubbed and fretted against the wood, how their bodies ached and itched and tormented them.

For two days we rattled on, with stops and starts, through this limbo. But on the third, though the halts grew longer, neither water nor bread came. Until late in the evening the doors were opened and the dishevelled sergeant in person was revealed. He had been drinking. Tzuica—sticky Rumanian plum brandy—no doubt. His boots crunched on the flints as he rocked on his heels, watching the surly escort throw in the bag of bread.

'You women are lucky tonight.' Our silence was solidly doubt-ful. 'There's a spoonful of jam each to go with the bread.'

Perhaps the Tzucia would induce further condescensions. Maria asked boldly: 'How much further to go, Sergeant-major?'

Flattered, the sergeant said: 'Another day.'

'And where are we headed?'

He hiccuped. 'To be shot, of course!' And roared with laughter.

The sliding doors crashed shut. And the carriage broke into noisy argument. Those who had not begun to weep and wail were again asking each other questions: Could it be true? But he was drunk. That was just why you could believe him! Sobbing Jewish women began to clasp one another and exchange kisses of farewell. To have escaped the Nazi camps, and now this!

The train moved on, with painful slowness. And stopped after an hour. And moved on again.

Mrs. Capoianu, who had been lost in a waking dream beside me, asked suddenly: 'Sabina—are we all simply the victims of a madman? What does it all mean? They say he sits behind locked steel doors, terrified, ordering more and more deaths. And when the foreign Ambassadors come, he never speaks, but draws and draws with a red pencil on a scrap of paper. Over and over again, drawings of women in postures of torture.' She shivered convulsively. 'And they all speak of him so, as if he were a god. "Full-of-genius" Stalin!" "Father Stalin!" '

I said: 'It wouldn't be the first time men had become victims of a dictator who tried to sit on God's throne. They accuse Him, and try to take His place. When I think of Stalin, I always re-member Pharaoh. The slave-labour, the pogroms, the terror—here it is all over again. A man has tried to steal God's place. You know how Pharaoh ordered all male children of the Jews thrown into the Nile. And then Pharaoh brought up as one of his own family the man who was to carry out God's plan against him. It's said, in the 2nd Psalm, that God laughs sometimes.' (After many years I thought I heard God's laughter again: Stalin's daughter, a convert of the underground Church in Russia!)

'I know he can't last forever,' Mrs. Capoianu said. 'But what makes a man into a fiend like that?'

'Often circumstances.' I said. 'They don't explain everything, but they explain a lot.' He was the illegitimate son of a police officer. His mother had to work as a servant in his house, and so she became pregnant with the future Stalin. His legal father was a drunkard who knew the boy was not his and he beat him mercilessly. Then Stalin entered an Orthodox seminary where the boys were more prisoners than scholars, and there was the aggravating circumstance that he was a Georgian at a time when the Russians had closed down and oppressed the Georgian Orthodox Church. So he became a revolutionary. Now we see how such revolutionaries are made.

It was a night of dread. At every halt we feared that the crunching boots would stop, the doors be opened and women dragged out to their deaths. For hours the Christian prisoners tried to calm and comfort the rest. Yet nothing happened that day, or the next. At sunset the peaks of distant mountains were seen, touched with gold. As darkness fell again, the women sank into a stupor of exhaustion and misery.

'Out! Everyone OUT!'

The bolts were drawn back to reveal a night as black as pitch. There was no station, no siding, even. Dear God, was it true, were they really going to massacre us all? Crying, screaming, swearing, the women leapt or fell out onto the flinty tracks. There were no steps down and I fell painfully on my knees. Several others were helped down—but not by the guards, who stood waving machine-guns and shouting like lunatics at the terrified prisoners. Probably a long wait in the cold and wet was to blame for their mood. But to us they seemed devils out of hell.

Women were punched in the face, flung aside, slapped, struck with gun-butts. We had not the faintest notion of what we were supposed to do.

'Line up, line up! Keep near the sergeant!' But there was nowhere to line up to. Women slipped and tumbled down a muddy embankment into a wire fence. One young guard assumed they were trying to escape and lashed out with his fists. Mrs. Capoianu caught a swinging blow and staggered into her neighbours.

After an hour of utter confusion, several hundred of us were herded into fields beside the track.

'Everyone down! Lie down on your bellies! Get down!'

We were forced to lie face down in the mud. A ring of swearing guards encircled us.

'Oh God, oh God, they're going to shoot us!' the woman next to me murmured over and over. 'Don't let it happen, don't let it happen. I'll never complain again.' She gabbled prayers and pleas. I think we all did.

'On the road! Bandits, are you all deaf?'

We marched very quickly through the darkness, spurred on by threats and blows. Struggling with our bundles. Falling, skidding, gasping for breath. Stunned with shock after four days of stiff-backed inactivity.

'Hold it! Get them into that field! Everyone down!'

Down we went on our faces or kness again. Half the column was lost, and we had to wait for it to catch up.

How long we marched, I don't know. It seemed hours before we saw the high walls of a new prison, long stretches of pallid blankness under the glare of electric lamps. The heavy steel and wood gates opened and we passed through in straggly rows of fives.

In the courtyard word went round: this was Tirgusor.

A new name, new guards. The same curses. The same routine.

The checking of names and numbers began. It was long past midnight when we reached our cells.

Why here? Why Tirgusor? everyone asked. It was a maximum security prison where murderers convicted of violent crimes were held. The name was famous in Rumania. What a mystery! What could it mean?

'That they have no other prisons left,' murmured Mrs. Capoianu.

But no one was comforted.

Tirgusor

I was put to work in the sewing shop at Tirgusor. Women worked round the clock in twelve-hour shifts, sitting at benches in a big high room with barred windows near the ceiling.

The sewing machines appeared to date from the last century and broke down at least once a day. I soon ceased to share Richard's pride about Singer, the Jew who invented sewing machines.

We stitched thick thread into prison mattresses. The heavy material had to be turned and twisted constantly, while the sewing-machine pedals were pumped by foot.

The night-shift women regularly fell asleep over their machines. (You couldn't sleep by day because of the prison noise.) So warders patrolled the rows, dealing out slaps and punches. Not a few women wondered, in the small hours of morning, if life had not been better at the Canal.

Tirgusor contained the country's most hardened criminals. Murderers, sex offenders, swindlers, sadists—some clearly insane.

On the machine next to me sat a hysterical woman. She had stabbed a doctor to death with a pair of scissors. Several times a day she borrowed the scissors shared by the whole bench. She seemed not to notice the nervous glances of her neighbours as she snipped away. Often she would stare at the scissors before putting them aside.

Poor 'Mad Anna' lived in a world of fantasy. She believed she'd had intimate relations with the doctor she had killed. Now she wrote, with a needle on soap, letters to herself from imaginary lovers. They were numerous, and had distinct characters. Peter's letters were high-flown. John's were passionate. Henry's were homely. All were read aloud to her startled cell companions.

Anna had occasional fits of hysterical weeping, but for most of the day lived happily in her illusory world. In prison or out, it made small difference to her.

How many tearful recognition scenes I saw in prisons: when the cell door opened it seemed to be always to admit the mother or sister or cousin of one already there. They had each thought the other was free, and looking after the children. With that hope gone, their grief was terrible to see.

We saw some very odd meetings too. One morning a new arrival announced herself: 'I'm Mrs. Cornilescu from Cluj.'

That was a coincidence. We already had one Mrs. Cornilescu from Cluj. Heads emerged from bunks to watch the confrontation. It seemed that both the Mr. Cornilescus were called Emil. And both were former Iron Guards. But the first was tall and dark. A charming man, so well-bred. The second Mrs. Cornilescu paled. Her Emil was also tall and dark. With such lovely manners.

'Pardon me,' said my neighbour. 'But in Cell 3 I happen to know there is a third Mrs. Cornilescu. Her husband also fits this description!'

Neither of our Mrs. Cornilescus could be called beautiful. One was small and sly with brown teeth, the other tall and haggard with legs thin as sticks. Both had snapped up the offer of marriage.

A furious argument began. The first Mrs. C. slapped her rival's face. The second pulled the first's hair. Guards rushed in to part them.

'My dear, it's an old story,' said my neighbour. 'The man's on the run from the Secret Police like all the old Iron Guards. He's got no home, no papers, no money. He lives off one woman after another, marrying them or promising to. Then the wives are arrested and meet in jail. I've seen some frightful fights in my time.'

Meetings between relatives also came about because entire families had been arrested for helping fugitives in the mountains. The resistance leader, Colonel Arsenescu, was a popular figure and hundreds of people were arrested for helping his men. His wife was in prison. She was told, by stool-pigeons, that her husband had been shot: the lie was fed to her in a bid to break her spirit.

We heard that General Eisenhower had been elected President of the U.S.A. Then, that several Communist leaders had been overthrown and purged from the Party. Was it the start of liberalization?

'What do such puppets count?' said Silvia, a woman journalist. 'Russia controls everything. Nothing will change until Stalin goes.'

But a rumour began to spread throughout Rumania: the Canal was to be abandoned. The great labour colonies were to be shut down. The basic plan was at fault.

Rumour hardened into a fact. An eye-witness from Camp K4

told us that the camp was closing. Officers were being arrested. The Canal engineers were to be tried as criminals for 'stealing State funds'.

The thought was in every mind: what use would they have now for these tens of thousands of prisoners? Would they set us free?

A young woman from Ana Pauker's ministry was put in our cell. She upset everyone with her bitter tirades. We were the bandits, she the suffering innocent. Jenny Silvestru couldn't believe it had happened.

'I'm a victim of injustice!' she declared, several times a day.

'For injustice, read Communism,' Mrs. Iliescu, wife of an Iron Guard officer told her.

'The Party should shoot the likes of you. You're treated too well!'

'My dear girl, I was in prison under Antonescu. I was freed for a few months before the Communists put me back. This is my sixth year in jail. Your threats mean nothing to me.'

Mrs. Iliescu was as troublesome as Jenny. Her contempt for the Communists was boundless.

'We must show our superiority to these scum by working above their wretched norms. Under Communism or not, what we do will benefit the Fatherland!'

She worked so hard in the sweatshop that the norms were raised and everyone suffered. It was a stupid and revolting attitude. Yet it was hard not to respect her. She had suffered so much. She had such courage.

One of her often-repeated stories was of a woman interrogator who had a sadistic taste for torturing men prisoners. She landed in Jilava after the first Party purge. 'Women whose husbands and sons had borne pain and indignity at her hands fell on her,' said Mrs. Iliescu. 'They threw a blanket over her head and beat her black and blue.'

Even when such unspeakable hatreds existed, reconciliation was still possible. There is a huge power in the word of God. Once, when asked, I refused to lead prayers in the cell so long as there were women present who would not make peace. I quoted Matthew 5:23:

'Therefore if thou bring thy gift to the altar, and there rememberest that thy brother hath ought against thee; leave there thy gift, and go thy way; first be reconciled to thy brother and then come and offer thy gift.'

Men and women were persuaded to end long and bitter quarrels with these words. Their lives were changed. As an apocryphal word of Jesus has it: 'You will never be happy until you look on your brother with love.'

But an atmosphere of intense fear and suspicion reigned throughout Tirgusor. We had no wall-tapping grapevine. The Communists were trying to use such things for their own purposes. In every cell stool-pigeons spied and tapped out false messages. The answers obtained from unsuspecting new arrivals were used in the intense interrogations then in progress.

The Communists in prison were sure they would be shot. They had been ruthless, ruthlessness would be returned.

In the meantime the loving and the lovable were executed.

A happening in Jilava.

The daughter of a high Communist official, herself a Christian, learnt one evening that she must face the firing squad at midnight. Executions were frequent, and death sentences were passed on paltry pretexts, often for revenge.

This girl, before going to meet 'the midnight bride'—as execution was known—held a last supper of oat-gruel and water with her cell companions. Calmly she lifted the earthenware vessel which had contained the food.

'Soon I shall be earth again,' she said. 'Of the same stuff as this vessel. Who knows what is was before? Perhaps the handsome body of a young man. Soon out of my body grass will grow. But there is more to death than this, and it is for this that we are on earth, to tend our souls regally while we live.'

As the girl was taken out, she raised her voice in the Creed. Passing through the vaulted gallery, it echoed from wall to wall. The words were those we say in church. But it was a different Creed, because she meant every word. She went to death for the one God, and was received into life everlasting.

Weeks passed. Twice daily at Tirgusor, we were counted. But few guards could count. Fewer still could add the front ranks to the rear. The business took hours. Then came cell checks. The bars were tested with wooden truncheons. It was very cold in the yard and we used to pray each morning that there would not be too many miscounts.

One day the count passed with amazing speed. And immediately after came the ominous call:

'Gather all your things!'

We were on the move.

The Pig Farm

In open trucks we drove towards the collective farm of Ferma
Rosie. We started work at once in the fields. We had no cover
vines with earth to save them from the cold. But the earth
was like iron and the poor plants were long since frozen dry.
The work had been left too late. There would be no vineyard
next year. And no one seemed to care. It was not their business.
They made a play of carrying out the useless work and sent in
their report.

This vineyard had been one of the most famous in Rumania.
Its owner was now in prison. But the victims of forcible collectivization were by no means only big landlords. Small farmers and
peasants were the hardest hit. Their attempts to revolt against
the system were ruthlessly crushed and they became sullen and
indifferent. They worked as little as possible. Then, for 'failing
to discharge their obligations to the State' they were jailed by
the thousand. The land remained untilled. The former 'granary
of Europe' faced famine. And the State's answer was to send
prisoners as slave labour on the collectives.

It was the same everywhere: the fields were cultivated so
badly that little grew. The guards put to watch over us were
often peasants themselves. One told how he had been ordered
to shoot the first man he saw in a village. Then the villagers were
gathered and invited to join the collective of their own free will.

Officials searched the homes of unwilling farmers. Always
they found that they were 'hiding arms'—guns the police had
planted.

Farmers' wives told how the collectivization teams had
taken everything they owned, cattle, carts, farming tools.

Mrs. Manuila, a big-boned peasant woman who worked beside
me, said: 'When everything was gone, my husband said, "Our
hymn book remains. Let us sing to the Lord and thank him for
the greater possessions we have in heaven."'

Mrs. Manuila possessed a favourite cow. She spoke of it tenderly.
How she embraced its neck on cold mornings. How its warmth
had spread through her body.

'Cows don't give good milk unless you love them,' she said. 'Now it's just a beast like other beasts.'

On the collectives, nothing was done with love: there was no blessing from God.

While working in the fields one morning, I collapsed. The sweatshop, the collectives, had ended my resistance. Guards put me on an improvized stretcher. I was carried to the truck and taken to Vacaresti prison hospital. On the way my head had swollen until I guessed it must have taken the shape of a melon.

I knew the prison well. Richard had preached there in the old days. I'd come at Christmas with parcels, to help prepare a tree. Instead of a hospital ward I was put in an isolated cell in which there was nothing except a dirty bucket in the corner. I slept on the bare concrete.

Next morning, looking out through the window, I saw male prisoners taking their exercise. When they passed my window I asked if they had heard anything about Richard Wurmbrand. The first and second man shook their heads. The guard was taking a nap. The third, when he heard my request said: 'Wurmbrand? The Pastor?' 'Yes,' I replied, 'he is my husband.'

He bowed to the earth as the Orthodox do in church. 'I met him,' he whispered. 'I do not regret my ten years in prison. They were worthwhile because the pastor brought me to Christ. And now I meet his wife!' He had to pass on, but he had not told me if Richard still lived.

He went around the yard, head down, hands behind his back. When he passed near the window again, he added: 'I met him in Tirgul-Ocna. He was in the cell for the dying. He always spoke about Christ.'

On his next trip round the yard I found my new friend was a school teacher. The guard yawned. His nap was over and he ordered the prisoners back to their cells. But I knew that Richard continued to be Richard, to exalt Christ, to win souls. Or was he referring to a past long ago?

As to the mark of high respect, I was not surprised. Rumanians generally had a deep respect for those who brought them to Christ.

I remained another day in the cell, no doctor calling to examine me, but I was happy to remain there, hoping to see the teacher again. I did not believe that Richard was dead. I cannot say why. But a verse from the Bible came like music to my mind. It concerned Jacob's son, Reuben, which is Richard's Hebrew name: 'Let Reuben live and not die.' It was to me a promise.

After forty-eight hours the hospital authorities remembered I had been admitted as an urgent case. I was put in a bed with sheets and blankets.

A woman doctor in clean white coat walked the wards.

'Now you must eat everything you're given,' she said. The kindness of her voice brought tears to my eyes.

Dr. Maria Cresin was fresh from medical school. With courage and patience, she worked in understaffed, overcrowded Vacaresti, adored by her patients.

I had an ugly skin trouble. A kind of scurvy, she said, resulting from malnutrition. I must eat: it was the only cure. She gave me injections, and the trouble began to fade. Sores and scabs on my body began to heal. The colitis and diarrhoea ceased. I could even see more clearly: lack of vitamins plays tricks with the eyesight, and many prisoners were blind by night.

In the next bed was a once-wealthy woman. She wasn't too upset at being in prison. She was sure she'd be free soon. Wasn't Eisenhower America's President? And Winston Churchill Britain's Prime Minister? Two great soldiers would not let East Europe remain in slavery.

'When the Americans come, they'll make the Russians pay war compensation. Taking into account my former income, I shall ask 5,000 lei a day for the six months I've been in prison. That is one million lei! I shall be secure for the rest of my life.'

I suggested that she might as well ask for 10,000 lei a day. Then she'd have two millions.

'What a good idea,' she said. 'You Jews are clever people!'

The other prisoners called her 'The Millionairess'.

We played games in the ward, which often ended in tears. We tried to imagine how life would be when we were deaf old women. A word was passed from one end of a row to the other. Each patient distorted it a little, so that it emerged as something different. But the laughter and the excitement upset us. And once it had changed to weeping the ward was caught up in a crisis of grief. Many were young, and they saw their youth passing away. The game would become reality.

Vacaresti was supervised by a political officer. (Medicine, like everything else, had to be practised in the spirit of the class struggle.) One evening he came into the ward with some uniformed colleagues and made a pompous speech about the joys of Communism. When such fine hospitals as this were freely available, who needed God? he asked.

I said, 'Lieutenant, as long as there will be people on earth, we will need God and we will need Jesus, who gives life and health.'

He was outraged. How did I dare to interrupt? How could I go on believing such stuff?

I said, 'Everyone who lives in a house knows it has been built by an architect, just as everyone who attends a banquet knows it was prepared by a cook. We are all invited to the banquet of this world, which is so full of wonderful things, the sun, the moon, stars and rain and fruits of all kinds; and we know that the one who has prepared this is God.'

The political officer laughed and scoffed and walked out with his friends, banging the door.

Next morning a guard came and told me to pack. The same day I was sent back to the labour colonies.

This time it was a State pig farm, where fifty women tended several hundred swine. The years had been hard, but this was the hardest of all. Food was at starvation level. We dragged ourselves from our beds at 5 a.m., still wearing the filthy rags in which we had lain down, and went out into the cold and darkness to feed the pigs.

The sties were ankle-deep in liquid filth—the one substance that never froze. A vile, nauseating stench hung over the place and penetrated every angle of our huts. It hung about the body and hair. The very skilly we slopped up with our wooden spoons savoured of it. We were better off than the prodigal son: we filled our bellies with the husks that the swine did eat.

The meaning fell away from things. Death stared me in the face. The whole world was made of tears and despair as never before and a cry rose from my heart: 'My God, my God, why hast thou forsaken me?'

Trying to clean their sties was as hopeless as trying to clean the world. Each day we started afresh, wet, hungry and half-dead, to cart away in barrows the mountains of filth.

I knew there was no hope for me, nor for the world, and expected only to die.

And perhaps, in a psychological condition such as this, I should not have survived for long. But happily it did not last for many weeks. I am convinced that the Lord heard my prayers and took me out according to his plan. I had only to learn a very deep lesson, to drink the cup to its bitterest dregs; and now I am thankful that I passed through this hard school, which teaches you the highest love, love towards God, even when He gives nothing but suffering.

From the back of an open truck I watched the pig farm re-

ceding, a dark huddle of huts in the white landscape. The wind
was like a cold, steel hand. It tugged at the flaps of our clothes
and sent fine skeins of snow skittering across the land. No one
knew or asked or greatly cared where we were headed. One
collective was identical with the next.

But unexpectedly we came to Ghencea, the transit camp
from which, over two years ago, I had set out for the Canal.

'What crowds of women! The place is busier than ever,' we
whispered among ourselves as we waited to be checked and
numbered. 'What's going on?'

It was after dark before they'd finished with us and we could
be marched off to the huts. The circulation returned to our stiff
limbs. Inside, in the comparative warmth, hope began to seep
through us like a thaw. The hundreds of women who packed
this and every other hut in Ghencea came from camps all over
Rumania. Either they planned some big new slave labour scheme,
or . . .

But no one dared to voice the hope. We'd been through
too much, we'd gulled ourselves too often.

On the second day a rumour spread; in the offices at Ghencea
ten men from Security H.Q. were working on dossiers. Our dossiers! They'd arrived from Bucharest two days ago. Could it
really mean freedom?

I looked around the hut. Under the dim, unshaded lights,
scarecrow-women sat and talked in low voices, turning over
the rumour, pulling it inside out, talking, talking—and all the
while our minds were planning for the future. The smell of sour
food and sour bodies hung like a miasma in the air. Loudspeakers
had been added to the camp equipment. From time to time they
gave forth vast, crackling sounds, like amplified frying eggs,
and roared out incomprehensible distorted messages. When the
first sensation had passed you saw women sitting blank-eyed,
for hours at a time, waiting. No, they didn't believe they would
leave it behind—ever.

Some of the gypsy girls I'd known at Cernavoda were there.
And one day I heard my name called.

'Sabina, Sabina!' It was Zenaida, who had queened it in
pre-war Bucharest, from K4. She had done a round of collectives,
too. We tried to clasp each others hands, then stopped. For all
our fingers were swollen and cracked with chilblains.

We laughed and told our stories, or as much of them as we
could bear. She insisted that I take a pair of men's trousers and
a warm jacket which she'd scrounged from somewhere. I did
so gratefully.

'It's Charlie Chaplin to the life!' The others stood back to take in the effect. 'Even her boots have tabs on the back! '

Soon enough, we came around to discussion of the vital topic. 'How much longer?'

'Does it mean what we think it means?'

Then guards began to take us for questioning at the camp offices. Zenaida was in one of the early groups. She told me:

'It was just like any old interrogation, really, only very polite. And instead of asking about you, they asked what *we* thought about *them!*'

The customary three officers in uniform sat behind desks covered with papers, Zenaida said. After a few questions about her health, and how we were enjoying our stay and did we have relatives outside, things took a more unusual turn.

They asked: Do you know how wrong you were to oppose the building of Socialism? What do you think of your re-education in prison? Do you understand that the State was right to give you this chance to reform? That nothing and no one will be able to turn back the tide of Communism?

'Naturally, I told them I'd enjoyed every minute,' said Zenaida. 'What a pompous ass in charge. Ranting on about national achievements and our fine farms and splendid camps. To *me*, dear, after three years and nine months of it!'

Like most prisoners, she did her best to give the impression that she had seen the error of her ways, and was now eager to work for a place in society.

Before the month was out, small groups of women began to leave Ghencea. As always, we didn't know where they might be headed. Lists of names were read out, parties were marched to the camp offices, then driven off in trucks. But it was one more small, hopeful sign.

Eventually, my turn came. The major behind the desk was stout and pink as a baby. He had hands like fat little bunches of sausages and with them he kept clearing the objects on his desk while he talked, as if he might need to jump up on it later to round off his speech.

There were a few special questions reserved for religious prisoners.

'In this place, Mrs. Wurmbrand (Mrs.!) you must know that I am more powerful than God. At least, he has not so far made any interventions in this office.' He took as his due the appreciative smiles of the two assistants. 'But have you really accepted this? Have you really seen through the sham of religion? Have you realized that in a Communist society, God is superfluous? That you don't need him any more? If you are ever released from here you'll be astonished at the achievements of recent years, and we are only beginning!'

The gold braid on his epaulettes was new and glittering. Under his sausage-hand was a buff file stuffed with papers which might be mine.

I said: 'I see that you are powerful. And probably you have papers and documents there about me that I've never seen and can decide my fate. But God keeps records, too, and neither you nor I would have life without him. So whether he keeps me here or sets me free, I'll accept that as best for me.'

The major banged both fists on the desk, as if it were something he could hurt. 'Ungrateful, Mrs. Wurmbrand, ungrateful! I'm sorry to see that you've failed to learn your lesson, and I shall make a report to that effect.' He shouted in mock-rage for a few minutes.

But three days later my name was read out. Higher authorities than the major were, indeed, deciding my future.

We stood waiting in the snow-covered yard outside the camp offices with our poor bundles. Even now we weren't at all sure that we'd be freed. It was only when we'd been marched out through the gates of twanging barbed-wire and stood shivering in the road that the guard began the long process of handing out slips of paper.

The wind carried his hoarse voice away.

'Wurmbrand, Sabina, born Cernauti, 1913 . . . resident at . . .'

I took the document ordering my release. 'Certificate of Liberation', was the heading, but it was growing too dark to read. The last bars of copper showed in the sky as we piled into a truck and drove off. Ghencea is only a few miles from Bucharest, but we were dropped well outside the outskirts of the town.

I walked with my greasy, smelly bundle through the suburbs. For the first time in nearly three years I saw people, hurrying home after work, shopping for their families.

'Home!' That was where I was heading. If it existed.

If anything existed. Homes, friends, family—I didn't know what had happened to any of them. Mihai would be fourteen now. What had the years done to him? I was almost frightened of finding out; and longed to see him at the same time.

How the lights dazzled my eyes, and the smells of food from restaurants shocked my senses! I wanted to cover my ears against the screeching metal of the trams, to cower from their plumes of falling blue sparks. As the stream of people hustled past indifferently a sense of dismay came over me. I looked for the No. 7 tram stop. Perhaps it didn't exist any longer. Yes, there it was.

I suppressed my panic and climbed aboard, then realized I had no money.

I said loudly: 'Would someone be so kind as to pay my fare?'

All heads turned to see who made this unusual request. And a glance was enough to know why it was made. A dozen people immediately offered to pay for me. They crowded around, their eyes full of sympathy. This kind of thing was a part of life now. Everyone there, it seemed, had a relative or friend in prison. They asked no questions—only mentioned names of their dear ones whom I might know.

We passed near Victory Street with sad memories of the police station where I'd first been held. Nothing had changed. The gigantic portraits of mankind's four geniuses—Marx, Engels, Lenin, Stalin—still stared down on the crowds who tramped through the slush. I left the tram near a block of flats I knew and climbed the stairs. The door was opened by a friend.

'Sabina!' She put her hands to her mouth and stepped back. 'Is it possible?' We embraced. 'I feel quite faint,' she said. And began to cry.

Someone ran to fetch Mihai. My heart seemed to stop as I saw him come through the door. He was tall and pale. And so thin.

But a young man, now.

As we embraced, the tears began to flow down my cheeks at last. He wiped them away with his hands.

'Don't cry too much, Mother,' he said.

At that moment it seemed to me that all my troubles were over and that I would never need to cry again.

PART THREE

Home Again

We walked together next day in Bucharest's big park, Cishmigiu. I had to discover my son again. I didn't know him any more. When Mihai was very young, we almost feared for him. He seemed consumed by religious feelings. He put such searching questions. He was precocious, a keen evangelist at the age of five. When he was seven he brought to Christ a professor who became a member of our congregation.

Would the good in him have been destroyed in our absence by the Communists—by men who did not know what kindness was?

I rejoiced to find in him at once fine traits of character. We spoke of my years of imprisonment and forced labour. He said, 'We don't criticize nature for the fact that it contains both day and night, light and darkness. So I accept the badness of men. Let us try not to call them brutes.'

I, still wondering, told him about the Way of the Cross. He listened attentively, until his eye was caught on our walk by a fruit tree bursting into bud. It was one of those heavenly spring days that come before their time, as if the fine weather can't wait to be born. Snowdrops were breaking through the neglected beds. Hyacinths were unfolding.

When I was done, he said: 'You, Mother, and Father, too, have chosen the way of the Cross as the best way to serve God. I don't know if I would choose it, too. I feel nearest to God in a place like this. Somewhere there is beauty. Not suffering and shame.'

He'd had so few of life's pleasures and he valued the little joys at hand. God's lilies cost no money to look at. He said: 'Why not just stay in a garden, smell the flowers and love God in that way?'

I replied: 'You know that when Jesus was crucified it is said that there was a garden nearby. What would you do if, being in a garden, you heard the shrieks of an innocent man being crucified? The jails of Vacaresti and Jilava are not far. People are being tortured in them as we look at the flowers, and in the Ministry of the Interior across the way.'

He asked, quietly: 'Was it very hard for you, Mother?'

I answered: 'Mihai, we are Hebrew and we are children of God. What oppressed us most was not the physical side. It was that we were put to labour for the illusory world and were taken away from the spiritual. The story of the Canal shows how illusory this physical labour can be if God is not behind it.

'The Canal came to nothing in the end. So did the Roman empire, the Greek republics, the first Jewish state, the Egyptian and Chinese civilizations. Now the British Empire is going, too. All belonged to the world of illusions.

'So this was our greatest suffering. To have to live in an illusory world—not in our own Hebrew spiritual one of "those who come from the other side", which is etymologically the sense of the name.'

One evening he came to my room and read to me from Plutarch's *Life of Cato*. It said that the tyrant Sulla's palace was nothing more than a place of execution, so many were tortured there and put to death. Cato was then in his fourteenth year, the same age as Mihai now. And when he saw the heads of illustrious persons carried out and observed that men sighed in secret at these sights, Cato inquired why someone did not kill Sulla. His preceptor replied that the people feared him even more than they hated him. Cato then said, 'Give me a sword that I may kill the man and deliver my country.'

Mihai put down the book.

'It's true. I feel a bit like that. I'd like just to enjoy life, but sometimes I wonder why so many young people don't do something. Just one boy like me could rid the country of a tyrant. That's what all the Old Testament is about. Is it not from God?'

I said I thought it wouldn't help in modern circumstances. And it wasn't the best way. We should try to kill the tyranny, not the tyrant. We should hate the sin, but love the sinner.

Mihai replied: 'Mother, that will be the hardest thing.'

In those first few days I was like a woman back from the dead. I was free! For so many years in prison, all problems had seemed trifling beside that. Blithely we said, 'If I could get out of here, I'd live happily on bread and water for the rest of my days. You'd never hear a word of complaint.' And live on bread and water most of us did.

Now the real problems began. The worries, large and small.

It was a shock to see the abject need and hunger all around. The people I called on were reduced to almost nothing. Worn blankets on beds, but no sheets and pillowcases. On many days they couldn't afford to buy black bread or use a little electricity to warm the place.

'We've had to sell everything,' a friend explained. 'Cutlery, linen, carpets. Even our books. No! Don't sit on that chair! The leg's broken.'

Most of the money had been used to buy precious medicines for her father, who lived with the family in that tiny flat.

'Sabina, do be careful what you tell people,' she begged. 'There are informers *everywhere*! The church is riddled with them.'

A stream of friends and strangers came to see me, all begging in the most heart-breaking way for news of relatives in jail. Only rarely could I help them or answer their question: Was it an amnesty? A thaw? A new policy? Why had I been released? Whom should they apply to?

I quickly learnt all about 'applying' to officialdom. The queues at Government offices were worse than at the food stores. I needed a ration card. Without one, I couldn't even buy bread. I waited in line four hours one morning. When I reached the small window, the girl snapped:

'Where's your work card? Without that you can't get a ration card.'

'But I'm an ex-prisoner.'

'I can't help that. No work card and number, no ration book.'

So I had to survive on the charity of others.

For a time we shared a room with a woman friend. But Mihai was a young man now. It wasn't possible for us all to live jammed together. I began a long, long search for another room.

Our old home had been confiscated. So had all its contents, furniture, bedding, books. But friends lived in the house where our flat had been once. They said there was a small attic free. Small it certainly was: one room was four yards by five, the other three by two.

After days of queuing and form-filling I was allowed to occupy this 'accommodation space'. The only furniture was some rickety old beds with broken springs. No water, no toilet. In winter it was bitterly cold, in summer too hot. The window looked out on to a blank brick wall.

Here we lived and cooked and slept. Mihai and I moved in. Janetta, when released, came to stay with us. We had no beds so we shared a sofa. Then there was Marietta.

She came to our door one day. And stood there, smiling girlishly, timidly, with dark blue rings under her eyes, in a mangylooking black coat. She held out a little parcel tied with string.

'It's nothing really,' she said. 'Two French pastries.' Which she had queued two hours to buy. And which were not very French.

Marietta was an old member of our congregation. She was a sweet, good-natured girl, but not too bright. People were a little afraid of her. She suffered from epileptic fits.

I was happy to see her. She had a quality of innocence that was always a delight.

'Come in and sit down, Marietta.' I stepped back to let her enter and the door banged against the end of Mihai's bed. 'We haven't been in long and we're very untidy.'

She squeezed past and sat down on one of the rickety chairs we had acquired. The back fell off. Mihai went to help Marietta.

'How cosy you are here!' she said, looking round at the stove on which I was frying potatoes in cheap fat.

'Pity about the roof,' said Mihai. The sloping ceiling was marked by big patches of damp on which a dark mossy fungus grew every day. Whenever one of us moved, we all had to move to make way.

Marietta shared our fried potatoes. Later, when Mihai had gone off into his bedroom to study, she told me that she had nobody in the world now and after a week would have no roof over her head. The family she stayed with had asked her to leave. Relatives were coming from Cluj, they needed the bed . . .

'Well, Marietta, as you see, this isn't a flat. It's just the old box-room we used to keep junk in when we lived downstairs. But if you like we could squeeze another bed in here. I expect we can find a mattress somewhere.'

Her face lit up with joy. 'Really? Are you sure the boy won't mind? I have a few things—blankets and some plates and cutlery. I'd so much like to be with you!'

So Marietta came to live with us in Olteni Street.

It was a week or so after my release. The air was sparkling, the tramcars seemed to swirl along as if in a funfair, the drab grey people moved in the streets with a lighter step. It had been a ferocious winter, one of the worst in thirty years. Now the mild, warm sunshine melted even our hearts.

Suddenly, church bells began to toll. How many years it was since I'd heard that sound. A deep, solemn note of mourning, that came first from the cathedral, then from St. Spiridion's, then from all the other churches in Bucharest which remained open.

The city has many bells. (Rumania in the Middle Ages was a bastion of Christendom against the Turks and the country is filled with monasteries and churches.) Now they all sounded together. But the lovely noise was also frightening. People stopped in the streets and asked each other what had happened. Despite the police ban on public gatherings, small crowds gathered in the squares and whispered together.

Then the loudspeakers on Victory Street crackled into life: 'Dear Comrades and Friends! Workers of the Rumanian People's Republic! The Praesidium of the Supreme Soviet of the U.S.S.R. informs the Party and all Rumanian workers with deep sorrow that on March 5th, 1953, the Chairman of the Council of Ministers of the Soviet Union and Secretary of the Central Committee of the Communist Party, Josef Vissarionovich Stalin, died after a grave illness. The life of the wise leader and teacher of the People, Lenin's comrade and faithful disciple, is over.' The speakers blared martial, funeral music.

The sound of bells meant not death, but the dawn of new hope to most of us. 'But why are they doing it?' everyone asked. Especially when they heard that religious services had been ordered to mark the demise of the President of the World Atheists' Organization, who had devoted so much effort to destroying Christianity.

Rumours spread that Stalin, in terror on his death-bed, had asked for the last rites and begged to be buried with a cross. The shadow of his millions of victims (the Soviet author Ilya Ehrenburg wrote later that if he'd spent his lifetime simply writing their names, he would not have had time to finish the list) fell across his bed, and he asked all Christians to pray for him. So it was whispered.

Schools and shops closed down. Mihai came home with the special edition of *Scintea*. Our one and only newspaper, the Party organ, contained of course nothing but columns of eulogy. All the vast slogans and banners in streets and cinemas and cafes hymned Soviet-Rumanian friendship. The radio trumpeted the same tune.

At great risk we could listen to foreign broadcasts. From one of these stations we heard a reading of Isaiah Chapter 14—a terrible chapter which describes the death of an oppressor. He goes down into hell, where he is mocked and told:

'Art thou also become weak as we? Art thou become like unto us? The worms cover thee ... how art thou cut down to the ground, which didst weaken the nations!' The chapter is triumphant and vengeful.

'What do you think of that?' asked Mihai, as it ended.

I said I didn't feel that way. In a man's last moments, as he sees death before him, great changes can happen. I recalled that Stalin's mother was a good and devout woman. How she must have prayed for him! A bishop told St. Monica, who wept over her son's sinfulness, 'The son of such tears cannot be lost'.

And now we have the testimony of his daughter, who turned Christian in spite of all his teaching and escaped to the West. Who knows what the dying Stalin meant by that 'incomprehensible and awesome gesture' Svetlana describes when 'he suddenly lifted his left hand as though pointing up to something ... the next moment the spirit wrenched itself free of the flesh'? The Pope said a Mass for Stalin's soul. Should Jesus have loved Stalin's soul less than the Pope?

The other side of the coin was joy at the start of what we hoped would be a new era, the end of slave labour camps and projects like the Canal. For all the rumours were coming true: the Canal was really being abandoned. After four years the scheme was dropped, with only a seventh of the work completed. More than 200,000 men and women had slaved there. No one knows how many thousands died. Billions were thrown away and the country's economy was wrecked. For nothing.

In *Scintea* we read that the State was now switching over from construction of major social works to producing consumer goods. Living standards must be raised. But the fact was that the Canal was a failure. It could never have worked. A final great survey was made by engineers. Some say they discovered that the Baragan plain would be flooded. Others that there would never be enough water to supply both Canal and irrigation projects.

What is certain is that the chief engineers and planners were arrested. Death sentences for 'economic sabotage' were passed. At least two men were executed on the spot. Another thirty received sentences of up to twenty-five years each.

I said to myself the Passover Prayer: 'We were slaves with Pharaoh in Egypt, and the Lord with a mighty hand freed us.' Again, it was true. Barracks and labour colonies were closed down. The huts crumbled away. Grass and weeds burst through the concrete. The huge, empty plain was given back to the wilderness.

It is a wild and lonely place today. Snakes rustle through the undergrowth, no longer hunted for food. And no one now lays out crumbs for migrant birds. Rusting equipment lies in the deserted vegetable fields and the cold wind from the Black Sea erodes the last traces of what was to be a wonder of the world.

Little by little I regained my health and some of my old strength. The ribs that had been broken when I was thrown into the Danube hurt me, but the doctor said that was only because they were not yet fully healed. He advised some weeks in bed.

And said it was a miracle that I had survived. But there was too much waiting to be done.

Walking one morning in Olteni Street, I saw a shabbly little man with thinning hair. He stared at me hard as we passed. When next I put my hand into a coat pocket, I found a little, folded leaflet. He had slipped it in without my noticing, then disappeared.

'And it shall come to pass that the Lord shall give thee rest from sorrow, and from thy fear, and from the hard bondage wherein thou wast made to serve ...'

I read the text, and I knew that the fight continued. Perhaps it was not on show, but everywhere around me was the love of God. In passing faces that betrayed nothing. In hearts that no Stalin could touch.

A new happiness flowed through me. I was a member of the Underground Church.

You won't find its title in directories, or its buildings in the cities of Eastern Europe. It has no cathedrals. Its priests are in worn working suits. They have no theological training. They know little of sectarian squabbles. The Underground Church has no name even behind the Iron Curtain. Only after we reached the West did I come to know that we were referred to by this title among the few people abroad who knew what we were doing. If I'd been asked earlier, 'Have you an Underground Church in Rumania?' I wouldn't have understood the question. Like Molière's Monsieur Jourdain, who'd been speaking prose all his life without knowing it. We simply did our Christian duty. We paid no heed to Communist laws. And we did not need to give our attitude a name.

For the next twelve years this was to be my life.

At first I'd been distressed by the plight of churchgoers. They were persecuted by the police, harried by informers. Through radio, schools, cinema, theatre and press the campain to stamp out belief was relentlessly pursued. The old could worship, with difficulty, and under observation. But the young might not believe.

I saw how many former friends, afraid of losing their jobs, didn't dare come near our house. Others wouldn't even admit they had once worshipped beside us.

Passing the university, I saw a teacher we'd known well and went to greet him. He was with a colleague.

'You're making a mistake, Madam. I don't know you.' He turned away, unable to look me in the face.

People were so frightened, while they were 'free'. In prison, even at the worst times, we'd seen God's hand at work. We came to know that although we suffered he would not leave us. We could trust him. So a vital part of work in our Underground Church was to teach people this. And, with a prison background, it was easier to win their trust.

I also had to keep myself in my place. Our church was now run by two young Lutheran pastors. But it was embarrassing to find so many of their people knocking at my door to ask advice or tell their troubles. Believers who had suffered for their faith were treated with something like idolatry by other Christians. Everything we said was 'gospel'.

It's a dangerous idea. Martyrs don't make the truth. The Truth makes the martyr. I had to be very firm and stop people from treating me with exaggerated reverence.

Keeping my opinions to myself wasn't easy, either. The two young pastors did their best, but they could only teach what they had learnt from Lutheran professors and from books often based on other books, written many centuries ago, in a world which did not look like ours. I didn't have as much respect for these ideas as I used to have. Not everything the books taught fitted the lessons I had learnt in prison.

Communist methods of brainwashing and indoctrination were new. They needed new answers. And these were found, by the Underground Church, as time went by.

'Mother, I've finished with school.'

Mihai came home early one day, with bright eyes and set mouth.

'What do you mean, finished?'

'I'm not going back.'

'But you must go on with your studies.'

'Not there!'

I got the story from him by degrees. The Communist Youth Movement was being built up and the best pupils were given the privilege of wearing a red tie. The children were told to propose a candidate for the honour. And they proposed Mihai— who refused. He said, 'I won't wear the red tie. It's the sign of the Party that keeps my father in prison.'

Consternation! The teacher, a Jewish girl, didn't know what to say. But she had to play the Communist. She scolded Mihai and sent him home.

But the fact was that the teachers, almost all of them, hated what they had to do and the people who made them do it. Next day Mihai's teacher smuggled him back into class and gave him a hug.

From that day on, he was the most protected boy in the school. Atheistic propaganda began in the classroom and time after time Mihai would stand up to argue with his instructors. He sometimes lost the arguments, because he couldn't follow their twists and turns, but he stood up just the same. And the teachers, knowing he was the son of a political prisoner, loved him for this. Rumania is not a Communist country, but a country oppressed by the Communists.

While I was in prison, Mihai had been cared for by our old friend Alice, a Sunday school mistress. Once she had been head of a department in an important Ministry, but when she refused to join the Party she was thrown out. She eked a living teaching French and coaching for examinations. After I'd been taken off, Mihai simply went to his 'Auntie Alice' and said: 'You'll be my mummy, now.'

She was very poor and also had to look after an elderly father. All three of them lived in a single room. Since there was simply no space for other children she wanted to take in, she helped them with love and such pennies as she could spare. They would have gone hungry but for Christian brethren who sacrificed for them.

Thanks to Alice, Mihai could resist all the blows which rained on him between the ages of nine and thirteen, and still tell me when I came back: 'Mother, I'm on your side and I love the Lord.'

But the propaganda in the schools was intense. With films and lectures the teachers had to work hard to prove that God didn't exist. So Mihai asked me often for proofs that He did.

I remembered what Richard had said, that nobody asks for proof that nature exists. It is there, and we're part of it. And spiritual things are just as self-evident as material things. A genius says he has been inspired—by what? By something higher than himself. A spiritual experience, a closeness with God.

In every school there was a 'godless corner' with pictures and books deriding the clergy. And Mihai knew that some of the stories were true. He had known pastors who behaved badly, who betrayed their brothers.

I tried to show him that the Church has a human as well as a divine side. And that every Christian has this dual nature.

Day after day, he'd come home with examples he'd been given of the Church's errors or the failings of priests.

I would say, 'But they never tell you about the remorse a pastor feels when he does wrong. They just show you the sinful side. They hide the good. Anyone can go wrong. It's when we're sorry

for it that we show what is divine in us.' So I dispelled his doubts.
Until the next onslaught.

Every Christian mother had this struggle. Life was a battlefield,
and every evening we made up the ground gained by the Communists during the day.

'Our professor says Joseph was a grain speculator.'

'Why did King David want to marry Uriah's wife?'

I replied, 'The Bible does not hide the truth. It tells of men
who can sin and make mistakes. But when you read these
stories for yourself, you see it's the Communists who are lying
and distorting.'

In this struggle for youth, they seemed to have all the weapons:
the schools, the radio, the press. But Mihai had always had
before him the example of Christianity in action.

When I was at the Canal in 1951, people from our church
risked their liberty to help him. An elderly couple spent two
days travelling—by roundabout routes to avoid detection—and
put a large slice of their savings in the hands of someone who
could help Alice.

Old Mrs. Mihailovici, who'd also been like an aunt to Mihai,
came hundreds of miles from her village after my arrest with
a bag of potatoes, all she had to offer. Her visit was reported by
informers, who always watch relatives of political prisoners.
When she got home she was summoned by the militia and so
badly beaten that she never recovered her health.

In spite of such treatment, the people of the Underground
Church never forgot their duty to the children of those in jails.

Sometimes we lost a battle.

I remember a woman who came to me in tears.

'My child is working for the Secret Police,' she said. 'He's meeting a man regularly who asks him about everyone who comes
to the house. I don't know what to do.'

She couldn't turn her son out. She couldn't let him betray
Christians who came to see them. I advised her to break contact
with us for some time.

Sometimes late at night a man—or more often his wife—came
to my attic and confessed that they were informing. 'We're in a
trap,' one woman told me. 'We love the Lord. We love you and
Mihai—but we can't resist all these threats and menaces. My
husband will lose his job or be sent to prison. We have to report
on everyone who attends church and what they say. We try to
tell them only what'll do you no harm—but you must beware!'

Others left Bucharest and moved from town to town to avoid
these weekly summonses to the Secret Police.

Your home under Communism is always divided. If they can't

find a child or a relative to tell how much bread you're buying, what you cook and who visits you, there's always a neighbour or a colleague who will. Girls are questioned about boys they go out with. And everything goes down in the file, to be used in one way or another against you.

From this system arises the phenomenon of thousands and thousands of secret Christians who wear the red tie or the Party badge. Some even hold high State posts while belonging to the Underground Church. They call a priest to baptize a child by night. They travel to a remote town to be secretly married by a pastor. And many informers came to me to tell of all they had to do and seek forgiveness for their betrayals.

I'd say to them, 'Prove the sincerity of your repentance by telling us now about how we're spied on. Let's have the names of the officers you took orders from. Tell us when and where you meet.'

If they were in the habit of handing over their information at a certain street corner, one of us would sit in a cafe nearby to take a snapshot of the Secret Policeman concerned. Then we'd follow him to see whom he met next. If their meetings took place, as often happened, in a 'safe' house of the Secret Police, we'd watch the place and photograph those who came and went.

It was risky work, but we were able by these methods to list most of the informers, including Colonel Shircanu, who headed police spywork against the Church. We watched him as closely as he watched us. We pinned down his chief informers.

Some we succeeded in bringing to repentance. Others had to be dealt with by sterner means. In these ways we defended the Underground Church and enabled it to continue its work.

I was lucky in having Mihai. My son was more than faithful. He was at a very difficult age for boys and we gave him the hardest tasks. On top of his own problems he had to be constantly on the watch. He had to take decisions that might land us both in prison. Yet we could often laugh together at the absurd things his teachers were obliged to say, and the strange things that happened.

One evening a few months after she'd come to live with us, Marietta came in much later than usual and all evening said scarcely a word. I'd noticed that she'd been late several times in recent weeks. And that she seemed—not happier, because she was a happy girl—but calmer, more self-assured.

All of a sudden, she said: 'There's something . . . I don't quite know how to tell you . . . Well, I have a boy I'm very fond of.'

She had met him on a hospital visit to a cousin. He was a cripple. The whole left side of his body had been paralyzed in a factory accident, and this had affected his speech. For months he'd been completely dumb, and unable to move without a wheel-chair.

'But now he's ever so much better and can get about with his sticks very slowly. He's not good at speaking, though. I understand, but other people can't at first.'

Next evening the young man came to see us. Laboriously, he climbed three flights of stairs. As Marietta said, it was difficult to understand him, and that night we had several friends from another town staying, sleeping on the floor. But it did emerge that Peter, too, had nowhere to go. He'd been sleeping in some-one's cellar since he came out of hospital, and now he'd lost even that.

The epileptic Marietta married the dumb cripple and Peter came to live with us. Now we were four, not counting the almost nightly guests who stayed in our tiny flat: wives of pastors who'd been arrested, Christians who didn't dare make contact with an ex-prisoner by daylight.

One of these was a youth who worked as cook in a police barracks. They never ran short of food there, and he often brought us his bread.

The Underground Church

Mihai came home with a story which he certainly had not been taught in his history class. Hitler, Napoleon and Alexander the Great took the day off from hell to watch a parade in Moscow's Red Square. As the columns of tanks rolled by Hitler said, 'If I'd known the Red Army was so powerful, I'd never have attacked Russia.' Alexander commented, 'If I'd had an army like this I could have conquered the world.' Napoleon, studying a Russian newspaper, looked up to say, 'If only I'd a newspaper as obedient as *Pravda* the world would not have known about Waterloo.'

Mihai was collecting jokes about Communism. Having finished his elementary schooling, he could go no further. No higher education was permitted to the children of political prisoners and he had time on his hands as he looked for a job. Then an old friend of Richard's heard him play the piano and offered him work.

'I look after the instruments at the State Opera House,' he said. 'I need an apprentice with fine fingers and a good ear.'

To get this job, Mihai had to fill up a sixteen-page questionnaire. He had to supply, among much else, the addresses of two neighbours in every street and town he'd lived in 'over the last twenty years'. He was fifteen.

'And you'd better be sure they know what to say when the Secret Police come round,' warned the tuner.

After receiving the form, Mihai went round to the personnel officer and said he'd spoilt it with ink blots—could he have another? Then he filled in the two copies, one to keep so that he could check on what he'd written in years to come. The questionnaire would follow him from job to job for many years, and if he contradicted it in any way there would be trouble.

There was a question: Has your father ever been arrested? He simply wrote 'NO', saying to himself: 'He was kidnapped in the street. That is not an arrest'. Was he wrong?

He was taken on, at a salary of £8 a month. It was a very big sum to us. And he had the ration card allowing him to buy bread.

The tuner found that Mihai had an excellent ear and could identify pitch and sound easily. 'He's better at it than me, and I've been doing this job for forty years.'

And he became expert at repairing every kind of musical instrument. So that when, after 18 months, he was discovered to be the son of a political prisoner after all, he had a small clientele of his own among Bucharest's musicians. In this way, though he lost his job he was able to earn a little for tuition and bought books to study at home.

I took on all sorts of strange jobs to keep the family going. First there was the Silkworm Rearing Co-operative.

Marietta read about it in a magazine. 'Rear silkworms at home. Supplement your income and help build Socialism.'

Mihai grinned. 'Marietta sees herself in a swishy evening gown all made from home-grown silk.'

'No, seriously,' said Marietta. 'Silk is worth a lot of money.'

Mihai reached for the magazine. 'Ah, but you have to take anything you produce to the State Co-operative. What do you suppose *they'll* give you for it? Anyway, where could we put them? If you think I'm going to eat my meals with a box of dirty old silkworms in the middle of the table you're wrong.'

'You could keep it under your bed.'

'Under *your* bed.'

'What do silkworms eat?'

'Mulberry leaves, stupid, everyone knows that!'

'Mihai, remember when you lived with Aunt Alice, and on the next corner was the hospital and across the street, facing the house, was the cemetery?'

'Yes. It really used to cheer me up.'

'But that cemetery was full of mulberry trees. At least we could always feed these silkworms.'

So we set up shop with a box containing 100 of the little grubs and a leaflet of instructions from the silkworm Rearing Co-operative.

Mihai read out passages. '"When the silkworm is ready to change into a moth, it spins around itself a cocoon made of matter from its own body." I say, I never knew they turned into moths. You'd better be careful, Mother. One day you'll take the lid off and they'll fly away.' He studied the leaflet. '"When the cocoon is unwound it gives a silk thread many hundreds of yards long." That's going to be a bit awkward in here, isn't it?'

We peered into the cardboard box, in which Mihai had pierced airholes. The caterpillars were not exactly handsome, being of an ashy-grey hue and about three inches long. And they were voracious eaters. The life of silkworms seems to be one continuous communal meal; at the end of which they roll themselves up in a cocoon made of their own silk thread. This you can wind on to a reel.

At first Mihai helped himself freely to mulberry leaves from the cemetery. But soon the caretaker spotted him and chased him out.

'We'll have to make a raid under cover of darkness!' Mihai said.

Next evening, armed with paper bags, he climbed the cemetery fence and came back triumphantly with several days' supply.

'The dead don't need them,' Mihai said.

I recalled that the Book of Revelation says that in the heavenly Jerusalem the leaves of the tree of life are used for healing.

'I'm glad,' Marietta said. 'Because that goes to prove that very sick souls can also have a place there.'

Silkworm larvae are fussy creatures, having been artificially cultivated for 4000 years. They don't like temperatures of more than 78°F. or less than 62°. They like light, but not too much. When they are moulting, which happens every few days, they must not be disturbed.

'Ssh!' whispered Mihai, quoting the leaflet: ' "The larvae must be kept free from noise during each period of change!" '

After about a month, and repeated raids on the cemetery, we had 100 little cocoons. These were taken to the Co-operative —and we were paid enough to buy two days' food. Well, two days' food was welcome. I took home another 100 newly-hatched grubs.

'Oh, no!' groaned Mihai.

But for several months our silkworm farm thrived.

Until one day I found the grubs looking pale and swollen, as if they might be about to burst. Mihai whistled Chopin's Funeral March, and went off to the library to check up in a book on silkworm cultivation he'd found.

'Yes,' he reported. 'It's quite common—they call it grasserie. It comes from letting the poor things stand in a draught.'

I said, 'But grasserie only means fatness.'

'That's right, it said in the book—"a form of dropsy".'

Jesus healed a woman sick of the dropsy, but there was no sign that he would repeat the miracle for my silkworms. So we had to throw them out.

I turned to other cottage industry ventures like sewing and knitting jerseys. And so between the small sums I could earn and the money gained by Mihai, we survived.

That was the year of the International Youth Festival. Young

Communists and sympathizers from many parts of the world came to Bucharest; and for three months before it began there was nothing, nothing in the shops. Queues for bread and anything edible were huge. Just once in a while, after endless waiting, you found a scrap of butter or a few ounces of flour.

Then the Festival began. And the shops were crammed with goods. For three wonderful weeks we saw a host of things that hadn't been seen in Rumania since before the war. Mihai would come in: 'I saw boxes of dates in the State Grocery! And there are chocolates wrapped in gold paper, too!'

Then the Festival ended. For months after, the shortages were worse than ever. They had squandered all the reserves on this prodigal display to deceive foreign visitors.

Mihai said that these young Communists from abroad were just as infected with the blight of spying as our own youth. Many Rumanians who made unwise remarks to youngsters from France or Italy were reported to the Secret Police. An acquaintance of Mihai's was arrested.

It was all so wrong and false and ugly! When I heard such things, I hated this evil system which had destroyed decent thought and life over one third of the world. Peasants forced to steal from land that was once theirs. Workers terrorized in the factories and deprived of their rights. The corruption went all through life from top to bottom. The managers of the big State stores were leaders of a black market in their own goods which was worth millions. Lies and spies filled our lives. It fell often to ex-prisoners, just those who had suffered most, to teach people that hatred towards the Communists was negative and wrong. Only understanding and love could triumph.

Mihai told a story that shows how the Communists were hated.

Two friends meet in a bus. In a whisper one asks the other, 'What do you think about the Prime Minister, Georghiu-Dej?' His neighbour puts a finger to his lips: 'Are you mad?' he mutters. 'People listen.' They get off the bus and walk through a park. 'Really,' insists the first man. 'What's your opinion?' Some strangers are sitting about 500 yards off. 'Hush,' says the neighbour. 'They may hear.' At last they reach a wholly isolated place with no one in sight. 'So now, tell me what you think of Georghiu-Dej,' says the first man. The neighbour replies, 'I have the highest opinion about him.'

The subterfuges and the way we scraped a living were not the truly important thing. That was to gather and keep in a life of prayer and trust our Christian brethren, and the wives and children of prisoners. This was Janetta's and my real work over the years while Richard was in prison.

Since so many honest and good pastors were by now arrested, it fell more and more upon their wives to build up the Underground Church. Dozens of us became self-taught 'ministers'; through talking to people we learned to preach. Women came from every part of the country to Bucharest to ask advice and report on how the church fared with them. Soon we found that nearly all our time went to this work.

The West is still arguing about whether women should be ordained. In the East this problem has found its own solution. For wherever, under Communism, pastors are imprisoned, their wives become pastors in their place, ordained by Jesus' pierced hands.

The Underground Church had innumerable secret meeting places in the city. Often in cellars and attics like our own. On dark nights a light would show in a window and people would flit up the stairs and give a special knock on the door. We crammed into spaces so hot and close that there wasn't enough air for the flame of the lamp by the window. It guttered, and the room was in half-darkness.

The ideas of using the tactics of the Communist cell against the Party arose in conversation with pastor Grecu, who sometimes joined us late at night. He was a minister of the approved church, and they allowed him some licence because he was known to drink. Drunken priests made good Communist propaganda. They did not know that he drank in order to stay on, and only as much as was needed to throw dust in their eyes.

Pastor Grecu's heart was with us. He was of enormous help. He carried on a secret ministry which went far beyond the limits imposed by the State. Many priests did this: there was no clear dividing line between the Show-Church and the Underground Church. They were interwoven.

Under persecution, sectarian barriers fell more and more: Catholic or Orthodox or Lutheran, we came down to the pure elements of faith. It was like the church of the first centuries.

Pastor Grecu and I had many discussions on tactics. Janetta had now become a pillar of our church. We'd both read Lenin's *What is to be done?*, in which he set out his plan to conquer the world. It was written in 1903, when all the Bolsheviks in existence could be seated on one sofa—in fact, there's a picture of them doing so. One of Lenin's first principles is to infiltrate rival organizations—this, at least, is a rule that works. After the Communists took power in Rumania we found they had long insinuated themselves into both 'bourgeois' Ministries and the leadership of anti-Communist bodies. Seminaries and the priesthood itself were infiltrated.

Now the roles must be reversed. They were the bosses. And we saw that the Underground Church could not work unless we infiltrated the Communist organizations which were trying to destroy us.

It seemed at first to be against our principles. But Pastor Grecu had an answer pat:

'Christ called the temple a den of robbers, but the Apostles deliberately worked there after his death and resurrection. Strange circumstances call for unusual actions. *A voleur, voleur et demi*—to catch a thief you have to be a thief and a half.'

Still, I was hesitant. 'Many of our brothers and sisters are going to have moral scruples. If they join Communist bodies they'll be asked to do so much that's wrong. People with Church backgrounds are bound to give themselves away. They'd be weeded out in a month.'

Pastor Grecu said: 'Some of them may be good actors. The younger people will find it much easier. No trouble in getting them into the Communist Youth. And from there into the militia. And then into the Secret Police and the Party.'

I agreed that we must take a lesson from the Russians. And apply it with the aid of those who came to our secret meetings.

The people who came to these services were all enthusiastic and eager to help, but as I went among them I mentally divided them into two groups.

Most would shrink from playing a false role. I knew what they would answer if I proposed infiltrating the Communists. They would reason that it would need a great deal of deception which could not be justified.

A second, much smaller group, would think like St. Paul, the great soul-winner. He made himself Jew with the Jew and Greek with the Greeks thus winning both. Even in this group, only a chosen few were admitted into our confidence. They agreed at once that they could not leave the Underground Church unprotected to preserve their own integrity. The selfish end, to be personally righteous, does not justify allowing innumerable Christians to go to prison. Only one in a hundred of our members knew what we were doing. That was our way of safety.

Pastor Grecu wondered whether parents would not object if they thought their children were taking on dangerous tasks.

I said: 'When I was at school they used to tell us about King Stephen the Great. Once he was wounded and came to the gates of his castle. His mother said, "Who's there?" He said, "It's your son, Stephen." She replied "You can't be my son. He would not leave the field while his army was still there. He stays and fights.

ı know no other son." Many mothers I know have been brought
up in this tradition.'

'They must be dedicated women.'

'I know how they feel, the mothers who come here. If the
Communists were to prove to me now that Richard had died
in prison, I wouldn't be simply sad. I'd be proud too. This spirit
is spreading day by day. If one can be proud of a son who dies
for his country how much more one could be proud of a son
who was a martyr for Christ.'

Pastor Grecu smiled, a shade bitterly. 'Dying is at least a quick
process. There are other martyrdoms.'

Janetta said, 'Yes, there are many. And it may be a higher
thing to sacrifice one's integrity in the cause than it is to sacrifice liberty, or even perhaps life.'

He stood up to leave and brushed some crumbs from his shabby
suit. 'How curious it must be to live in a world where one is called
on to give up none of these things.'

Marietta had a friend, a pretty girl from a country town whom
I shall call Trudi. She was eighteen, with dark, fluffy hair and
sparkling eyes. When she'd visited us several times, I said: 'In
prison the guard used to tell us before we got a beating, "You
wanted to be martyrs, so now suffer!" And we did. But even at
the worst times there was the joy of knowing that it was for
Jesus. Like early Christians. But now there is something that
goes further. And, Trudi, you can help us here.'

She looked at me with her brown eyes. Trudi was a quiet, intelligent girl. She wasn't frightened by work. Her large, but
shapely limbs, the deliberate way she handed you a plate or closed
a door, encouraged you to believe that here was someone who
wouldn't easily break. She was the eldest girl of a large family.
For years, she had been their nurse and guardian spirit.

I explained that I'd been watching her, and how we were
looking for girls to join the Communist Youth.

'Now something new has come up. It may be a wonderful
opportunity. A Colonel Shircanu, who works for the Secret Police,
has been asking his sergeant if he knows a girl to help in the
house. They have a big place in one of the best quarters of the
city. His wife seems rather extravagant and silly, but kind
enough. If you were to apply for this job through their special
employment office you might find out a lot that would help us.'

She didn't speak and her face didn't change. But the brown
eyes gleamed. I went on: 'They wouldn't suspect anything. The

sergeant has asked his wife to ask her friends, and one of them comes to our services. Nobody knows she's a Christian.'

'What would I have to do?'

'Nothing, at first. Get the feel of the house. Get to know everyone. I've noticed that people enjoy telling you their troubles. Look how old Mrs. Tomaziu was showing you her varicose veins yesterday.'

Trudi laughed.

'As if you were a nurse.'

She thought about it for a while. Then she accepted.

One evening Pastor Grecu told me he'd found a curious passage in the Gospel of St. John which hinted at some kind of infiltration of the high priest's court by the disciples.

'It says that one of the disciples was known to the high priest Caiphas—so well known, in fact, that on the very night that Christ was on trial, this disciple could enter the temple precincts and even get Peter in, too.'

He suggested it was something to tell young people starting on this secret work of ours, if they objected. But few of the youth did.

I sent a few girls to join the Communist Youth, but I did not let Pastor Grecu know their names. The clergy of the official church were under constant pressure to inform on congregations. It was best for him not to know.

We'd seen such tragedies caused by this endless spying. Once in our rooms Mihai's 'Aunt Alice' asked: 'In the Bible it says that "all things work together for the good"—but what good, I'd like to know, is served by informers? I'm afraid to open my mouth these days.'

At first I had no answer. I could think only of the terrible harm they did. But the question worried me. Lying in bed that night, I saw that there was spiritual significance even in this. Informers taught us that while we live we are constantly surveyed. Angels watch all we do and say; but they are invisible, so we do not care. These informers reminded us that our every action counts.

I had my own detecting system. Police agents came to our rooms to spy, pretending to be believers. The first time it happened I suspected the man at once.

He stopped me in Olteni Street.

'Excuse me—you *are* Sister Wurmbrand?'

'Yes, but I'm afraid I don't remember where . . .'

His raincoat was rather too new, and he was a little too anxious. The eyes were furtive. In his early thirties.

'At Cernavoda. I was in Gang 4. I used to see you some days

for a month before I was moved to Cape Midia. You were a great help to us—people you've never met still talk about your speaking out for Christ!'

He paid some fulsome compliments. As we walked along, I asked a few questions about his time at the Canal. His answers were vague. I was sure he'd never been there. But I couldn't catch him out.

He asked where I lived, what I did, how I made a living, and so on.

He said, 'I'm a believer, you know. I was converted in prison.' He told a rambling story about a Christian who persuaded him at the Canal to return to the faith of his childhood.

The upshot was that he invited himself to our rooms. I let him come up the dingy staircase and said: 'Welcome to our home.'

He began asking questions about my political feelings and those of my friends which only a provocateur would have put. So I asked a question of my own.

'Do you read the Bible much?'

'Yes, yes. Very often.'

'Perhaps you'd like to read something to us, then.' And I gave him my Bible. Mihai, Janetta, Marietta, Peter and a woman visitor were there.

He read something from the Psalms, and even managed to add a few sanctimonious words of his own.

'Now let us pray,' I said. 'Will you lead us in prayer?'

And we knelt around him, and waited for him to start.

He muttered a few words and stopped. He coloured, and there was a long silence. He couldn't find anything to say. He knew we all were aware of his job now.

It was Janetta who finally spoke. 'What you are doing is very wrong!' she said, angrily. 'You'd do yourself a favour if you dropped it.'

Richard gave me a Bible in 1938, the year of my conversion. Every other page was left blank for notes. And as often as we came together to read and study it in the early years, I wrote down thoughts, comments and spiritual experiences; so that after a time I had a whole book of precious words and memories, which brought in friends living and dead from every part of the country.

Many of my notes were in a private code, making it doubly an article of suspicion. But even after my own arrest Mihai was able to rescue it and keep it safe.

When I opened and read so many thoughts of Richard I had noted in the past, it was as if he stood in the room with me. I had the strongest sense of his presence, leaning over me, encouraging and comforting. I noted these visits down in my shorthand. And when I open my Bible now I live these years again. It has become worn and tattered over thirty years, but it is always with me; for it is the sum total of my wealth. A courier of our Mission smuggled it out.

Bibles were rare in Rumania (then as now), and many came to our rooms to hear readings. I could not go easily to Underground Church meetings elsewhere. I was watched and not allowed to leave the town.

But Mihai could attend both secret and open meetings. They were held under the guise of parties. As many as thirty young people would turn up at the home of whoever had the biggest flat. They'd greet each other noisily at the door. Then the record player would be turned up. A pop tune blared out and passers-by could see them dancing. After a time, the record-player was switched off. Someone would speak about the gospel. There were prayers. Then they'd play a few more records, and make party noises for the neighbours' benefit.

'Emil's had three birthdays already this year,' Mihai laughed. 'And his sister's had two wedding anniversaries. Next time we're going on a picnic.'

And they took the record-player with them into the countryside for Sunday excursions—which became a prayer meeting. Lookouts were posted at all paths approaching the spot. If anyone came near, they'd give a warning sign.

All this gave great intensity to the services. Every detail was planned in advance: the place, the hour, the password. Those who went knew they might never come back. It was very unlike a service in the free world. And every preacher spoke his sermon as if it were his last: the words could mean prison and death, and there was weight in them.

Most of our pastors were members of the official church. Faced with controls that made a mockery of 'religious freedom', they carried on a secret ministry. It was the only way they could reach the young, the only way they could preach freely about Christ. Every word they said in church was liable to be reported.

Mihai told us the latest joke: 'The Housing Ministry has ordered that all new blocks of flats are to be built with specially thin walls so that neighbours can spy on each other.'

But was it just a joke?

At meetings, I was often asked about my life in prison and at the Canal. At first I couldn't talk much about it. I couldn't find the words.

Little by little, Mihai got me to talk. When he learnt how we'd been beaten, or forced to eat grass to stay alive, he asked: 'How could you bear all this without giving way and denying Christ?'

I answered by telling him of a peculiarity in the Hebrew language. In Hebrew, amazingly, some future events are described in the perfect tense. Now the perfect tense is so called because it refers to actions completed, perfected, at the time of speaking. So, in the great 53rd chapter of Isaiah which foretells the coming of the Messiah and his sufferings, the writer speaks of these events as belonging to the past, not the future. Yet the words were written 800 years before the coming of Christ.

When Jesus read the prediction of his heavy sufferings, they had already begun. He was then rejected and despised of men. It was his present, and his future. But he read of them in Hebrew as if they'd happened in the past.

Now that is exactly how I felt in the midst of suffering. I tried to explain: Joy is the everlasting present of the Christian spirit. I was in a heavenly place from which no one could move me. Where was the affliction through which I passed? To that most inviolable part of my mind, it belonged to the past. I lived the suffering long ago, while the present reality was delight in the closeness of the Lord.

This certainty that it had already happened saved me. Catastrophes come to us all, but once they're over, they're done with. That is taught in this oddity of Hebrew. We experience now past dramas.

Years later, I discussed this with Richard. In solitary confinement he said, he had felt the same thing in exactly the same way. I wondered if it wasn't another example of communication in the spirit between us.

A month after Trudi had installed herself in Col. Shircanu's home, after interviews with Secret Police officers and much form-filling, she sent me an urgent message. She came to our rooms no longer, but left information at a certain house. Miss Landauer, a teacher, passed it on.

The news was bad. She had heard Shircanu mention the name of Pastor N., who often came to our meetings, on the telephone. 'I'm sure he'll help,' he said.

Challenged, the pastor told us he had been threatened with a long prison sentence. His health was failing. He could not face it. A few days earlier he had promised to 'co-operate' with Shircanu. But he had done nothing for him yet.

Deeply ashamed, Pastor N. left Bucharest for a provincial town.

Then Trudi gave us the name of a girl student whom Shircanu had mentioned in similar terms.

At first she denied everything. I put my hand on hers.

'Please, be truthful. We know well the kind of pressure they'll have used on you. Many people have told us before—of their own free will—how they're forced to inform. You owe it to your real friends to let them know what happened.'

She broke down and knelt beside me.

'I was just walking in the street,' she sobbed, 'when a car drew up and two men said, "We're police. Get in". They didn't take me anywhere, just drove me around for hours. They kept telling me I had to report every week about everything that was said and done in your house and in the church. If I didn't, they said, awful things would happen to my family.'

So she agreed. But swore to me that she had reported nothing very damaging. I could only hope not.

Again and again, Trudi turned up valuable information. But her most spectacular coup was to turn the colonel's home into a secret refuge for the very people he was trying to hunt down.

Now that he'd 'arrived' in the Communist hierarchy, Shircanu began to enjoy its privileges. He took his family off on leisurely holidays to the mountains or the sea. The trusted Trudi was left in charge as caretaker. Mrs. Shircanu called her, 'My little treasure'.

One day a message came through Miss Landauer: 'Why not have a meeting here, in the Shircanus' home? They're away for several days and it's a big house with several exists. No one will suspect.'

And, indeed, who could suspect that Christians would hold a secret meeting in the home of the man who headed the spy work against them? I thought it was worth trying. Rather nervously, half a dozen leaders of the Underground Church arrived on the appointed evening, one by one, at spaced intervals. We were received by a smiling Trudi. Everything went off perfectly.

From then on, we met quite regularly at Shircanu's house whenever the colonel was away.

Trudi played her double role well. As time passed, more and more of our people learned to do the same. They had to sing Red songs and the Party's praises. Most of them succeeded. Several rose high in the ranks.

We learnt from the experience of the Underground Church in Russia, which had survived thirty years of persecution. Brethren from Bessarabia, a province stolen from us during the war by the Soviets, told how Christians resisted there. So we knew how to act in similar conditions.

We had our failures, inevitably. For some workers the strain of a double life proved too heavy. Others became too bold and paid the price.

One of our men was manager of the State book store, a huge place of several floors. He had, of course, no Bibles for sale, but he did have large stocks of anti-God textbooks, which contained a great treasury of texts and verses from the Bible. These were accompanied by comments holding them up to ridicule, but most readers simply laughed at the criticisms. Many were sold.

It was this success, perhaps, which stimulated the manager to go too far.

On August 23rd, 'Freedom Day', his window display drew appreciative crowds. But when people continued to gather around it, smiling and even clapping, the Secret Police grew curious. It was Colonel Shircanu, Trudi told us later, who solved the riddle. Pushing his way to the front of the crowd in Victory Street, he inspected the portraits of Marx, Engels, Lenin and Stalin which took up most of the window space. Nothing to smile at there. Then he noticed that under the pictures was a poster advertising a cheap edition of Victor Hugo's masterpiece. Two words stood out in large black letters: LES MISERABLES.

He had the manager arrested and sent to a labour camp where he was put to cutting reeds—another State project of the day—at the mouth of the Danube.

Fighting Back

Up the dank staircase some months after my release came an official from the Ministry of the Interior. A fat man with a booming voice and black hair parted in the middle. He carried a briefcase, bursting at the seams, full of papers.

Was I a mother? he wanted to know. I was? But what sort of mother could I be? Didn't I care for my child at all? Didn't I want to see him get the very best in education? Didn't I want to see him placed in jobs with good pay and state pensions and ration cards? Of course I did, so WHY DIDN'T I CHANGE MY NAME? HOW DARED I CALL MYSELF A MOTHER!

He shouted and ranted in this vein for several minutes. I sat silent and looked at him. The less I said, the sooner he would get to the point. And I knew what it was.

Divorce. What possible use, he said at last, was it to remain tied to my husband? A counter-revolutionary whom I should never see again? It was only a question of commonsense for an intelligent young woman like myself to get a divorce from an enemy of the State. If I didn't do so now, I certainly would later. How long did I think I could stand up against the State in this blind, stupid disobedience?

So he bullied and cajoled and painted heartbreaking pictures of our ultimate fate. Love, he jeered, *love*! It was all rubbish, didn't exist. What I needed was a new husband and father for my children. There was no love for counter-revolutionaries.

I thought: You dare say this to me in my home.

But my best defence was to be silent.

'I didn't marry my husband only for happy times. We were united for ever, and whatever may come I will not divorce him.'

He argued and urged for another half-hour and in that time I answered nothing. Even God cannot contradict someone who remains silent. Finally the man retreated, shaking his round head.

'Sooner or later you'll come to us,' he said. 'They all do, you know.'

I heard him go noisily down the stairs. Off to his next victim. With whom, as likely as not, he would have more luck.

Every effort was made to force prisoners' wives to ask for a divorce. Firstly, a prisoner's will to resist, even to live, was often shattered when he heard he had been abandoned. Secondly, it helped to get the wives involved in the Communist way of life. Once the divorce was accomplished, women were anxious to forget their husbands and the easiest way to do this was to swallow the Party line. I knew scores of divorced women who parroted slogans mocking political prisoners—the men they had loved and whose children they had borne. Thirdly, the fatherless children were at the mercy of the State, to be indoctrinated from the earliest age.

Only one word was needed to make the break. You said 'Yes' when the official called. He would see to all the rest.

A few days later, the husband would be informed before his cell companions: 'Your wife has decided to divorce you.'

The man would think: 'Who cares about me now? I'm a fool not to give in and sign whatever nonsense they want, and so go free.' But even if he did sign, he might not be released for several years, and meanwhile his wife had children by another man. So homes and families were destroyed. One book couldn't hold the many tragedies of this kind which I found after my release.

In prison, women used to say, 'How stupid I was, quarrelling with my husband over nothing. What a good, loving wife I'll be—if ever we get out!'

But outside, they often changed their tune. 'Why shouldn't I divorce him, if that's what they want? He may remain in prison all his life. How can I feed the children without ration cards, how can I get work? He didn't really care . . .' So they would talk themselves into saying 'Yes' to the Ministry.

I told women like this that we must love men as they are, not for what we think they should be. I advised them to think of the happy moments of their married life, and use them to overcome temptation.

All too often, I failed. The pressures were too severe.

But sometimes I could help people to see matrimonial troubles in a new light wth a simple joke. I remembered an old Jewish story. A bewildered husband came to a rabbi complaining that his wife had given birth to a child three months after their marriage. 'She must have betrayed me!' he said. The rabbi answered, 'Not at all. You have lived with your wife three months. She has lived with you three months. You have lived together three months. This makes a total of nine months. Everything is in perfect order.'

Often I had recourse to compromises a little bit like this in attempting to patch up a marriage.

Or when women came to me saying that they meant to divorce a husband in prison, I would tell them the beautiful story of how it is with the Malagasy, the people of Madagascar. There, when a couple wish to divorce they come separately before the judge who inquires in great detail about how they have lived. He writes from this two declarations and when the day comes for judgement the judge says that a divorce is possible, but first the couple must read what he has written.

The wife reads: 'My beloved—On this day when we must divorce I remember the beauty of the day when we first met. How I longed to be in your arms, how I longed to become your husband! I couldn't wait for work to end so that I could be near you. Do you remember our first kiss . . .' And so he describes all the happiest moments and memories of a shared life. Meanwhile the husband is reading a similar declaration made up of his wife's memories of the marriage, which ends with deep thanks for all the good times, despite the present conflict. More often than not the couple end up in tears, and they go home in peace.

You never reach the end of marriage or the break-up of a friendship when you recall the beautiful things that happened. But too often we don't remember.

Janetta and I knew an attractive young woman, Maura Dalea, with two young children, and a husband in jail. A political prisoner. For seven years she heard nothing. She became involved with another man. The children grew up, filled with Communist propaganda.

Then, at last, a postcard came from prison. She sent him a parcel. But said nothing of her affair.

After eleven years, he was released. He traced his family. The children, a boy and a girl, were now twelve and thirteen. 'We don't know who you are,' they said, cruelly. 'Father? We've got a father already!'

He tried to win Maura back. But it was too late. She divorced him and married the other man.

It broke the husband. I saw him sometimes in the street, with his terrible, wounded face. But he avoided me. A few years later, crushed by years of prison and disappointment, he died.

Janetta said: 'What is happening in the prisons is the lesser part of the tragedy. Hundreds of thousands of people, this whole generation and the generation conceived in these years, will bear the marks of what Communism has done to us.'

Sometimes I could help people escape from these troubles, because I knew them myself. More than once I was tempted during Richard's fourteen years in prison.

The most serious occasion was about a year after my release.

A man who came to our meetings fell in love with me. I was then aged forty-three, alone, with a son to help through the most difficult stage of adolescence when boys need a father. The years were flashing by at alarming speed. And of Richard there was no word, no news.

He was a bachelor of about my age, a solid, steady man of whom Mihai was very fond. A Jewish Christian, he lived in a single room with his elderly parents. We exchanged visits and sometimes he'd take Mihai to the cinema or help him with his studies. Mihai was working very hard over his books at home now.

He was a kind and gentle man, who knew how to make me laugh. The thought crossed my mind: here is someone with whom a woman could live in love and trust. Sometimes he caught hold of my hand while he talked, and looked into my eyes with such longing. I couldn't take my hand away. It never came to what the church or the law would call adultery. But it was adultery in God's eyes. And in my heart.

Luckily, Pastor Grecu saw what was happening and spoke to me as I wish all who see a friend about to fall into such trouble would do.

'You know how much I love and appreciate you,' he said. 'And that couldn't change, whatever happened.'

He spoke with rare emotion and sincerity.

'I've known both you and Richard for many years. And I hope you know that whether you sin or you don't, whether you lose faith or keep it, I would still care for you in the same way. Because of what I know you are, not what you do.

'So forgive me if I ask—how is it between you and Paul?'

For a moment I was silent.

He went on: 'Don't imagine that I haven't had such trials, too. Please answer my question.'

'He's in love with me.'

'And are you in love with him?'

'I don't know. Perhaps.'

He said: 'I remember something Richard used to say: "No passion resists before the bar of reason. If you delay, if you give yourself time to think, you see all the harm you could do to your husband or your wife, to your children, too." I want you to make a hard decision—the hardest there is. Don't see this man again.'

I knew that he was right. With some difficulty, I avoided Paul week after week. Then he stopped trying to see me.

Later I learnt that Pastor Grecu had spoken to him, too, reminding him of Richard, in prison. Only then did I see how close I'd come to betraying all the years of waiting and trust. I knelt and prayed.

There were other temptations. Fourteen years is a long time. Sometimes I came near to yielding. Sometimes it was merely a passing weakness of the flesh. Sexuality is a remorseless driving force and one must, at times, not accuse oneself too harshly. One can remember to have understanding for one's own weaknesses as well as for those of others.

One morning I was in church, scrubbing the floor, when Marietta rushed in, waving a postcard.

Tears ran down her cheeks. 'I think—I think it's from . . .'

She could not continue, but knelt on the damp boards beside me, breathless.

I turned the cheap little card over. It was signed 'Vasile Georgescu'—but Richard's handwriting, large and irregular and beautiful, was unmistakable. My eyes hazed over.

I knew that political prisoners might write only ten censored lines. What could he say, after so many years, not knowing if his wife and family lived? I looked.

This dear, long dreamed-of message began: 'Time and distance quench a small love, but make a great love grow stronger . . .' And he asked me to come and see him on a certain date in Tirgul-Ocna, the prison hospital.

Soon the news spread through the Underground Church. The message was learnt by heart by people all over the country. It became a talisman of faith.

In prison, they had taken away even Richard's name. He was 'Vasile Georgescu'. The guards weren't allowed to know his identity. If the secret leaked out, questions might be asked abroad. He had to vanish without trace. But that was in 1948.

Now Khrushchev was working his way towards supreme power in Russia and there were signs of great changes to come. Throughout 1954, after Stalin's death, we hoped the West would do something for us. But with 1955 came the Geneva Summit conference, then Rumania's entry into the United Nations. We were shocked at the news. Tens of thousands of political prisoners filled the country's jails. No one imagined that Rumania could be welcomed to U.N. membership before they were set free.

But if the U.N. charter binding members to religious and political freedom was ignored, the summit conference brought some improvements in the prisons. We heard that food was better and medicine available. There were rumours of an amnesty. More visits were allowed.

Richard's postcard was the best news I could have had. But

I, who so longed to see him, couldn't go. Every week I had to present myself at the police station. They refused to revoke the ban on my leaving Bucharest. So Mihai had to take my place.

Tirgul-Ocna is a small town far to the north, on the other side of the Carpathians. The train makes a journey of several hundred miles around the mountains. I arranged with 'Aunt Alice' to go with Mihai. Not that she could meet Richard—the only visitors permitted were wife and child.

I waited behind. They were away two days, and all the time the worries went through my head: Would they see him? (I remembered how Mihai had travelled so far to visit me at the Canal, and then been turned back.) Would Richard be allowed to receive the few warm clothes and food I'd packed? Since he was in a prison sanatorium, he must be very sick. Would he be able to stand, or even talk to Mihai?

They came back, late on a December evening. We heard them climbing the stairs.

'We saw him! We saw him!' Alice called before she was through the door. Following it up with, 'He's alive. He's up and about!'

They came in with snow on their shoulders.

'Mihai!'

'Mother! Daddy's well and he says to tell you that he knows he'll come back to us soon. If God can perform one miracle and let him see me, he said, then he can perform two and bring us all together.'

Soon we were all in tears. And then we made them something hot to drink, and they told the story. Marietta and Peter were there. We became quite gay. To be a dumb cripple, an epileptic, a prisoner's wife and son, are no hindrances to joy. Alice's cheeks coloured and her thin hands fluttered with excitement as she talked.

'We had to wait hours and hours in the snow. They let us in through the main gateway, then we stood about in a wired-off compound away from the sanatorium buildings. The prisoners had to cross an open space to get to a big tin hut where they received their visitors. It was terrible to see them. Frightening! Gangs of muffled shapes against the dazzling snow. Like grey ghosts. And among them, going along, I saw Richard. You couldn't miss him, he's so tall. I waved like a mad thing, but he couldn't pick me out. We were all in a huddle, and everyone waving. Only Mihai was allowed to speak with him.'

When at last they got away there was no train back, and they stayed with peasant friends in the little town.

Mihai had been so overcome at seeing his father that at first I couldn't get much from him. But I was too happy to mind. He'd been allowed to leave the food and clothes.

Only later did I realize what a shock it must have been for him. To see the father he loved and respected behind bars, shaven-headed, skeleton-thin.

Mihai had burst out immediately with the words he'd been preparing: 'Mummy says not to be afraid, because if we don't meet again on earth we will in heaven.' Comforting words! Richard smiled and asked, 'Have you enough to eat?' Mihai replied, 'Oh yes, Our Father looks after us!' The political officer of the jail, who was listening, grinned at this. He thought it meant that I had married again.

In such conditions they could say little. Richard's last words were: 'Mihai, the only gift I can give you as a father is to tell you this: always seek the highest of Christian virtues, which is to keep the right measure in all things.'

I put Richard's postcard between the pages of my Bible. Now and then I went to look at it, and read for the hundredth time. In prison he became a master at writing these miniscule letters. He told me later that others came to him for help because he could squeeze in so much meaning. They also asked each other what he'd said, and Richard's words went around. The result was that dozens of prisoners began their postcards: 'Time and distance quench a small love, but make a great love stronger.' So messages of love and hope were going out far and wide.

The year 1956 began with the whole Communist bloc in rebellious mood. 'Five Year Plans' had got nowhere. Food was as short as ever. Wages were kept low. All the hopes raised after Stalin's death had faded.

Then, in February, at the Twentieth Congress of the Communist Party, Khrushchev made his secret speech denouncing Stalin and his works. The Russians never published it, but before long in every country of Eastern Europe people felt the warm breeze of the thaw from Moscow.

Faster and faster came the signs of de-stalinization. The huge forces of militia and Secret Police were reduced in size. Million-dollar trade contracts were negotiated with Western countries to rescue the economy. Collectivization was relaxed. Struggles began in several Communist bloc countries for the Party leadership. And most wonderful of all, hundreds of political prisoners were being freed under an amnesty each day.

I didn't dare to hope that Richard would be among them. We had no hint, no news. He had still almost twelve years to serve.

One lovely morning in June 1956 I went out to visit friends.

And when I returned, there he was. He put his arms around me.

It was an evening of laughter and tears and greetings to friends who came from all over Bucharest. Long after midnight, we borrowed a mattress from a neighbour and made up a bed. Richard is so tall we had to put a cushion on a chair for his feet.

He didn't sleep. I know because Janetta and I couldn't sleep. In the small hours he got up and walked quietly to look for a long time at Mihai, as if to make sure that he was really there.

Richard had suffered beating and doping in prison. He had eighteen torture scars on his wasted body, but had not talked. Doctors found that his lungs were covered with the healed scars of tuberculosis. They simply couldn't believe he had survived eight and a half years (almost three of them in solitary confinement in an underground cell) virtually untreated. He was now given the best bed in a hospital ward. All released prisoners were treated with kindness and generosity by the people wherever they went. They were the most privileged group in Rumania, which infuriated the Communists.

Richard had to move continually. Brethren gathered from all over the country to see him. So he had to go from one hospital to another to avoid attracting the Secret Police.

Soon after he got better we celebrated our twentieth wedding anniversary. Richard hadn't a penny to buy me a present. But he obtained a pretty, bound notebook and in it, every evening, he wrote verses, love-poems, addressed to me. Mihai and other close friends also wrote little messages in it. And on the day of our anniversary, he gave it to me. But this lovely gift was not mine for long.

In the first flush of the political thaw, Richard was allowed a licence to preach. Persecution had brought the churches much closer, and he was invited first to speak in the Orthodox cathedral at Sibiu, where the priest was an old friend.

'The only trouble is that I've the Metropolitan to think about,' he said. 'You'll be expected to make the sign of the cross and so forth.'

Richard said: 'I'll make however many signs are prescribed in Orthodox ritual so long as I can speak about His cross.

I went to Sibiu with him. He was still weak and they had to find something for him to sit on while he spoke. They decided to bring out the Metropolitan's throne. And when this was seen the rumour went around that the Metropolitan himself was to preach. And instead there came this man. Who was, people said, a Jew.

Richard not only made the sign of the cross, he preached

about the cross, and its meaning. It was a sermon without political content, on the surface. Nevertheless informers in the church
reported every word, and the Secret Police understood its hidden
meaning, sometimes better than some Christians.

When next Richard spoke, giving a series of talks to students
at Cluj University, one of the top men from the Ministry of Cults
was sent to listen. This man reported that Richard's lectures
were a 'torrent of sedition'. The sedition consisted in the fact
that he answered one after another all the Marxist arguments
against religion and defeated them. The Lutheran bishop was
pressured, unwillingly, into depriving Richard of his right to
preach in Rumania. He had possessed it for six weeks.

The representative of the Ministry of Cults said at the next
meeting of Lutheran pastors, with hatred in his voice: 'Wurmbrand is finished, finished!' And walked from the building.

A few minutes later there was a screech of brakes and a terrible crash. The man had been knocked down and crushed against
the wall by a car that inexplicably mounted the pavement.

Richard went on preaching in secret. He sped from place to
place. He spoke briefly in small churches and at underground
meetings and left at once before anyone could report to the local
police. He left the house without telling even me where he was
going, and I lived in constant fear.

Mihai called him 'The Phantom Preacher', but knew it was
not much of a joke. At any moment he might be arrested.

Before the year was out the risings in Poland and Hungary
blazed briefly and were stamped out. The 'thaw' had been short-
lived.

But in the four months between Richard's release and the
October revolutions, we had a respite. A small theological seminary at Sibiu was allowed to train a few new pastors. Mihai
decided he would join.

He was now eighteen, and had a character of steel. He bore
little resemblance to the boy Richard had left behind so many
years ago. He had gone through intense spiritual struggles as
well as physical hardship in that time. But, through all the doubts
and in spite of indoctrination, he remained a Christian.

Richard helped now to strengthen his belief. But from the
start he said, 'Father, I love and respect you, but you're you and
I'm me. We don't think alike on everything. I've a personality
of my own!'

Mihai had passed all his high school examinations without a
day's schooling after the age of fifteen. Now he was set on entering the ministry.

Richard said, 'Are you sure you want to go to this seminary? I seriously don't recommend it. For any young man.'

'Why ever not?'

'Because the way seminaries teach in these days is mostly destructive. You won't be taught love towards God, or to the Bible, or the best way to follow the saints. You'll dissect the Bible, you'll pick away at the word of God. It could be poison to your soul. Some of the professors are saints, others are far from being so.'

But Mihai had decided.

When he came home for the Christmas holidays I had a bad shock. At family prayer, Richard read something from the Gospels in which Jesus quotes the Old Testament.

'Oh,' said Mihai later. 'I don't think it means that. Anyway, Jesus didn't have the knowledge and background needed for a correct interpretation of the Old Testament by scientific standards.'

'He didn't?' I said, wanting to burst into tears. 'Let us be thankful for that.'

Mihai overcame this early brashness. We talked to him, and in the end he opposed the Communist-inspired teachings of his professors. Which got him into much trouble.

His ideal was to become a missionary in India at that time. He studied Indian religions and Hindu practices. I was a little afraid when I saw him standing on his head for several minutes, according to the rules of Hata-Yoga. I asked: 'Don't you think God made the legs to stand on?'

For his thesis he began work on a study of British nonconformist preachers, Booth and Spurgeon, men who cared little about official theological studies.

The Communists wished to keep the school open to impress the West (Rumania had just entered the World Council of Churches) but with as few students as possible. When 400 applied to join, the authorities were alarmed. They let the boys know that if they insisted, their fathers might lose their jobs. So many withdrew, 'voluntarily'. By 1965 the Lutheran seminary in Cluj had only five students left. There were six students in the Baptist seminary of Bucharest.

But for three years Mihai managed to carry on his studies at Sibiu. There was a fine library and some of the professors were excellent men. So he was not at home when they came to arrest his father for the second time.

We knew it was coming. The new wave of terror began in 1958. And we all saw now how we'd been tricked. Many really thought the Communists were interested in coming to some kind of terms with the West. That they would mellow. People had lived through all the deceit of the past yet even now they did not realize the depth of the lie.

In July 1958 a series of laws was enacted tougher than anything yet seen in the satellite countries. The death penalty was ordered for scores of minor offences, and was being liberally applied by the autumn. Mass arrests returned. Thousands were sent to new slave labour projects, such as the clearing of the Danube Delta marshes. All juvenile delinquents (i.e. young people who criticized the Government) were sent 'to the reeds'.

A new purge began in official ranks. All those of socially doubtful origin who had found jobs in the 'thaw' were now sacked. A rule forbade them, and their children, from working for any branch of the public services.

The fight against religion was renewed. On Khrushchev's orders churches were closed and priests arrested throughout Eastern Europe as part of a seven-year drive 'to eradicate the vestiges of superstition'.

Our attic was now more than ever a centre for the Underground Church. It could not escape attention for much longer. Every evening Richard prayed: 'God, if you know some prisoner to whom I could be of use, send me back to jail.' To this prayer, I said a hesitant Amen.

One Tuesday evening in January, 1959, a woman from our church arrived in tears. The week before she had borrowed some copies of Richard's sermons. Hundreds of these, cyclostyled, were circulating throughout Rumania. It was strictly against the law. Now the police had raided the woman's flat and taken off the copies.

We also learnt through an informant in the Party that Richard had been denounced by a young pastor who claimed to be his friend. He may have been blackmailed—made to sign the denunciation under threat of prison. Anyhow, he did this and it is not for me to judge his motives. We were fond of him, and it is better simply to continue to love.

On Wednesday, January 15th, at 1 a.m., the police battered on the door and burst into our attic before we could get out of bed. The light came on.

'You're Richard Wurmbrand? Get into the other room. And stay there.'

Our tiny flat was full of men opening cupboards, turning out drawers, throwing papers on the floor. On Richard's desk, where he wrote, they found pages of notes, typewritten sermons, worn Bibles. All were seized.

Then they found my anniversary gift, the notebook in which Richard and Mihai had written verses to me.

'Please don't take that. It's a personal thing, a present. It's of no use to you.'

They took it.

The captain in charge brought Richard out of the other room. He had been handcuffed.

I said, 'Aren't you ashamed to treat innocent people like this?'

Richard moved towards me. They caught his arms. He warned, 'I shan't leave this house without a struggle unless you allow me to embrace my wife.'

'Let him go,' said the captain.

We knelt together in prayer, with the Secret Police standing around us. Then we sang the hymn, 'The Church's one foundation is Jesus Christ, her Lord'.

A hand fell on Richard's shoulder. 'We've got to get going. It's nearly 5 a.m.,' the Captain said. But he spoke quietly and his eyes glistened.

I went after them down the staircase. Richard turned his head to say, 'Give all my love to Mihai and the pastor who denounced me.' They pushed him into a van.

When it started up, I began to cry out, 'Richard! Richard!'

I ran after the van, calling out and weeping. Along the icy street. Then it vanished around a corner. I had to stop, breathless, confused.

Back at the attic the door stood open. Weeping, I fell on the floor.

I cried out, 'Lord, I give my husband into your hands. I can do nothing, but you can pass through locked doors. You can put angels around him. You can bring him back!'

I sat in the darkness, praying. Until the new day arrived. Then I began to remember what I still had to do. Alice came to see me. I told her, 'Again they have stolen my Richard.'

The New Terror

First, Mihai had to be told. It wouldn't be easy. He'd been through so many tragedies. And the news had to be kept from informers at the university, or he would be expelled. So I couldn't go myself to Sibiu. They knew me there.

Early next morning Alice took the train, and waited in a small park near the theological faculty for Mihai to pass. She dared not ask the other students. If they reported her visit (and it was an offence not to do so) the news would come out.

She could only hope that Mihai would pass that way. It was bitterly cold in the park. Snow clung to the branches of trees and lay thick on the benches. Towards evening, he came.

'Yes,' he said. 'I've been expecting it. Tell Mother I'll come home at once. They may take her, too.'

'But your studies,' said Suzanne. 'Nearly three years you've worked . . .'

'What does it matter? It's sometimes the pastors with degrees who betray and destroy what the real "fishers of men" have built. Better without a degree. I'll be thrown out soon, anyway. When they feel like it.'

It was very late when Alice returned to the attic, and told me all they'd said.

I did see Richard once more before he vanished for another six years. There was a trial. Relatives could attend. The Party had grown a little more formal since the heady days of 1948. We don't jail men for nothing, they said to the world; we have our tribunals, our judges.

There they sat, five of them, on a raised platform under a red banner which read: JUSTICE FOR THE PEOPLE IN THE SERVICE OF THE PEOPLE. Above this were portraits of Gheorghiu-Dej and other well-fed Party faces.

Enemies of the People came through one door and went out of another—case heard, defence offered, sentence given within minutes. Priests, peasants, gypsies, journalists moved through as if on a conveyor belt.

A sweeper had got drunk and shouted, 'Gheorghiu-Dej is an old idiot. He ought to go back to driving his puff-puff!' (Dej was a former railwayman). This insult was tossed about the court until the sweeper's lawyer asked for clemency. 'Two years,' said the President. Out went the sweeper. And in came Richard.

I did not hear one word of what followed, and nor did he. We simply looked at each other. For the last time, it might have been.

Mihai told me afterwards that it was a re-hearing of his old, secret trial, which took place in 1951. The amnesty was cancelled, the old sentence restored. And as he went out he turned his head and gave us a last, cheerful smile. It had taken a couple of minutes.

The clerk, a small, exhausted man, came and handed me a piece of paper. It said that Wurmbrand, R., born 1909 etc., etc., was sentenced to twenty-five years. An increase of five years.

Later we discovered that the sentence also included a heavy fine, plus 'legal expenses'. And all our property was once more confiscated; this happened to every political prisoner's family. We had no money, so two officials from the tax office came and wrangled about it. They went off with the few precious things we'd collected since my release in 1953.

They left us the beds, a table and two chairs. We thought ourselves quite lucky. But over the next six years they came again and again, demanding money, confiscating. Winter and summer, I battled with bureaucracy over our few poor sticks.

It was a time of frantic fear. Every day friends were arrested. Nearly all our dear ones were back in jail. Night and day ceased to exist for us. People came from every part of the country with stories of terror, of churches closed and menfolk kidnapped.

While all this was happening to us, Khrushchev paid his 'ice-breaking' visit to the U.S.A. and there was talk of a major Summit meeting in Paris for May 1960.

We were discussing the prospects in Miss Landauer's flat.

'You'll see, Sabina,' she said. 'After this conference your husband will be freed. They'll come to an agreement. The prison doors will open!'

Then the telephone rang—a neighbour to say that the police were in our attic.

'Don't come back tonight! You'll be arrested for certain. They've already taken Alice.'

Alice was perhaps the most unselfish, generous woman I know. All she had she gave to others. She cared for the children of political prisoners. Children who were literally turned out on to the street. This was her crime.

Because she refused to inform on friends during her interrogation she was terribly beaten up. Her teeth were kicked out, bones broken. Then she was sentenced to eight years imprisonment.

The police searched our attic for two hours that night. Besides Alice they arrested a girl who happened to call in—a common practice.

We came back later to the wrecked flat. Clothes and papers were strewn about. The beds upended. Even the mattresses slashed.

Mihai said, 'D'you know what they've taken? The Great Rheumatism Cure!'

Old Mrs. Tomaziu had copied out by hand pages and pages from a book by a German doctor which gave a rather dubious course of treatment for rheumatism. She'd insisted on lending them to me. 'It's a very rare book, dear. I could only borrow it for a day. So don't lose my notes, whatever you do.' I had a hard time explaining to her that they had been seized by the Secret Police. I don't think she was ever fully convinced.

Hours and days were spent in trying to get news from the police of Alice and other friends who were arrested every day. Success was rare. They'd vanished into the bottomless well of prison. Perhaps, one day, we'd hear of them again. (It was a long time after Alice's arrest that we discovered what had happened to her.)

All our closest friends seemed to be going.

Elderly Mr. Trifu, who had been like a grandfather to Mihai. He was a poet in the mould of W. H. Davies—without a formal education, a countryman who wrote lyrics of heavenly simplicity and depth. Mihai was, so to speak, brought up in his lap.

And Nailescu, perhaps the greatest composer of religious music in the country. He left a wife and four children, who were turned out of their home on to the street.

And Pastor Armeanu. I've told people in the West his story. They think I'm joking. He was sentenced to twenty years for preaching on the text: 'Cast your nets on the right side . . .'

'Aha!' they said. 'Why not on the left side? Imperialist propaganda!'

An informer reported this sermon. It was made the pretext for his arrest.

Pastor Armeanu left behind a wife and five young children. They were deported to a desert place, the Baragan. One day, Mrs. Armeanu came to our door, exhausted and sick. We took her in. She was no trouble. On the contrary, her sweet nature, which bore everything without complaint, helped us all.

But now we were five.

The man we all suspected of denouncing Pastor Armeanu came to an Underground Church meeting.

Mrs. Armeanu whispered: 'Leave him be. He was forced to do it.' She wanted to forgive and forget.

But I didn't. I taxed him: Why had he done it?

He blustered. 'They pestered me for months. Anyway, I didn't say anything that wasn't the truth. He did say the things I reported and even if I agreed with them, they were counter-revolutionary. I did my duty, as I saw it.'

'But then you're on the side of a regime that stops at nothing? That kills and arrests innocent men, that poisons children with atheism?'

He shifted uneasily. 'Oh no. Of course not.'

'Then why didn't you inform them that you yourself are against the regime, instead of saying that your brother is?'

There was bitterness in my heart. I knew that pastors and friends and even a bishop had some guilt for Richard's arrest. They loved themselves more than the principles they preached. I fought with myself, feeling hatred enter me towards those who had taken my husband. And so many husbands. I prayed, but could not find peace.

Then Marietta cut from somewhere a picture of Christ on the cross, by one of the Italian masters. Often my eyes strayed to where it was pinned on the attic wall. And each time I remembered His last words: Father, forgive them, for they know not what they do. And also: I thirst.

How they thirsted, the betrayers, for forgiveness! Which I would not give them. Which in my bitterness I withheld.

And with that thought something changed in me. I knew that even for saints a time may come when self-love is stronger than love of God. The Lutheran bishop Mueller, a good friend, used to say that those whom others call a traitor might be seen by God as a weak saint. He said it not minding at all that others might consider him a weak bishop for this. I resolved to give love and expect nothing in return.

In the winter of 1960 snow came early. The streets were deep in it and no one went out if they could avoid it. A pane of glass had gone from the window. Mihai nailed a piece of old carpet over the hole, but nothing stops a determined wind. It whined mournfully under the door.

'We might as well be sitting outside,' Marietta said. 'It isn't a bit warmer in here.'

The carpet blocked the light and in spite of the draught our leaky little attic was horribly stuffy at night, with five people in it.

When I wasn't busy with the Underground Church I tramped the streets from Government office to office, trying to win a respite over the fine imposed on Richard. Unless so much was paid within a certain time, they would come and take all we had left. I waited on benches in draughty halls to see officials, and filled in dozens of complicated forms.

It didn't do us any good.

One day two tax department officials hammered on the door. Mihai opened it and called to me. They wanted more money. I couldn't pay? Too bad. They'd make a list of all furnishings and household goods, so that I might reclaim them when I found the cash.

I said, 'That won't take you long.'

They noted down chairs, tables, cutlery, the cabinet of an old gramophone with its works missing (a relic of Mihai's musical repair days). The beds we could keep. They were, anyhow, too broken to move.

'Carpet, brown, small,' said the first man, and gave it a tug. It came away from the window, letting in an icy, hissing wind.

'No. Better count that as part of the window,' he said. 'They've got people sleeping here.' And they put it back.

I thanked them. But that was a mistake. They were reminded of their duty.

'You've got three days to pay. Otherwise you've had it.'

And off they went.

I spent the next morning trying to see the correct functionary. At last my turn came. He sat in a cubicle with pasteboard walls.

'You mean they haven't cleared you out yet!' He was furious. 'What business is it of mine what you do next? The court instructions are clear. Either you pay immediately, and pay it all, or your property's confiscated. You can't pay? That's it. They'll be round tomorrow, first thing.'

I walked down the stairs. I couldn't stop the tears running down my cheeks. Shivering and coughing, I paused in the big hall a moment before taking the plunge into the icy street. Then someone touched my arm.

A tall, bespectacled man in a dark suit had followed me down. I supposed he was another official, with some new threat. He glanced quickly round.

'I know your case,' he said. 'Here. Take this.'

And he vanished, hurrying back the way he had come.

I looked at the folded notes he'd slipped into my hand. Enough to stall them off for weeks!

Walking home, I didn't notice my sodden shoes, my frozen hands, my exhaustion. My heart was filled with glowing calm. That kind, that generous man, who had shown me a sign of God's love. Who could he be?

Mihai made discreet inquiries and found he was from a department of the tax office. One of the many friends of the Underground Church. We could not meet — it was too dangerous — but every month from then on, as long as Richard was in prison, he sent a sum out of his small salary.

Mihai had been duly expelled from his seminary. Our friend Bishop Mueller did all he could to keep him in. Dr. Mueller was despised by many of his Lutheran flock because of his open collaboration with the Communists, who even honoured him with decorations. They did not know that he reported to the Underground Church every discussion with high officials. He also secretly protected and helped families of Christian martyrs. I can say this now openly, because he is dead.

Mihai managed to make his way into the engineering and construction faculty of the university. Not admitting, of course, that he was the son of a political prisoner.

'They'll find out in a few months or so,' he said. 'Then I'll be thrown out and can join something else.'

I was trying to earn a little money by working at home. I'd found an old knitting machine, designed to turn out jerseys and pullovers. The trouble was that when I wanted to work, the machine didn't.

The friend who had given it to me soon discovered that he'd given himself as well. He was a mechanic, and hardly a day passed without my calling on him for some repair.

At last he said, 'Bearings have gone.'

'What does that mean?'

'It means we throw it out. Scrap it. I can't get spares.'

'Oh dear.' My pullovers, if sometimes a little unusual in shape, had sold well.

'I'll look around. Perhaps I can get you another cheap.'

A week later he arrived with a pair of simpler machines for making socks. Now Mrs. Armeanu and I were busy. Needles were the problem. They broke often, and replacements were simply unobtainable in the new Rumania. All supplies went into the factories. The mechanic tried to take a few from his place of work. But employees were searched as they left. I couldn't let him risk imprisonment for a needle. So sock production often stopped for months at a time.

We had a socks black-market. Since no one could sell goods without State permission (it was illegal to make them privately, come to that) our friends sold them at factory gates. Or in the flea market. Or at bus stations. Anywhere that offered the safety of a crowd.

Finally, we gave it up. In the sixties, economic barriers with the West were eased. Rumania got Western machinery and know-how. When nylon socks appeared, mine had to disappear. I was quite happy about it.

After this, I kept my money-making ventures to language-teaching.

'Comrade Sabina Wurmbrand?'

A young man in a dark raincoat had come to the door after dark.

'I am Mrs. Wurmbrand.'

'Tomorrow at 9 a.m. you're to report to the Ministry of the Interior. You'll show this card to the guards and ask for the room indicated on it.' He gave me a cold stare. 'Good night!' And clattered down the stairs.

There was no more frightening summons. Visitors to the Ministry usually became guests for an indefinite spell. Had someone denounced me? We were a sad little family in the attic that night.

Early next morning I packed a small bag with toilet things and warm clothes. I said goodbye to them all, and set off.

The office was rather grand, with a carpet and curtains and pretty girl secretaries. The portraits of Lenin and Co. were in colour and well-framed. Behind a desk the size of a grand piano sat a plump man in civilian clothes, about forty years old.

'Sit down, Comrade Wurmbrand.' He waved to an armchair. 'We've asked you to come here because we're taking an interest in your case. Tell me about yourself and your family. Don't worry! Nothing will go beyond these walls. You have a son (he glanced at the papers on his desk) Mihai ... How are his studies proceeding ... ?'

I'd caught the drift. It was another attempt to persuade me into divorce. Politeness would be applied where pressure had failed.

He was suave and confident, leaning back expansively in his chair.

I answered, 'I love my husband, and whatever happens I shall stay married to him. We are united for ever.'

'Well now, let me make a little proposal. You want your child to complete his education. You want the right to work, to live your own life. You can have all this, very simply. Just leave your identity card with me. And in forty-eight hours we'll send it round to you endorsed in your own name. Forget about big words like divorce. This is just a simple formality the State asks of you. Isn't it the intelligent thing to do?' He paused playing with a pencil. 'Of course, if you don't co-operate, there are other ways. When we want something, we get it . . .'

I looked at the political officer. Into his eyes.

'Suppose one day *you* are in prison, like so many other officials? Would you want your wife to divorce you?'

At this he sat up with a jerk. Then he exploded.

'Don't you know where you are, who I am? How dare you put questions to me!' He flung the pencil into the fireplace. 'Now get out, get out! And don't forget what I've told you! Understand?'

I picked up the little bag and went to the door without answering.

'Understand?'

But he had understood, too, for that was their last attempt to make me divorce Richard.

Instead, they told me: he is dead.

It happened on two occasions.

First, a couple of haggard young men came to the door saying they were ex-prisoners. I believe they were. But they couldn't look me in the eyes. When they began to describe seeing Richard in jail, I knew at once that I was dealing with provocateurs.

'Poor Pastor Wurmbrand,' said the bolder of the two. 'We don't know exactly what happened to him. He became very moody before the end. Wouldn't talk to anyone. Or so we heard in Gherla prison.'

'What are you trying to tell me? That he committed suicide?'

'You can never be sure. But we know he was taken out feet first. And who could blame him if he did?'

He tried to be cunning. But could not have chosen a stupider lie.

'Poor Pastor Wurmbrand. A real saint, he was. Everyone said so.'

'Please go, now.' I couldn't find anything else to say.

'We want to say, Mrs. Wurmbrand, how sorry . . .'

'Please go.'

They looked horribly guilty and ashamed. Probably they did it just for the sake of a ration card, or the promise of a job.

The second time, it was officially stated that Richard was

dead. But not directly to me. A plain-clothes man called at a friend's house. They didn't want to break the sad news to Mrs. Wurmbrand personally. Would the friend oblige? Then just say Pastor Wurmbrand had died after some weeks of illness and was buried in prison.

I was glad to be spared another sickening interview.

But they didn't stop there. Richard's name was by now being whispered all over the country. He was becoming a legend. Children would not go to bed without praying for his safety. To put an end to it released prisoners were sent to Christian homes in several of the bigger towns to persuade people that he had died in prison by his own hand. Nobody believed them.

Then Mihai was expelled from his faculty. He had refused categorically to comply with Communist teachings and practices. Now he discovered that they knew all about him: his hours, his friends. They kept files on every Christian. You had to be a virtuoso of underground work, which few of us were, to keep things hidden from the Secret Police. We knew people informed on us. It was an inevitable part of life. But Mihai said the church had been too deeply infiltrated.

'Mother, I hate to say it, but you're too soft-hearted. You let all these people come to the flat: they've only got to say "Praise the Lord!" and they're in. But we've got to be hard with these informers.'

I would have liked to argue, but he went on: 'I'm frightened they'll arrest you again, Mother. And me. They know I'm up to the neck in your secret work. But it isn't just people like us, who at least know the risks and have a purpose in life. I'm thinking about the boys I used to know in Sibiu who got taken in twice a week and beaten up until they promised to inform. About the kids in Brasov who tried to form a freedom party. It was a childish game. They even kept a diary and records of their meetings. But the Communists like to play, too. They're all in jail now. Perhaps being beaten to death.'

I thought of Alice. That sweet, gentle woman. Stretched out on a bench with her feet and hands tied and her teeth kicked in. Richard had been horribly tortured, too, on his first arrest. Though he never spoke of it. What was he suffering now?

We knew that although several Underground Church meetings had recently been broken up by the police, others had been left alone. Deliberately, so that informers could work in peace. Now we made a new effort against them.

Our meetings were increasing in size. Up to fifty or sixty people at a time. We had to be specially careful if someone at a meeting had rank—a university professor, or a Party member.

They would be watching him. Then we kept numbers down to half a dozen trusted friends.

One way of spotting informers was to plant false news. Word was passed to a suspect that a gathering was to be held at the address of a friend. If an unusual number of plain-clothes snoopers were seen near the house, then we knew he was guilty.

Generally, we kept our knowledge from him. Sorry the house was empty, we smiled. We had to change the address at the last minute—didn't have time to tell you.

A known informer is valuable. You can mislead him. If you drive him out of the church, he's replaced at once by one you don't know. So the rule was: keep friendly.

Sometimes we traced informers through information from arrested men. The questions which interrogators didn't ask them were often more important to us than those they did.

One of our members had been secretly printing Russian gospels. Yet he was never asked about it during interrogation. We guessed why—his fellow-printer was the informer. He was a Christian —caught in the net of blackmail and threats.

He still worked and prayed with us in love; and yet was their agent, out of fear.

So it went on. On the one hand the struggle to keep out wind and rain, tax-collectors and Secret Police; on the other the battle to hold together the Underground Church. We lived dangerously. And were never bored.

In November I made a trip to Cluj. A show trial had been arranged there for leaders of the Army of the Lord, the forbidden religious organization which Richard had done much to help. I heard that a close friend of ours, a teacher, was among them.

The Army is made up mostly of countryfolk and hundreds of them came to Cluj on the day of the trial. They stood in a silent mass outside the gates of the military tribunal. It was raining heavily.

They'd come from all over Rumania, in spite of the dangers of being noted and denounced, to show their loyalty to those who were to be court-martialled for their faith.

When the prison vans arrived, the crowd surged forward to catch a glimpse of their dear ones. In dirty, coarse prison clothes the accused men and women were hustled into the court.

Wives and families called out to them, clutching bundles of warm clothes and food.

'Get back! Get back!' The militia brandished their rifles. A couple of younger soldiers, rattled, made as if to shoot. There was a moment of panic.

An officer was shouting to someone in the building, 'Phone for reinforcements!' Using their guns as staves, the guards pushed the crowd out of the yard, into the street, men, women and children, then tried to close the gates. The cry went up: *Take us too, We are their brethren. We believe like them!*

At the end of the street a car appeared, full of police with threatening guns. People ran and scattered into doorways. But the moment the car passed, they churned out again and pressed against the gates.

In the end the police, who were totally unprepared for such a demonstration, agreed to let in close relatives only. A handful of wives and children were admitted. The rest stood all day outside the gates, trying to persuade the guards to let them in. Late at night the crowd was big as ever.

The court was trying to avoid further trouble by rushing through all the trials at a single sitting.

At dusk the prisoners were led out, back to their cells. An officer emerged to say that sentences would not be known until next day. Those who'd come from out of town were found beds for the night by the local people who sympathized with them. Most of us were in tears. None of the wives had a chance to say a last word to their husbands or to give them the precious bundles.

I was taken to the home of an Underground Church member, with half a dozen wives of arrested men. We decided to spend the night in prayer for them.

'Announce it or not tomorrow,' sighed one wife, 'it will be heavy.'

It wasn't the first trial for Army of the Lord followers. Far from it. From twenty-year-olds to people in their sixties, they had been hunted down for years.

Next morning I went to the courts. A list had been nailed to the gates, which were locked, and a sad group stood around it. My friend's sentence was eight years.

I walked to the railway station in the rain and sat down to wait for the train back to Bucharest.

I was asked to come urgently to the house of a secret Christian. Trudi was there. Not the smiling, capable Trudi who welcomed us to Colonel Shircanu's house and eavesdropped on his telephone, but a crumpled, woebegone girl. For a moment I thought they had found her out.

'What is it?' I asked. The others were out and we could talk freely.

It was about her fiancé, a young man of the same age. They had not yet money to set up a home and in any case Trudi felt that she must keep to her post of danger, at least for the time being. Now the boy was pressing for proof of her affections. 'If you really loved me,' he said at every meeting, 'you would not hold me off like this.' She was desperately afraid of losing him. What could she do?

So with Trudi, as with so many other girls, the problem of purity arose. To touch, or not to touch? Now, looking back over thirty years towards the question I'd faced as a girl in Paris, and having seen so much, and had so long to think about it in prison and while waiting for Richard, I knew the answer.

To ask *Why purity?* is as wrong as to ask *Why life?* It is one of the great gifts of nature. Since life began, the ideal put before man in the great religions everywhere, in China, in the Greek mysteries, has been purity: the dream of a pure woman. The Gospel begins with the story of a virgin, as opposed to the Messalinas of that time. Joan of Arc had to be a virgin to save France. Reading the life of St. Thérèse of Lisieux, you love her for that virtue. Would Spinoza or Beethoven have produced such exalted work if they had not been pure?

To ask, Why be pure? is like asking, Why be honest? Ask, and you reveal a little of your soul.

In all the world of literature I have two favourite characters: Solveig in *Peer Gynt* and Gretchen in Goethe's *Faust*.

Peer Gynt was a scoundrel and a drunkard, but he met on his way one pure and devout girl. Peer was sure she would wait for him. Decades passed, in which Peer went from bad to worse, but he always remembered that he had known a pure girl. Her image was continually before his eyes. When he returned to her he was old, but she had been the means of his salvation.

Gretchen was seen by Faust walking to church and she, too would not lift her eyes to him. In a moment of madness, tempted by Mephistopheles, she fell into sin with him, but she atoned for it in prison (which she called a holy place) and won back her purity. She longed for Faust in heaven, and the thought of her put him on the way to salvation.

Why should a girl keep herself pure? Because in this way she can inspire mankind and lead humanity higher. I saw the value of purity in jail, where the purest women could most deeply help others.

We live as it were in the cellar of this world far from God. Every time we expose our soul to His light and love, it may grow.

But we must have understanding for human failure (in ourselves as well as in others). The Talmud says that God is long-suffering towards every sin except unchastity. The rabbi who thought this did not know God. Just the contrary is the truth.

There is no sin which Jesus so easily forgave as this. Jesus knew the almost irresistible drive of sexuality. Therefore he did not condemn the adultress. He tells us to do our utmost to beware of this sin, but keeps us at his loving bosom if we do commit it, notwithstanding. We might succeed later where we have failed today. There is no limit to the long-suffering of God and there is no sin for which the Church does not have full understanding and forgiveness.

I could give young people like Trudi one piece of practical advice. When you strive to get rid of erotic thoughts or sinful sexuality, the results are often the contrary of what you expect. Concupiscence is a huge power. Struggles to escape it only tighten the bonds.

It is the indirect way that succeeds. Don't try to eliminate thoughts which you abhor. They will not go. They have come to stay. But fill your mind with beautiful and pure ideas. Throw yourself into whole-hearted, time and energy-absorbing religious, social, political, philanthropic or educational work. The taking upon yourself of Christ's responsibilities in some field will make you Christlike in time.

New ideals have this great expulsive force. But if you fall remember that there is no limit to forgiveness. Nobody becomes a saint in three days. It took St. Anthony thirty years.

In 1962 a warmer wind began to blow from Moscow. We sniffed it cautiously. There was talk of a new 'thaw'. We received more letters from abroad. Rumours spread that Rumania was trying to break away from Comecon, the Soviet-controlled common market. There were even rumours of an amnesty.

People joked more freely:

Khrushchev: Mr. Kennedy, what can I do: I've tried brain-washing, I've tried prison but these stupid Christians still go to church. How can I stop them?

Kennedy: Try replacing the ikons in the churches with your portrait.

To Freedom

On every Communist festival we listened intently to the radio, hoping for some announcement about a release of prisoners. I couldn't sleep at night for thinking about it.

May 1st, 1962, Labour Day. Nothing.

August 23rd, Freedom Day. Nothing.

November 7th. Russian Revolution Day. A few hundred criminal convicts were set free. No news of the politicals.

And yet, the small signs continued to multiply. A huge trade deal was made with Yugoslavia. The 'Institute for Russian Studies' became a lesser part of the 'Institute for Foreign Languages'. The 'Russian Bookshop'—a big State store—became the 'Universal Bookshop'.

In August, 1963, jamming of Rumanian language broadcasts from the West stopped.

How breathlessly we sat by the radio that August 23rd, longing for news. There was none.

Early in 1964, without an announcement, a handful of politicals were released. A few were our friends.

We asked them: *What does it mean?*

They didn't know. 'The guard came in and read out a list of names, and that was that!' *How many names?* About eighty.

Eighty! So many! Now we were sure that an amnesty was on the way. It had happened just like this in 1956. Would it be on May 1st?

But there was no news that day.

One morning I was in my attic when Marietta rushed in, out of breath:

'Alice is home!' After four years! We snatched up our coats and ran outside and jumped on a tram.

There she was, thin and worn and smiling. How many things she had to say! But she had nothing, nothing. Just the patched rags on her back.

'Tomorrow we'll bring you some things,' I promised.

'But I know you haven't anything yourself,' she said.

'Oh, but we live in the lap of luxury,' laughed Mihai. 'You should see our penthouse flat.'

'Carpets on the walls,' said Marietta.

'On the windows, too!'

'Running water.'

'Straight through the ceiling!'

How lucky we were, I thought, compared with so many other women. We were surrounded with love. Everywhere it was working for us, running secretly like sap in the great tree of the Underground Church.

All night I couldn't close my eyes. In the morning we gathered a few things and took them to Alice, to the cousin's flat where she had slept.

Now, indeed, we had reason to hope that our dear ones would come home. But weeks passed, and months.

Every few weeks a friend named Marcia came running to the attic.

'The amnesty! It's coming next week! This time it's really true.'

Soon she was nicknamed Sister Amnesty. Marcia worked hard for the church, and she had a husband in an official post. So her rumours were taken more seriously.

The real amnesty, when it came, took us all unawares.

I'd risen early and gone out shopping for the family. It was a Wednesday in June, warm and blue. When I came home I found the daily paper waiting for me. A friend had brought it on his way to work.

In a modest space on page 1 was the news: AMNESTY.

It was not for every political prisoner. In fact, it was not clear who it was for at all. I read and re-read it. The announcement was hedged about with protective phrases. They couldn't admit that thousands of people, having been unjustly locked up for years, would now be freed. It made them look too silly. And Moscow was watching.

I hurried round to a friend's room. A little group had already gathered to discuss the news.

'Oh, it'll be like last year. Criminals only!' said Miss Landauer.

But Sister Amnesty was there, too.

'No, no! Haven't I told you so often! Let us pray and thank God, and you'll see!'

So we prayed, and returned home. I hadn't been back five minutes when a neighbour came running. A telephone call had come from an old friend who'd been released that morning from Gherla.

'He says your husband was on the list for today! He saw him waiting in the yard! He's coming!'

When she'd gone, I tried to peel the potatoes. But my heart was beating so fast I had to sit down. Hours passed.

Another knock on the door. Mr. Ionescu, an old friend who lived on the floor below and had a telephone, stood there smiling.

He took my hand, and said: 'It's someone calling you from out of town.'

So I went down and picked up the receiver and on the other end was Richard. When I heard his voice, I couldn't speak. I felt myself falling, falling, and a noise roared in my ears like the sea and then darkness poured over me.

I opened my eyes again on worried faces staring down.

'She's all right!'

'You fainted!'

They'd brought Mihai down now. He was laughing and talking on the telephone. Richard was in the home of friends in Cluj. 'I didn't know if I still had a wife and children,' he said. 'I thought I'd better find out!' He was well, and free. He was coming home as soon as he could. Gherla was hundreds of miles away in the western provinces. He'd catch a train from Cluj, the nearest railway point. But not today. His first underground meeting had already been arranged there that evening.

During the afternoon other friends came home, from prisons all over the country. A score of us, wives and friends, waited and talked in the attic, anxious, hopeful. There was a commotion on the staircase. A telegram. I tore it open.

'Richard says he's coming on the overnight train. He'll be here at 8.30 tomorrow morning!'

With a moan, Sister Amnesty slipped to the floor. This time she had fainted! They crowded round, slapping her cheeks, sprinkling cold water.

Of course we had no sleep that night. Every hour news came of fresh releases. Men and women we hadn't seen for ten, fifteen years walked in through the door. As if back from the dead. The whole house was full of people greeting each other, remembering, making plans in a fever of talk. Flowers kept arriving. Big bunches of summer roses that had cost the earth. From friends who could not come themselves, because of the danger.

They couldn't be seen at the station, these people—so we took their flowers instead, to show their love. I hadn't realized there were so many. Sister Amnesty had her arms full of gladioli. Marietta carried roses. Mrs. Armeanu and Alice had big white michaelmas daisies. The sun shone down with the lovely freshness of early morning light.

Crowds of anxious, expectant people were meeting every train. Hoping against hope that their prisoners would come. They had no news.

Then the train arrived. The big, droning diesel engine slipped past and my eyes searched the carriages. A loudspeaker announcement blared. The crowd churned round, pushing and jostling.

I saw Richard before he saw me. He was leaning from a carriage window. Thin and pale, with a shaven head.

God had given him back to me.

His clothes were very shabby. His boots had no laces—they weren't allowed—and they were too big. He came towards me, walking so slowly, tall and smiling, swimming about in his boots, and embraced Mihai and me. The station rocked with the noise of shouts and greetings. Someone with a camera lined the three of us up for a photograph.

People crowded round asking Richard for news of their friends and relatives, the ones who had not come back on that train.

Then I remembered how many had not come back, and never would, for they had died in prison.

'Don't speak,' Richard said. 'Let me just look at you.'

Day and night the attic was packed with friends and strangers who came from all over the country to see Richard again. Standing, sitting, squeezing in the ever-open door—everyone had to have a word with him. The Secret Police didn't try to break it up, because they could only have done so with a machine gun. They watched and made their little notes in the background.

Richard was thin as a stick and weighed about seven stone. He'd survived beating and brainwashing. He had to go into hospital at once. But even there, people continued to flock in to see him, until the director said apologetically he'd have to move. The Secret Police were complaining. He went from hospital to hospital, and finally landed in the sanatorium at Sinaia, one of the most beautiful mountain towns, where the Royal summer palace was once. But still people came, by motor-cycle and bicycle and bus. The Secret Police sent another warning. He decided to leave. There was nothing else to do.

In Bucharest, things were chaotic. Tens of thousands of political prisoners were freed that year. They sought jobs and wives and children, and they tried—sometimes with terrible results—to fit into a life they hadn't known for fifteen or twenty years. There were tragedies in hearts and homes and on the streets.

The police couldn't cope with all the confusion. And so Richard seized the chance to preach, secretly, in any church where the pastor would have him. And we were able to help many friends.

We sent Mrs. Armeanu down to Constanza for a Black Sea holiday. Her husband had not been released.

Richard even managed to obtain a licence to preach. But it was limited to a church in the village of Orsova, which had an officially restricted congregation of thirty-six members.

'If there's one more,' the Secret Police warned, 'there'll be trouble. We know you, and we're watching you.'

Richard told me, 'I don't think I can speak there. Other people are bound to turn up when the word gets round that I'm preaching. We'll only harm the people at Orsova.'

So we decided for the time being not to go. In any case, the Underground Church work in Bucharest was keeping us too busy to permit it. In secret gatherings here and there—because meetings in houses were illegal—Richard brought hundreds of souls to Christ. But still he didn't seem to think that he was doing enough and we didn't know how long he would be able to keep out of police hands. When I asked him what his plans were for the future, he said:

'Ideally, I'd like to be a recluse, to retire into a desert place like the hermits of old and spend the rest of my life in contemplation of God and in meditation. But things are very far from ideal.'

Once more he saw how little freedom the church had, how it was infested with informers—from the highest bishops to the humblest members of the congregation. Priests told him that if they failed to report on their flocks, their churches would be closed. Children and young people were indoctrinated with atheism more fiercely than ever.

But what disturbed Richard most deeply was to learn how ignorant and how naïvely credulous, people were in the West over Communism and its attempts to destroy religion.

At this time I began to have contact with certain high dignitaries of the Russian Church, by means which I cannot disclose. Many were Party tools, and they told us so openly and with sorrow. They had no choice, they said.

Other prelates from behind the Iron Curtain who went to international conferences, men chosen by the Party and playing the role ascribed to them by the Communists, were in fact working for the Underground Church.

When they got back, we were given their impressions. They were horrified to find what dupes some of the British and American delegates to these conferences are. 'They believe absolutely anything they're told,' they said. 'Some are more enthusiastic about Communism than any real Communist.'

What could be done about it?

Leaders of the Underground Church met and decided that Richard should make the attempt to reach the West. His task would be to make people understand the reality of what was happening to us—and what might happen to them.

Since 1948 Rumania had been selling Jews to Israel. Our hopes of leaving were pinned on this traffic. Thousands upon thousands of Jews were still trying to get out. Long lines of them waited at militia H.Q. for application forms. The exodus had already offended Arab nations and the Government was cautious; but official scruples could be overcome on payment of a large sum to the authorities.

Negotiations were long and tedious for us. And all they produced was a tip from a high official that our dossiers were stamped NEVER TO LEAVE. But we didn't give up. Friends suggested Mihai should go ahead of us. At that time he seemed to be in the greatest danger. Others said I should try to leave alone and raise money in the West to 'bail us out'.

Now that the first confusion of the mass release was over oppressive measures returned. Richard was watched everywhere. He could not enter a church without its pastor being warned or threatened.

Our own former church was closed and turned into a cartoon-film studio. Pews and altar were torn out, windows blocked. In one way it was a blessing in disguise: it made our attic on the top floor of the block very difficult to watch closely. Studio technicians, musicians, secretaries and so on came and went all day and couldn't be distinguished easily from our brethren.

Through secret channels we got word to our friend Anutza in Norway. She set to work raising money towards our ransom. Our families abroad also did their best. But it was through Anutza more than anyone that we were finally able to leave. She persuaded the Norwegians to grant us visas. She raised $7,000 from the Norwegian Israel Mission and the Hebrew Christian Alliance (to which I express here my thankfulness). Another source supplied $3,000. My family also contributed and helped in many ways. They were all love.

Our first visitors from the West, the Rev. Stuart Harris, chairman of the British Mission to the Communist World and American Pastor John Moseley arrived secretly by night bringing the first relief for needy families. Mihai spotted police outside. We'd been informed on! The visitors stayed with us until 1 a.m. By then the agents, believing that it had been a false alarm, had left. Next day we collected some Bibles from the two men in a park. We were spied on even here. An informer came later to the flat asking insinuating questions. Harris and Moseley were also permitted to hand out Bibles next day at the Baptist seminary. They heard afterwards from me that the students were obliged to return them all the day after Harris and Moseley left.

Our next visitors came out of the blue, some Americans and a Swiss. They didn't even know Richard's address. So they went to an official church organization to inquire.

Pastor Wurmbrand? Goodness gracious yes, they knew Pastor Wurmbrand. They'd send one of their men along as a guide. Oh, no trouble at all, pleased to help. So this man came along with them to the attic. Obviously, he'd go straight back and inform on all we said.

But the meeting took a comic turn. The guide spoke French but no English. So Richard talked to the visitors in English and I had to translate for the informer.

'Now my husband explains what liberty the church has here, and now he speaks about the great possibilities for tourism and now about the weather ...'

Richard meanwhile was talking like a runaway train about everything that happened to us and the real condition of the church. He was lively and brilliant and made them laugh with his account of things which had not been so funny at the time.

Then one of the Americans said, 'Well, this is very interesting, Mister, but our time's short and we'd like before going to have a word with Pastor Wurmbrand.'

'But I am Pastor Wurmbrand!'

'Impossible!'

'But true!'

'If you say so, it must be. But after fourteen years in prison! We expected to meet someone in the last stages of depression. And instead, we find a happy man.'

At last, after more than a year's work and pressure from friends in the West, we were told: *Your exit visas will be granted, the dollars have been received.*

Richard was called for a last encounter with the Secret Police. They told him: 'Now you can leave. Preach all you like abroad. But speak against us—and you'll be silenced.'

We have had evidence since then that the threat has not been forgotten.

I, too, had a last meeting with officialdom. It was the bailiff, knocking on the door, a list of property to be confiscated in his hand. 'This is absolutely your last chance to pay!'

'Come tomorrow,' I said. 'And you can take everything.'

Brethren and sisters came from far-off villages and towns to say farewell. Friends in Bucharest arrived every hour to wish us well.

Early next morning we were at the airport.

It was December 6th, the feast of St. Nicholas, patron of prisoners in the Rumanian Orthodox calendar. A damp mist seemed to dissolve the buildings and the grey aircraft out on the runway.

Ours was an old DC 7 and there were sixty of us, all ransomed, and nearly all Jews. We'd been there since dawn, and a warm sense of oneness, of deep gratitude at our good fortune in escaping from Communism, and of deeper grief for those whom we left behind in its grip, held us together. The officials, the passport men, the girls in uniform with lists in their hands, looked at us with envious eyes. We were going to live in the West. In the West!

They had tried to stop a crowd gathering at the airport. But a crowd had come to see us off just the same. Looking back, waving towards them through sheets of plate-glass, we trooped out over the wet, grey asphalt. The mist was lifting.

We boarded the plane. Mihai found himself next to the only foreign passenger, an Italian businessman, who at once began to talk. Cheerfully, he asked Mihai a score of questions. He hadn't thought it was as bad as they said. All those stories one heard about life under Communism. He'd had some very good meals at the Athenée Palace (Bucharest's most luxurious hotel, dating from pre-war days).

Mihai was silent.

They went down the steps together at Rome airport.

Mihai asked: 'This is really Rome? Not East Berlin or somewhere?'

'Sure, sure!' laughed the businessman. 'See that sign over there: *Bevete Coca-Cola*. You're on Italian soil.'

'So. Then I am a free man.' And he began to weep.

Finally, he said, 'Now, if you like, I'll tell you how it really is in Rumania, but I don't know if I could ever make you, or anyone else, understand.'

And with that, we advanced towards the customs. My brother and sister-in-law waited for us at the airport. Love had urged them to come specially from Paris.

Epilogue

From Rome we flew to Oslo. Richard would have liked to stop at Geneva, to report on the persecution in Rumania. But a secretary of the Lutheran World Federation begged Richard over the telephone not to come, 'because the Russians will know it'. I wondered why someone should fear the Russians at the World Council of Churches, when we had not feared them where they ruled.

In Norway, the lovely country which offered us a home, we were met by members of the Israel Mission which had paid part of the ransom, and by other church officials. But first and foremost by Anutza. She had worked fifteen years for this reunion. Nor had we been forgotten by Pastor Hedenquist, head of the Swedish Israel mission. He came specially from Stockholm. Over the years he had prayed for us every day. The Hebrew Christian Alliance, which had paid another part of the ransom, inquired immediately about our needs.

Then we went to Britain. Here our friend Stuart Harris opened to us the doors of universities and a multitude of churches of all denominations. People heard at last about the martyrs and victories of the Underground Church, which had been almost unknown until then. British Christians were not aware of the facts: the persecution of their brethren in the third of the world under Communist domination had been barely mentioned to them. In most places my husband spoke, in some, I did. An awakening took place in Great Britain.

As they made acquaintance with the unknown world of 'God's Underground,' we made acquaintance here, and later in America, with the Anglo-Saxon world. We could understand, now, Pope Gregory the Great. As a youthful deacon he noticed the fair faces and white bodies of some young people standing bound in the slave-market of Rome, and asked: 'From what country are they?' He was told that they were English (Angles in Latin). 'Angels,' he said, 'not Angles. Their faces are so angel-like. What is the name of their king?' The reply was 'Aella'. Gregory said, 'Alleluia shall be sung in Aella's land.' When he became head of the church, he saw to this. Now we heard the Alleluias sung by thousands who showed towards the Underground Church an angel-like love. The first mission to the Communist world was founded.

Friends made in Oslo, Pastors Sturdy and Knutson, saw to it that we should go to America. Richard and I spoke again in churches, at big rallies, seminaries, ladies' guilds.

Richard was called to testify before committees of the U.S. Senate and later of Congress. I sat near him when he spoke. Not only senators, but representatives of newspapers and radio-stations around the world were there. Batteries of T.V.-cameras were turned on him as he spoke about the suffering of the Underground Church:

'One third of the world is entitled to one third of your prayers, of your concerns, of your gifts . . . In prison I saw men with 50lb. chains at their feet, praying for America. But in America you seldom hear in a church a prayer for those in chains in Communist prisons.'

Asked by a senator if he bore any marks of torture, he stripped himself to the waist and showed eighteen scars on his body. People wept at his words, 'I don't boast of these scars. I show the tortured body of my church and my country. I speak for the heroes and saints who cannot speak for themselves, Protestants, Catholics, Orthodox and Jews who died under torture for their religion.'

Tears flowed down my face as I sat near him. I had before my eyes the farm women, the nuns, the many young girls, the Protestants and the Catholics, the Zionist ladies who slaved over new Pharaonic works because they had wished to see God's promise to the Jewish people fulfilled. I remembered those who had died. I knew that by death they had passed into the loving hands of the One who made lilies and carnations. But still I could not stop weeping.

Richard said later, 'Your tears made a greater impression than all my words. Tears undermine the strongest walls.'

Richard dictated his first book, *Today's Martyred Church Tortured for Christ.* I listened, sitting on a sofa, trying to knit. He wept. I wept, too. It was a very simple book. But written not with ink, rather with the tears and blood of martyrs. Unexpectedly, it became a best-seller in a score of languages. This book and our visits to different countries and continents became the starting point for the creation of nineteen missions in the free nations of Europe and Asia, in Australia and America. They work together to bring to the Underground Church Christian literature, radio-broadcasts in their language and relief for families of martyrs.

One book after another came from Richard's pen. He was tireless in preaching, but didn't simply talk—he created efficient organizations to work secretly in the Red camp. Some questioned his methods, but their criticisms came always too late. Richard acted, considering that there would be time enough for justifications later.

We were happy among all peoples, in every country we saw. We felt at home with our German Brethren. Between the German and the Jewish people there are rivers of blood. But perhaps it was not by accident that the sea which God parted for the Jews was called the Red Sea. Those who love can come through even a sea of blood. Only those who persist in hatred are drowned in it. We were happy with our Australasian, with our Maori brethren, with white, black and Indians in Africa. We had meetings without apartheid in South Africa. Intermingled, Christians of all races and colours of skin listened in tears to the message of Christ as taught in the Underground Church.

I remembered a sad reflection of Mihai's, made years before: 'Even if Father returns, he will be no more the man we knew, but a ghost, incapable of serving anybody.' In Africa, a newspaper wrote of our visit: 'We were hit by a hurricane called Richard.'

Richard's teaching, 'Hate Communism, but love and win the Communists for Christ' was accepted by millions everywhere. There is now prayer, concern and active help for the Underground Church. Its oppressors are embraced in Christian love, though a fight against their evil conduct goes on. In this fight, Richard attacks also church leaders who compromise with Communism, or even become its stooges.

Richard is Richard and I am I. For me, his fighting against so many people is too much. I would like him to be quieter. I tell him sometimes, 'In the Song of Solomon, Christ is compared with a flower. The flower is plucked, or it withers, having done nothing in all its life other than to delight onlookers with its perfume and splendour. It does not oppose those who wish to kill it. This, I think, is the ideal Christian life.'

Richard replies, 'If we don't fight Communism and its infiltration of the churches, the oppressors will defeat us.' I wonder why he worried about this. Wasn't the church born crucified, defeated? Was it not more beautiful in the catacombs than sharing the throne with emperors? Did not our underground services compare favourably with those in Western cathedrals, where no one wept when the passion of the Lord was mentioned, nor shouted with joy on hearing of his resurrection?

My husband couldn't be reached by such arguments. He

asked, 'To what flower is Jesus compared in the Song of Songs?' Mystified, I said, 'To a rose.' He answered promptly, 'The rose has thorns. Don't touch her, She will prick you.'

I have known him for thirty years. I will not change him. So I chose the quieter part. I organize the affairs of couriers of our mission who go to Communist countries and return. You have to instruct them, to gather information about the state of the church from them, to provide them with Bibles, literature and tapes, with money for relief.

Hundreds of thousands of Christians are in Communist prisons. In Rumania, many of our friends are there. And news of what people are suffering elsewhere daily makes me live again the past. In June 1969, the Soviet press boasted of arresting, for their faith, a man named Rabinchuk and all his five sons. I could not take my mind off Mrs. Rabinchuk. How terribly she must suffer in her empty house. In Albania, clergy have been rolled through streets in barrels and thrown into the sea. In North Korea, forty-five Christians were killed in one day in 1969. The families of these people, and innumerable others, are starving; and everywhere thirsty souls ask for the Word of God.

Taking many precautionary measures, I meet couriers and hear these things from them personally. The work has been going on for four years now, but not one of our couriers, nor any of their contacts in Communist countries, has yet been arrested.

I had also other people to meet. Clergy come to the free world, to conferences of the World Council of Churches, to Baptist and Orthodox conferences, or simply to preach and to deceive the West about non-existent religious liberties in the Communist camp. They are a special breed of men, these leaders of the official churches in the Red camp. Richard calls them 'traitors'. I would not call them so. Who am I to judge? They are unhappy beings. They are Red puppets. But what choice did they have? Some waited decades in the hope of seeing their countries freed. Much was promised by U.S. Presidents, but not performed. Despairing of help from the West, they have learned to live with the regime. Their brethren chose the martyrdom of prison. They have chosen the martyrdom of the conscious lie in order to keep a few churches open, to be able to perform a few baptisms, marriages, burials. They travel around the free world telling of the full liberty they enjoy in the Soviet Union, hoping that beneath their forced cries of enthusiasm Christians in the West will perceive how bad things really are. (Do British or American Christians go around the world asserting that they have liberty?) But Western church leaders cannot look into hearts. They are

unaware of the tragedy, and propagate what they hear: 'There
is liberty in the Communist camp!' That these unhappy creatures
must denounce to the police those whom they know to be faithful
is not known. It is part of the Communist 'morality', which the
West seems unable to understand.

With many of these official church leaders from the East
I and certain other women friends of mine meet, usually by night,
in their hotel rooms. I am no longer young. But the Communist
agents who spy continuously on these. delegates assume that
bishops with beards and robes cannot be choosers. So they interpret our visits in their own way.

We pray with them. Some become very helpful. The Communists cannot guess who has been won over to our side. It
could be the bishop. It could be the K.G.B. agent sent to watch
him. It could be the Soviet Ambassador. Or even the member
of the Government to whom one of these reports. An Underground Church that has won Svetlana Stalina, Mrs. Kosygin
and the greatest contemporary Russian writer, Solzhenitsyn, has
proved that it knows how to work.

Our personal life has also changed a great deal. Richard had
been for years a prisoner treated with contempt, accustomed
to mockery, and beatings. Now he is given adulation which
might turn another man's head. But Richard has passed through
the fiery furnace. He knows that the applause is not his due, that
glory belongs only to God. The publicity helps those who have
few other spokesmen. Fame, as well as shame, can be borne
humbly.

At first I feared the great wealth around us in the United
States. Though in the beginning ours was the poorest house in a
California suburb, it was palatial after the attic in Bucharest.
Some furniture was bought. We received a car as a gift. I worried about these 'luxuries'. But Richard quoted the German
mystic, Meister Eckhardt: 'If you despise money, try to be rich,
because you will be able to use your possessions well. Why not
be rich? The Bible says, "The Lord was with Joseph and he
was a prosperous man". Let us just have, knowing that what
we have is not ours but the Lord's. And he allows us to give not
only to others, but also to ourselves. Whence is the stupid idea
that God created the bees to produce honey only for sinners?
Saints have also the right to enjoy dainties. We have known how
to be abased: let us know how to abound.'

I love the asceticism of chosen souls like St. Thérèse of Lisieux. I think about Russian brethren in the town of Nijnaia-
Tagila, who have fasted uninterruptedly for a whole week, praying to be spared payment of heavy fines (already to pay such

fines they have sold furniture, tools, homes). The food stays in
your throat when you remember them. Richard cares for many
like them in every practical way he can. In prison there was a
time when he fasted four days a week.

But, knowing Richard as I do, I see in him also what I have
seen in everyone who has passed through terrible years of torture.
The inevitable laws of reaction come into play, and after such
deprivation of life, of even simple sunlight, you have a fierce im-
pulse to taste at once every joy there is. I wasn't afraid: God is
not unrighteous, he doesn't forget old sacrifices. Richard is aware
of the danger. And every danger of which you are aware
ceases to be a real danger.

I told him this much: 'I'm pleased to hear you despise money
—mind you don't stop when you've made the first million.' (There
is no danger of this for the moment.)

We have the help of Mihai and his young wife Judith in our
mission work. What a consolation they are for us. They had been
friends in Bucharest, when he was sixteen and she was ten.
Her parents took her to Israel, where she was converted by a
woman whom Richard had brought to Christ thirty years before.
After we reached the West, Judith came to visit us. Mihai said
to her on the first day, 'Is it not so that you will stay with me for
ever?' She answered, 'Of course.' And so it happened.

We have had great joys. We have also had our anxieties.
Within the past year, six men from Iron Curtain countries who
have fought against Communism in the West have been killed.
Four in Germany, one in Italy, one in Spain. A Catholic prelate,
Mgr. Draganovic, has been kidnapped from Trieste and is now
held in a Yugoslav prison. Documents forged by the Communists
have been put out to show that others have been in prison not for
their faith, but for embezzling church money or homosexuality.
Whenever I am away from Richard I feel fear. But if it is
dangerous to do God's work, how much more dangerous it is to
leave it undone. No man can stop a hurricane. Neither can I
stop Richard from exposing more and more the cruelties and
subtle infiltrations of Communism, so rousing the fury of Communist leaders and their tools in the church. May the angels of
God protect him.

Those whom Richard attacks certainly don't remain passive;
they put barriers in his path. If they had studied his character
first, they might realize it was hopeless! The higher the barrier,
the greater his leap. He started his Christian life facing grave
external obstacles, and turned them into assets.

My travels on behalf of the mission led me also to Israel. I saw there the holy places. I saw many of our former congregation, my family and my cousin who had told me on the day of my arrest: 'Leshanah habe-Jerushalaim!' (Next year in Jerusalem.) Nearly twenty years had passed.

In Israel men walk on holy ground. There is a seemliness that stops you from saying what you experience when you worship where the cross of Christ once stood. Magdalene wept silently here; never did she tell anyone what she had felt then. I surely cannot compare myself with her. But I also prefer to be silent.

I was grieved to see that part of the chapel belonged to one denomination (word that sounds to me a little like 'damnation'!) and part to another. I have my evangelical faith, but it will never make me quarrel with a Christian of another conviction. Roses spread their fragrance in every country, though they are called by different names. So do Christians.

I left a free Israel, free though surrounded by enemies. Czecho-slovakia had a mighty 'friend' near it, but it is in chains. Which should teach me to value the enemies of our work: they make it prosper. The dream of Zionists has been fulfilled and my Jewish prison friends had not suffered in vain. Their dream is my dream, too—I feel one with them, for Christianity has taught me to love my own people more and to work for their good.

What these friends did not know was that in a different country God was performing another mighty work through the Jewish people. Boris Pasternak risked his all, and just he, a Jew, brought Jesus back into Russian literature, from which He had been banished since the Communist revolution. Daniel and Ginzburg, Jewish writers, and Litvinov, a Jewish political fighter, went to prison for Russian liberty. There Jews lead the struggle against Communism. Two Orthodox priests (both of Jewish descent) dared to protest against the Patriarchy's collaboration with the Soviet Government. The greatest hero of the Rumanian Under-ground Church is a Jew, Milan Haimovici. He passed through seven years of prison and torture. How often I spent nights with his wife Monica, talking of our lost husbands. Now the Lutheran Church has rewarded him. He is caretaker of a church building in West Germany. He was considered one of the best pastors and preachers in Rumania. But in a German pulpit he could be 'dangerous': he might expose the atrocities of Communism. He had to be silenced.

God gave Israel back to the Jews. He will give them also great men dedicated to Christ, King of the Jews.

And now I am back at work. The work of a smuggler. Not a nice word, except that the smuggled goods are Bibles. The work of helping the families of Christian martyrs and underground pastors. The work of fighting the Communist poison in Western youth.

This work grows every day. The names of martyrs are known now throughout the whole world and children go to bed remembering them in their prayers. Will not these prayers be heard?

As the pastor's wife, I have often told youngsters a story of the boy who stood on the shore and waved to a ship at sea. A man beside him said, 'Don't be silly. The steamer will not change its course because you wave.' But the ship turned, came to shore and picked up the boy. From the bridge he shouted, 'Sir, I'm not a fool. The captain is my father!'

We also know that he who steers the universe on its course is our Father and that he hears our prayers.

The author welcomes correspondence concerning

the Underground Church, and letters should

be addressed to

Jesus to the Communist World, Inc.,

P.O. Box 11, Glendale, California 91209